Rosenne's The World Court: What It Is and How It Works

Rosenne's The World Court:
What It Is and How It Works

7th Revised Edition

Dr. Daphné Richemond-Barak

BRILL

LEIDEN | BOSTON

International Court of Justice. Photographed by Nils van Houts With the kind authorization of the Registrar.
Copyright: ICJ-UN. Reproduction is prohibited.

Library of Congress Cataloging-in-Publication Data

Names: Richemond-Barak, Daphné, editor. | Rosenne, Shabtai. World Court. |
    United Nations Institute for Training and Research.
Title: Rosenne's the World Court : what it is and how it works /
    Daphné Richemond-Barak.
Other titles: World Court
Description: 7th revised edition. | Leiden, The Netherlands : Koninklijke
    Brill NV, [2020] | At head of title: UNITAR. | Includes bibliographical
    references and index. | Summary: "Rosenne's The World Court offers a
    contemporary and interactive take on the UN's main judicial organ. The
    International Court of Justice, which has remained largely unchanged
    since its creation in 1945, operates within a growing network of states
    and international bodies. The book analyzes the institution via the
    prism of its relationship with states—the Court's natural constituency
    —as well as UN organs, international and domestic courts, academia, and
    non-state actors. It offers topics for class discussions, moot court exercises,
    and model syllabi. Direct engagement with the writings of leading
    scholars in international law and international relations helps uncover
    the Court's political and legal role in a complex international order.
    The book's novel and multidisciplinary approach make it an essential
    resource for students, teachers, and scholars"—Provided by publisher.
Identifiers: LCCN 2020030067 (print) | LCCN 2020030068 (ebook) |
    ISBN 9789004221550 (hardback) | ISBN 9789004226968 (ebook)
Subjects: LCSH: International Court of Justice. | International courts.
Classification: LCC KZ6260 .G55 2020 (print) | LCC KZ6260 (ebook) |
    DDC 341.5/52—dc23
LC record available at https://lccn.loc.gov/2020030067
LC ebook record available at https://lccn.loc.gov/2020030068

Typeface for the Latin, Greek, and Cyrillic scripts: "Brill". See and download: brill.com/brill-typeface.

ISBN 978-90-04-22155-0 (hardback)
ISBN 978-90-04-22696-8 (e-book)

Copyright 2020 by Koninklijke Brill NV, Leiden, The Netherlands.
Koninklijke Brill NV incorporates the imprints Brill, Brill Nijhoff, Brill Hotei, Brill Schöningh,
Brill Fink, Brill mentis, Vandenhoeck & Ruprecht, Böhlau Verlag and V&R Unipress.
All rights reserved. No part of this publication may be reproduced, translated, stored in a retrieval system,
or transmitted in any form or by any means, electronic, mechanical, photocopying, recording or otherwise,
without prior written permission from the publisher. Requests for re-use and/or translations must be
addressed to Koninklijke Brill NV via brill.com.

This book is printed on acid-free paper and produced in a sustainable manner.

Contents

Foreword   IX
Acknowledgments   XI
List of Figures and Tables   XIII

Introduction   1

1 The International Court of Justice and Its Predecessor   4
  I   Early Beginnings: the League of Nations and the PCIJ   4
    A   *Early Forms of International Adjudication*   4
    B   *From Arbitration to Adjudication*   8
    C   *The Permanent Court of International Justice*   11
    D   *The PCIJ's Achievements*   16
  II   Legal Underpinnings   20
    A   *The Establishment of the United Nations*   20
    B   *The UN Charter and the ICJ Statute*   23
    Conclusion   28

2 The International Court of Justice and States   30
  I   Access to the Court: States Only   31
  II   The Principle of Consent   35
  III   Admissibility and Jurisdiction   45
    A   *Legal Disputes*   45
    B   *Conferring Jurisdiction on the Court*   47
      i   Jurisdiction Conferred by Treaty   48
      ii   Jurisdiction Conferred by Optional Clause Declaration   52
      iii   *Forum Prorogatum*   59
  IV   Arguing before the Court   61
    A   *The Principle of Equality*   61
    B   *The Value of Legal Precedents*   63
  V   How a Case is Tried   66
    This section is supplemented with interactive material, available at
    DOI: 10.6084/m9.figshare.15093243
    A   *Preliminary Objections*   67
    B   *Provisional Measures*   73
    Conclusion   78

VI   CONTENTS

3 The International Court of Justice and the United Nations   80

    I   Advising the UN as an Organization   80
        A   *Nature and Scope of the Advisory Function*   80
        B   *Facilitating UN Activity and Cooperation*   87
        C   *Developing International Law*   88
        D   *Safeguarding the System*   90
    II   Advising on Disputes   94
    III   The ICJ's Relationship with Other Principal UN Organs   99
        A   *Relationship with the Security Council*   99
        B   *Relationship with the General Assembly*   105
    IV   A Timeline of Advisory Proceedings   108
    V   Comparative Practice   110
        A   *The European Court of Human Rights*   111
        B   *The Inter-American Court of Human Rights*   113
        C   *The African Court on Human and Peoples' Rights*   115
        Conclusion   117

4 The International Court of Justice and the International Community   121

    I   The ICJ and Other International Courts and Tribunals   121
    II   The ICJ and National Courts   134
        A   *Compliance with ICJ Decisions*   134
        B   *The Decisions of National Courts in the ICJ's Jurisprudence*   135
        C   *The ICJ in the Jurisprudence of National Courts*   138
    III   The ICJ and "the Most Highly Qualified Publicists"   142
        A   *Academia at the ICJ*   143
        B   *Scholarly Critiques of the ICJ*   147
    IV   The ICJ and Non-State Actors   148
        A   *Contentious Proceedings*   149
        B   *Advisory Proceedings*   150
        Conclusion   153

5 An Assessment   155

    I   What States Use the Court and for What   158
        A   *Applicant*   158
        B   *Respondent*   159
        C   *Application v. Intervention*   161
        D   *Optional Clause Declarations*   163

CONTENTS   VII

    E   *Advisory Proceedings*   165
       i   Voting on Requests for Advisory Opinions   165
       ii   State Participation in Advisory Proceedings   168
II   Avoiding the Court   171
    A   *Not Using the Court to Settle Disputes*   172
    B   *Not Depositing an Optional Clause Declaration*   173
    C   *Filing Preliminary Objections*   174
    D   *Non-Appearing Respondent*   176
III Compliance with the Court's Judgments   178
    A   *Defining Compliance*   179
    B   *The Timing Issue*   180
    C   *Additional Issues with Compliance*   181
       i   Compliance for Other Reasons   181
       ii   Compliance or the Appearance of Compliance   182
       iii Compliance and Legitimacy   183
    Conclusion   186

6 Bringing the Court to the Classroom: Student's Guide   190

    A facilitator's guide is available upon request at worldcourt@brill.com
I   What is a Moot Court?   190
II   Written Pleadings Phase   191
    A   *Written Pleadings Overview*   191
    B   *Memorial*   191
    C   *Judges' Notes*   192
III Oral Hearings Phase   193
    A   *Oral Hearings Overview*   193
    B   *Room Setup*   193
    C   *Oral Hearings*   193
    D   *Timekeeper*   194
    E   *Addressing the Court*   194
    F   *Conclusion*   195
IV Recap   196
V   Moot Court Problems   196
    A   *Problem #1: Amaliland v. Raviland (Case Concerning Space Debris and Environmental Protection)*   196
    B   *Problem #2: Abalonia v. Rodonia (Case Concerning Diplomatic Protection of Beta Boop)*   199
    C   *Problem #3: Arraticus v. Remonicus (Case Concerning the Tig Population, Species Endangerment, and the Law of the Sea)*   202

VIII CONTENTS

7 Teaching the International Court of Justice 206

I   The ICJ for Law Students 206

    A   *Public International Law Course, 2 Credits*   206

    B   *Public International Law Course, 4 Credits*   208

        Lesson 1 – The Court and Its Jurisdiction   208

        Lesson 2 – The Role(s) of the Court   209

II   The ICJ for International Relations/Political Science Students   210

III   A Full Course on the International Court of Justice, 2 Credits   212

    A   *Lesson 1 – The Court and Its Predecessor*   212

    B   *Lessons 2 and 3 – The ICJ and States: Contentious Jurisdiction*   213

    C   *Lesson 4 – How the Court Works*   214

    D   *Lessons 5 and 6 – The Court and the United Nations: Advisory Jurisdiction*   216

    E   *Lesson 7 – The Role of the Court in Advancing Peace and Security*   217

    F   *Lesson 8 – The Role of the Court in Developing International Law*   219

    G   *Lesson 9 – The Relationship of the ICJ with other International Courts and Tribunals*   220

    H   *Lesson 10 – A Need for Reform of the ICJ?*   221

    I   *Lessons 11 and 12 – Moot Court Exercise*   222

Index 225

Foreword

On 6 December 1988 Professor Shabtai Rosenne wrote me a rather formal letter asking me to be his Literary Executor. He asked me to see to it that after his death certain of his books should not be allowed to 'fall into disuse', but that new editions should appear from time to time, continuing to be associated with his name but, and here I quote, 'without detracting from the appropriate recognition due to whomsoever produces new editions.' Both the language and the generosity of spirit were marvellously typical of Shabtai.

Thank God, more than twenty years elapsed before I was called upon to fulfil my task, and those two decades proved to be among the most productive of Shabtai's long and exceptional career. Each year which went by seemed to enhance his academic and professional stature.

Following his death in 2010, his Obituary in The Times of London put him at the very peak of the international lawyers of his generation. Few would dispute that assessment.

No words of mine could add lustre to the recognition which he received during his lifetime from his most distinguished peers, including membership of the Institut de Droit International, the first Hague Prize for International Law and the Manley O. Hudson Medal of the American Society of International Law – when he received that Medal, the then President of the International Court of Justice informed those present that no Member of the Court would ever dare to suggest any procedural step without first looking to see what Rosenne had said on the matter!

It was at the Peace Palace, the home of both the International Court of Justice – the World Court – and of The Hague Academy of International Law, that Shabtai's brilliance was best displayed, and there more than anywhere were his qualities understood and celebrated: understood and celebrated by generation after generation of Judges, Registrars, librarians, academics and diplomats. But perhaps pride of place in the array of his admirers should go to the young: he was never too busy to engage with students and up-and-coming academics, and his General Course at The Hague Academy in 2001 was a huge success.

So it was natural that when Shabtai and I began to discuss who would be a suitable person to work with him on a revision of his unique introductory book, 'The World Court: What It Is and How It Works', our minds turned to up-and-coming academics. I was pleased when he agreed with my suggestion that Dr. Daphné Richemond-Barak would be an ideal choice, given her already considerable academic output and her practical as well as theoretical knowledge of the Court and its workings. Several meetings took place and Daphné set to work.

Between that time and today two significant changes occurred with respect to the progress of the book: as mentioned above, and to our great regret, Shabtai passed away in 2010, and Daphné can no longer be described as 'up-and-coming,' having established a solid international reputation for ground-breaking research and writing, for teaching, and for organizing and participating in important meetings and panels. Her creativity has been demonstrated in several fields of law, as evidenced, inter alia, by her recent, pioneering publication on underground warfare.[1]

This new edition of 'The World Court: What It Is and How It Works' displays Daphné's innovative approach at its best, and her revision has been strikingly extensive and thorough. As was true for previous editions, the present edition offers the politician, the diplomat, the journalist, the teacher, and the student an unrivalled guide and introduction to the International Court of Justice, but it is to the last of these categories, the teacher and the student, that the book is now primarily addressed. And it is no longer simply 'a book.' The new edition carries with it an online package of materials which make it a trailblazing resource for all those teaching or participating in courses on The World Court.

I have no doubt that Shabtai would have approved of the changes that Daphné has introduced as he always welcomed new developments in information technology and improvements in computer hardware and software, and to the end of his days adapted rapidly to the use of new online resources and technical improvements in accessing them. In addition to this, he would have been very glad indeed to know that his introductory book, as updated and re-cast by Daphné, would be highly likely to lead to more courses on the International Court of Justice being introduced at universities all over the world. He himself taught such courses in both the USA and Europe, using his own materials and experience, but other teachers may have been daunted by a lack of easily accessible publications and documents. This new edition changes that, and all those involved in this project: Daphné, Brill Nijhoff, the Rosenne Family and the undersigned, have every hope that the new edition will meet a significant need and will lead to a substantial growth in the number of students studying the many fascinating and important aspects of The World Court.

Finally, it seems to me proper to note that, in accordance with Shabtai Rosenne's request, this book certainly remains 'associated with his name,' while 'not detracting from the appropriate recognition due to' Daphné Richemond-Barak.

Alan Stephens
Zichron Yaacov, November 2019

---

1 Daphné Richemond-Barak, *Underground Warfare* (OUP, 2018).

Acknowledgments

My deepest thanks go out to Shabtai Rosenne himself. I had the privilege of meeting Shabtai on numerous occasions. On one of these occasions, he told me that he had stayed up all night in order to read the latest ICJ decision that had just been released. His face lit up as he proceeded to share details and insights. As I prepared this new edition, his enthusiasm stayed with me and strengthened my determination to pass it on to future generations.

I would also like to thank Shabtai Rosenne's confidant and friend for whom I have utmost respect and admiration – Alan Stephens, for his trust and friendship. His role in making this project come to life and, more generally, in carrying out Shabtai Rosenne's legacy is fundamental. We are all richer as a result of his dedication.

The Interdisciplinary Center (IDC Herzliya), my home for over a decade, where this project was born and completed, provided me the priceless opportunity to write this book. I was lucky to enjoy the support of the institution, its founder and President Professor Uriel Reichman, and the Deans of the Lauder School of Government, Diplomacy and Strategy (Professors Alex Mintz, Boaz Ganor, and Assaf Moghadam) who all showed support for project. I would like to mention in particular the Lauder School Fund for Academic Advancement, which allowed me to carry out quantitative research on the Court. Insights from this research were helpful in sharpening the book's claims and providing a ground-breaking analysis of the relationship between the Court and states. I am immensely grateful for the show of confidence and open-mindedness that enabled me to use innovative research tools.

My colleagues at IDC deserve all my gratitude as they keep me going when it is tough. Their daily encouragement, presence, and genuine interest create the peaceful and supportive environment one needs to write, think, and create. None of this would have happened without them. I am particularly grateful to Dr. Amnon Cavari and Dr. Maoz Rosenthal who encouraged me to explore new research methods and shed light on previously unexplored aspects of the ICJ's role.

I am forever indebted to Professors Christopher J. Borgen of St. John's University School of Law, Chiara Giorgetti of the University of Richmond School of Law, and Marko Milanovic of the University of Nottingham School of Law who took the time – their most valuable resource – to read over the manuscript.

Chelsea Zimmerman played a key role in bringing this project to completion, and I cannot thank her enough for her professionalism and attentiveness to details. Naama Strul, Tsurit Rips, Achinoam Harel, and Guy Freedman turned a dream into reality by helping me code state interaction with the ICJ – a tedious task that is essential to the assessment carried out in Chapter 5. A number of additional people helped along the way, and I would like to thank them here: Adam Broza, Brandon Weinstock, Akiva Fund, Ezra Friedman, Tamar Sacerdoti, Ella Drory, Aviva Strauss, Ira Ryk-Lakhman, Chanoch Berman, and Shay Gurion. In spite of the help and support I received, any remaining mistake is of course mine and mine only.

I also received significant support from within the International Court of Justice, without which this project would not have seen the light. My relationship with the Registrar at the time, Mr. Philippe Couvreur, and current and former judges goes back many years ... I had the privilege of clerking at the Court in 2003–04, and have kept in close contact since then. Special thanks go to Judge Bruno Simma, who has always been available and supportive. I am a staunch admirer of his career, academic rigor, and endearing personality. Finally, I cannot thank enough Boris Heim, formerly the Head of the Information Department of the International Court of Justice, who spent countless hours providing information about the Court in the archives, allowing me to make the Court come alive with the help of original pictures and sketches.

I must acknowledge with endless gratitude the faith placed in me by Brill Martinus Nijhoff and I am thankful for the understanding of my editors, Hans van der Meij and Marie Sheldon. You backed me when I told you that I wanted to make this book into *the* academic support for studying and understanding the ICJ. You supported the difficult undertaking of remaining true to Shabtai Rosenne's vision, while answering the needs of students in a highly interactive, technology-based, and changing world. Today, I hope you are satisfied with an outcome intended to carry on Shabtai's life work. Thank you for everything. It has truly been a pleasure to work with you.

Last but not least, I would like to thank my husband. For years, the Court and The Hague have carried a major significance in our lives. The International Court of Justice has been a part of my family history going back to the first years of the Court's existence and *The Minquiers and Ecrehos* case, in which my grandfather, Prosper Weil, represented France against the United Kingdom. Later, life brought my husband and I to The Hague where international law, our own personal lives, and this family history all came full circle. The Court has played an important role in the life of our family, and I hope it will continue to do so for many years to come.

Figures and Tables

Figures

1.1 The formalization of international adjudication also contributed to the development of a community of experts engaged in the interpretation of international law   10

1.2 ICJ activity by decade   20

1.3 Judges   24

1.4 Office of the President, picturing President Dame Rosalyn Higgins (the first woman appointed as a Judge, who also served as President between 2006 and 2009)   25

1.5 Office of the Registrar   26

1.6 The Peace Palace, in The Hague, is the home of the ICJ   29

2.1 States that appeared in case brought jointly but never as Applicant   51

2.2 View of the Great Hall of Justice   58

2.3 A preliminary objection file   67

2.4 Sealed judgment in *Barcelona Traction*   79

3.1 Bodies requesting advisory opinions   82

3.2 Floor plan in *Continued Presence of South West Africa in Namibia*   109

3.3 Sealed advisory opinion   118

5.1 States that appeared as Applicant more than five times   158

5.2 P5 appearing as Applicants   159

5.3 States that appeared as Respondent more than five times   160

5.4 States that appeared both as Applicant and Respondent   160

5.5 The more states appear as Applicant, the more they appear as Respondent, and vice-versa   161

5.6 Deposit of optional clause declaration does not affect preliminary objections   163

5.7 States that failed to renew, withdrew, or never filed optional clause declaration yet appeared as Applicant   164

5.8 Voting record of P5 on advisory opinion requests   167

5.9 States that submitted written statements but did not participate in oral hearings   168

5.10 States that filed preliminary objections more than once as Respondent   174

5.11 Trends in filing of preliminary objections   175

5.12 Non-appearing Respondents   176

5.13 Number of judges per state   189

Tables

3.1 Timeline of advisory proceedings 109
3.2 List of advisory opinions and requesting organs 118

Introduction

In Loving Memory of My Grandfather, Prosper Weil

• • •

Justice, justice you shall pursue.
Deuteronomy 16, 20

• • •

I am writing these words with great humility, and mindful that I have stepped into a giant's shoes: Shabtai Rosenne is, after all, the scholar most cited by the International Court of Justice.[1] Taking over Shabtai Rosenne's book is more than an honor, it is a commitment to stay true to the memories, the experience, and, perhaps most importantly, the man.

Shabtai knew the Court better than anyone else. He was an outstanding lawyer, and his loss is still felt by the many practitioners and judges who benefitted from his unparalleled knowledge and experience.

"THE WORLD COURT: WHAT IT IS AND HOW IT WORKS" holds a very special place in the study of the International Court of Justice. Shorter and more accessible than its sibling, "THE LAW AND PRACTICE OF THE INTERNATIONAL COURT OF JUSTICE" (edited by Professor Malcolm Shaw), "THE WORLD COURT" provides an overview of the world's main judicial body and its role in the international legal order. When teaching international law, I have struggled to find material that presents the *institution* of the Court in an attractive, contemporary fashion. Teaching about the Court and teaching its jurisprudence are two very different things. This book encourages the former, in order to enhance the understanding of the latter.

The present book facilitates the study of the ICJ and students' understanding of its role in the greater web of international institutions. It walks the student through its corridors to explore the inside of its chambers and halls – even if the student has never visited the Peace Palace in The Hague. It engages

---

1 Sondre Torp Helmersen, *Finding 'the most highly qualified publicists': Lessons from the International Court of Justice*, 30 Eur. J. Int'l L. 509 (2019). (In a study that included judgments and minority opinions appended to judgments, the author found that Rosenne was cited 233 times, with the second most-cited scholar, Hersch Lauterpacht, coming far behind with 119 citations.)

the student thanks to its interactive style and the supplementary virtual content. It sets the stage for lively discussions about the Court and its workings. Among other things, this book provides a template for conducting moot ICJ trials, sample syllabi, and interactive material (some available to teachers only). Though firmly anchored in international law, the book's insights also borrow from the field of international relations to allow the reader to grasp the important role played by power and politics inside the Great Hall of Justice. Finally, novel research methods shed light on how states prefer to interact with the UN's main judicial organ.

When the International Court of Justice was established – and even more so when the Permanent Court of Justice was created under the auspices of the League of Nations – the international legal system was embryonic and quite simple. As the world became more globalized, the number of international and regional judicial networks grew and, consequently, a fragmentation that stole some of the limelight from the ICJ. At the same time, the growing pace of globalization imbued the international stage with ever-increasing importance and responsibilities. The Court became an essential (but no longer the only) component of the international legal and judicial system. As a result of these developments, the Court had to adjust, redefine its role, and assert its position vis-à-vis a broader array of actors, institutions, bodies, agencies, and constituencies. There were 51 member states when the Court was established; today there are 193. International and regional institutions, with which the Court interacts on a regular basis, have also multiplied. Yet, the Court is expected to continue to fulfill the same role it was created for back in 1945.

This book analyzes how the proliferation of states and international institutions, and the growing influence of non-state actors, have affected the Court's function, states' perception of the Court, and the Court's view of its own role in the international order. True to Shabtai Rosenne's fascination for backstage political considerations, this book also explores some of the political underpinnings of the Court's institutional features: the political battles behind the rejection of compulsory jurisdiction, the Court's attempts to achieve "win-win" settlements, and the ambiguous yet fundamental function of advisory jurisdiction.

The importance of defining "what the Court is" cannot be underestimated – especially given the title of this book – yet the proper terminology and adequate theoretical framework to achieve this goal may still be lacking. Magritte's painting "The Treachery of Images" famously proclaims "*ceci n'est pas une pipe*" ("this is not a pipe"), thereby hoping to separate the image of a pipe from a real pipe. Only the real pipe, not its image, can be packed. The International Court of Justice, for its part, looks like a court, speaks like a court, is called a court, and operates like a court. Yet, it is both more than a court, and less than a court. It is its own thing. Paraphrasing Magritte, I would therefore say "*ceci n'est pas une cour*" ("this is not a court"). So what is it? How can we define an institution that aspires to pacify state-to-state relations, develop the corpus of international law, and preserve the international constitutional order established in the UN Charter – all at once?

In order to answer this difficult question, each chapter of the book examines the Court's interaction with a different actor. After the opening chapter sets up the historical and theoretical background for the rest of the book, the second chapter centers on the Court's relationship with individual states, the third on its function within the UN, and the fourth on its position within the international community. By placing the emphasis on the Court's relationship with various international, regional, and non-state actors (states, UN bodies and tribunals, domestic courts, and even academia), this book hopes to give justice to the complex yet fascinating role the Court plays in the international legal and political system.

It is my sincere hope that this book will serve as a much-needed platform to teach about the ICJ. Designed with all students in mind (law and non-law, undergraduate and graduate), it is a working tool that can be adapted by teachers to their own needs. For those who want more, it includes additional avenues for thinking, debating, and researching. Teachers in search of a solid and timeless platform from which to teach about the ICJ may use the book to engage with students and create assignments. Academics in search of insights on the Court specifically and on global governance more generally, may use the book for its tackling of international law and politics, its institutional focus, and its use of quantitative research methods to shed new light on the Court's role. Ultimately, this book aspires to uphold Shabtai Rosenne's wish to spread knowledge about the Court and disseminate its wisdom as widely as possible – and share our common fascination with this great institution.

CHAPTER 1

The International Court of Justice and Its Predecessor

The International Court of Justice (ICJ), often known as the World Court, cannot claim full credit for the advent of international adjudication. The Permanent Court of International Justice (PCIJ), its predecessor, was the first permanent court established to resolve state-to-state disputes. The League of Nations, the entity created by states following World War I that set up the PCIJ, must instead get credit for an initiative that still bears fruits decades later. Even before the PCIJ, seeds had been planted for the establishment of a permanent institution that could serve as the neutral arbiter of state-to-state disputes. This chapter retraces the historical evolution that led to the creation of the ICJ as one of the principal organs of the United Nations.

A   Early Beginnings: the League of Nations and the PCIJ

1   *Early Forms of International Adjudication*
International adjudication existed long before the word 'international' was coined in the eighteenth century by Jeremy Bentham, and centuries before the Treaty of Westphalia edified the walls of national sovereignty. Examples of international arbitration can be found from antiquity and medieval Europe to the eighteenth century. Although the creation of the PCIJ in the early twentieth century marked the institutionalization of a permanent institution, the origin of modern international adjudication can be found in arbitration between ancient cities and states.

Arbitration by a neutral and mutually accepted third party was used in Ancient Greece to resolve disputes between city-states and individuals who were engaged in commerce in foreign countries.[1] At the time, "arbitration did serve a valuable purpose, alike in averting war or armed reprisals between state

---

1   Derek Roebuck, *Sources for the History of Arbitration: A Bibliographical Introduction*, 14 Arb. Int'l 237, 260 (1998); Derek Roebuck, *A Short History of Arbitration, in* Hong Kong and China Arbitration: Cases and Materials (1994), at xxxiii–lxv, xxxvii. *See also* Jackson H. Ralston, International Arbitration, from Athens to Locarno (1929).

© KONINKLIJKE BRILL NV, LEIDEN, 2020 | DOI:10.1163/9789004226968_003

THE INTERNATIONAL COURT OF JUSTICE AND ITS PREDECESSOR

and state, and in bringing to a speedier end conflicts which otherwise might have ended only with the destruction of one, or the exhaustion and ruin of both, of the belligerent powers."[2] When a dispute arose between two cities, a third city would often act as the neutral arbiter. It was a peer-based justice.

> ### Peace Treaty between Sparta and Argos 418 B.C.[3]
> If any of the cities, whether inside or outside Peloponnese, have a question whether of frontiers or otherwise, it must be settled, but if one allied city should have a quarrel with another allied city, it must be referred to some third city thought impartial by both parties. Private citizens shall have their disputes decided according to the laws of their several countries.

These mechanisms differ from international adjudication in that they were not carried out by a court of law.

> ### The Politics of International Arbitration and Adjudication[4]
> International arbitration and adjudication share three general characteristics. First, a third party, not the disputants, determines the terms of any settlement. Second, unlike mediation, states agree to honor the ruling before the third party actually hands down a decision. Finally, the arbitration or adjudication settlements incorporate principles of international law that are not necessarily invoked in other types of negotiations. The two methods primarily differ with respect to the identity of the third party. In arbitration, an individual, state, NGO, or panel of states hands down a decision. On the other hand, adjudication is conducted by an international court, such as the International Court of Justice.

The turning point that many laud as the genesis of *modern* international arbitration is usually identified as the Jay Treaty – a treaty signed between the United States and Great Britain in 1794, not long after the end of the American War of Independence.[5] The treaty set up three joint committees, comprised

---

2 Marcus Niebuhr Tod, International Arbitration amongst the Greeks (1913), at 190–91.
3 Thucydides, The History of the Peloponnesian War, 431 B.C.E., (translated by Richard Crawley), available at http://classics.mit.edu/Thucydides/pelopwar.mb.txt.
4 Stephen E. Gent, *The Politics of International Arbitration and Adjudication*, 2 Penn. St. J.L. & Int'l Aff. 66, 67 (2013).
5 Georg Schwarzenberger, International Law as Applied by International Courts and Tribunals, vol. IV (1986), at 22; W. Evans Darby, International Tribunals (4th ed., 1904) at 769.

of equal numbers of American and British delegates, tasked with the resolution of legal issues between the two states that negotiations had not resolved, such as compensation for loss of private property and questions concerning the normalization of political and commercial relations. The joint committees were comprised of one commissioner appointed by each the United States and Great Britain; both commissioners then appointed the third commissioner. The mixed composition of these joint committees and the use of legal and judicial techniques to achieve settlement were not common at the time. Importantly, the mechanism did not include a neutral third party; rather the third party (i.e., the third commissioner) was either from the United States or Great Britain.[6]

> ### Georg Schwarzenberger, Present-Day Relevance of the Jay Treaty Arbitrations[7]
>
> Both Contracting Parties considered the maintenance of peace between them on the basis of the equilibrium established by the 1783 and 1794 Treaties as more important than any of the issues entrusted to the three Commissions. This overriding objective was symbolized by their willingness, if necessary, to leave to chance the choice of the uneven commissioner in each Commission. Their joint resolve found further expression in the effective settlement by diplomatic means of the difficulties in which any of the Commissions landed itself.

Although the Jay Treaty only addressed disputes related to boundaries, compensation owed to the British, and the British treatment of American shipping in the war with France, it caught the eyes of diplomats, statesmen, and legal professionals.[8] Inspired by the example set by the Jay Treaty, states became more willing to agree upon a method for resolving future disputes. Many subsequent treaties featured mixed committees in their arbitration clauses. In most situations, however, the arbitration process was contingent on the parties' ability to agree on both the procedural and legal frameworks in the context of a given dispute. Two nations that arbitrated a previous dispute and wished to settle another dispute through arbitration negotiated a new arbitration agreement, starting from square one.

---

6 *Id.*

7 Georg Schwarzenberger, *Present-Day Relevance of the Jay Treaty Arbitrations*, 53 Notre Dame L. Rev. 715, 733 (1978).

8 *Id.* at 732.

> *Developments in Dispute Settlement Inter-State Arbitration Since 1945*[9]
> Studies of the vast mass of treaty provisions in inter-State arbitration show certain clear developments since the 1794 Jay Treaty. From the end of the nineteenth century the early bilateral provisions for arbitration were supplemented by multilateral treaties – as a consequence of the general growth in multilateral treaty-making. At the same time the early provisions for *ad hoc* arbitration were followed by treaties establishing institutional arbitration (...) That is, States agreed that all, or a particular category of, future disputes should be referred to arbitration.

...

Questions

1. Why do you think the decision was made to not include a neutral arbiter in the Jay Treaty and instead resolve disputes between commissioners from the United States and Great Britain? What advantages does such a mechanism offer the parties? Under what conditions could it be replicated today?
2. Why would states opt for arbitration over mediation? Why would states prefer mediation over arbitration?
3. Reflect on the relationship between international law and international adjudication. Can you have one without the other?

Further Reading

Manley O. Hudson, International Tribunals: Past and Future (1944).

John Liddle Simpson and Hazel Fox, International Arbitration: Law and Practice (1959).

Henry King and James Graham, *Origins of Modern International Arbitration*, 51 Disp. Res. J. 42 (1996).

Charles H. Bower II, *The Functions and Limits of Arbitration and Judicial Settlement Under Private and Public International Law*, 18 Duke J. Comp. & Int'l L. 259 (2008).

Jan Paulsson, The Idea of Arbitration (2013).

---

9 Christine Gray and Benedict Kingsbury, *Developments in Dispute Settlement Inter-State Arbitration since 1945*, 63 Brit. Y.B. Int'l L. 109 (1992) at 101, 106.

2   *From Arbitration to Adjudication*

As part of the arbitration process, the parties to the dispute had to negotiate the choice of the arbitrator(s), identify legal questions to be submitted, and designate the applicable law.[10] It was rarely simple to reach a mutual agreement on such complicated, and at times extremely technical, matters in the heat of a political controversy, which left little room to maneuver. States were only willing to take part in arbitration in relation to a narrow list of issues: land and marine time boundaries, questions pertaining to sovereignty rights, and financial affairs.[11] Disputes that could affect national honor, vital interests, or other similarly vague concepts were excluded by reservation from the arbitrator's jurisdiction and acted, in essence, as broad exit points from the process.

Yet the prospect of war, and the need to find means to avoid it, grew in importance. The arms race of the nineteenth century and the introduction of conscription by European militaries along with the rapid expansion of both democratic and nationalist ideals, rendered the prospect of war in the eyes of the public and among many of its leaders imminent and fatal.

> *Helen May Cory, Compulsory Arbitration of International Disputes*[12]
>
> In Europe, the increasing size of armaments furnished an argument for a barrier against inevitable conflict. But the existence of huge armies also caused governments to feel that there was no security in arbitration and that the sword would always prevail. It was felt that to arbitrate certain cases would be an admission of weakness. The great powers believed that no court of arbitration could be trusted to determine cases involving their closest interests; no portion of the regulation of their foreign affairs must slip from their grasp; they relied more on their own efforts to gain a coveted prize than they did on the so-called justice of an arbitral tribunal; they did not fear war as much as they feared a loss of the attributes of sovereignty, and they had no faith in arbitration as a means to end war.

A bit more than a century after the signing of the Jay Treaty, Tsar Nicolas II of Russia initiated a collaborative international effort to fend off the impending world war. His efforts bore fruit and, in 1899, the Hague Peace Conference was convened to discuss issues pertaining to the control and regulation of

---

10   David D. Caron, *War and International Adjudication: Reflections on the 1899 Peace Conference*, 94 Am. J. Int'l L. 4 (2000).

11   Helen May Cory, Compulsory Arbitration of International Disputes (1932), at 3.

12   *Id.* at 41.

THE INTERNATIONAL COURT OF JUSTICE AND ITS PREDECESSOR

warfare – including disarmament, the reduction of military expenditures, and the treatment of prisoners of war.

The 1899 Hague Peace Conference agenda also included the peaceful settlement of disputes. Although some suggested the establishment of a permanent court of arbitration or even a permanent international court at the disposal of states, others went further, suggesting it be *compulsory* for states to have recourse to arbitration or adjudication for at least certain types of international disputes.

Proposals to establish an international court with compulsory jurisdiction on certain matters were rejected both at the first conference in 1899 and the second conference in 1907. The objection to compulsory jurisdiction centered on two particular problems: the composition of the tribunal and its jurisdiction. Many states were unwilling to commit on such important matters in advance of a dispute. They were concerned that some disputes, especially when vital interests were at stake, were not suitable for judicial settlement. However, attempts to distinguish between what was suitable to compulsory jurisdiction and what was not were fruitless.

Instead, states established a permanent institution – the Permanent Court of Arbitration (PCA) – as part of the 1899 Convention for the Pacific Settlement of International Disputes. It was the first international adjudicative body with *some* permanent features: a permanent location, a permanent secretariat, and an administrative body composed of representatives from the different contracting parties. The creation of the PCA cemented the institutionalization of what had been, until then, an exclusively *ad hoc* process.[13]

> **1899 Convention for the Pacific Settlement of**
> **International Disputes**
>
> **Article 15**
> International arbitration has for its object the settlement of differences between States by judges of their own choice, and on the basis of respect for law.
>
> **Article 16**
> In questions of a legal nature, and especially in the interpretation or application of International Conventions, arbitration is recognized by the Signatory Powers as the most effective, and at the same time the most equitable, means of settling disputes which diplomacy has failed to settle.

---

13   Geoffrey Best, *Peace Conferences and the Century of Total War: The 1899 Hague Conferences and What Came After*, 75 Int'l Aff. 619 (1999).

Article 20
With the object of facilitating an immediate recourse to arbitration for international differences, which it has not been possible to settle by diplomacy, the Signatory Powers undertake to organize a Permanent Court of Arbitration, accessible at all times and operating, unless otherwise stipulated by the parties, in accordance with the Rules of Procedure inserted in the present Convention.

FIGURE 1.1   The formalization of international adjudication also contributed to the development of a community of experts engaged in the interpretation of international law

The PCA, which remains an important institution to this day, provides an institutional framework for the conduct of international arbitration proceedings between states, and between states and non-state actors. Recourse to arbitration via this institution is not mandatory; it is facilitated. States that designate the PCA as a venue for the resolution of their dispute remain free to choose the arbitrators (amongst a list established by the PCA), the type of procedure, and the applicable law. The PCA mainly provides logistical support. This flexibility allows states to adapt the process to the needs of the specific dispute.

Many fundamental rules and principles of modern international arbitration crystalized thanks to the PCA's work, including the tribunal's competence to settle claims regarding its own jurisdiction, the equality of the parties and their right to a fair hearing, and the finality and binding nature of arbitral awards. The codification of arbitral procedures proved useful even for proceedings conducted before panels other than the PCA, and by the eve of the First World War, the main lines of international arbitral procedure were firmly drawn. These procedural principles significantly influenced the conduct of subsequent international adjudication, and still do today.

• • •

Questions

1. Why did states choose not to endow the Permanent Court of Arbitration with mandatory jurisdiction? Was this, in your view, the right approach?
2. What elements of flexibility characterize the PCA? Why was it deemed important to maintain such flexibility?
3. What distinguishes the PCA from the Jay Treaty mechanism?
4. How did the establishment and work of the PCA contribute to the development of modern international law?

Further Reading

David D. Caron, *War and International Adjudication: Reflections on the 1899 Peace Conference*, 94 Am. J. Int'l L. 4 (2000).

Yulia Andreeva, *International Courts*, 46 Int'l L. 129, 138 (2012).

Manuel Indlekofer, International Arbitration and the Permanent Court of Arbitration (2013).

3 The Permanent Court of International Justice

The First World War left Europe in ruins with over 15 million deaths, including 6.8 million civilians.[14] The prevailing world order – set by European empires – dissolved, leaving behind much uncertainty.[15] Out of this general despair, the idea of an international organization that could serve as a safeguard against future wars gained momentum. The establishment of the League of Nations embodied the first attempt at creating a system of international governance for the purpose of maintaining peace and security.[16]

---

14 World War I: People, Politics, and Power (Britannica Educational Publishing 2010), at 219.
15 Malcolm N. Shaw, International Law (8th ed., 2017), at 22.
16 The League had two central political organs: the Council and the Assembly. The Council, the League's executive body, was composed of a number of permanent members of the

Covenant of the League of Nations

Article 8

The Members of the League recognize that the maintenance of peace requires the reduction of national armaments to the lowest point consistent with national safety and the enforcement by common action of international obligations.

Article 11

Any war or threat of war, whether immediately affecting any of the Members of the League or not, is hereby declared a matter of concern to the whole League, and the League shall take any action that may be deemed wise and effectual to safeguard the peace of nations.

Shabtai Rosenne, The Perplexities of Modern International Law[17]

It is no accident that Grotius' classic work, *De Jure Belli ac Pacis*, places war before peace. It is no accident that today's classic, Oppenheim's International Law (whatever edition), is divided into two books, the first on peace and the second on war – reversing Grotius' order. Classic international law as it developed in the Westphalian system accepted war and the violent use of force as permitted conditions of international relations, regulated by international law. That is not the approach of international law today (...)

The nineteenth century pacifist movements (...) supported the movement to develop the potentialities of international arbitration as an alternative to war. But they were not strong enough to persuade governments to outlaw war and make recourse to arbitration compulsory (...)

The Covenant of the League of Nations (1919) was a start in controlling the use of force and the right to go to war. It did not prohibit recourse to war, but tried to control it. It provided that any war, or threat of war, whether immediately affecting any of the members of the League or not, was a matter of concern to the League which should take any action that it deemed wise and effectual to

---

League – the surviving Great Powers – and a number of elected (rotating) members. The Assembly, the organization's deliberative forum, included delegates from all member states. The League was also equipped with a permanent administrative organ, the Secretariat, and endowed with its own budget.

17   Shabtai Rosenne, The Perplexities of Modern International Law: General Course on Public International Law (2001), at 118–119 (references omitted).

> safeguard the peace of the nations. The members of the League agreed that if a dispute should arise between them likely to lead to a rupture, they would submit the matter either to arbitration or to judicial settlement or to inquiry by the League Council, 'and they agree not to resort to war until three months after the award by the arbitrators or judicial decision, or the report by the Council.'

The PCIJ was created not long after the League of Nations with a similar objective in mind.

> ### *The League Council's Letter of Invitation to the Members of the Advisory Committee of Jurists*[18]
> But the court is a most essential part of the organization of the League of Nations. If it is established on sound and statesmanlike principles, it can contribute perhaps more than any other single institution to maintain the peace of the world and the supremacy of right amongst the nations.

Unlike the PCA, the PCIJ was endowed at the outset with an adjudicative function. It was, so to speak, a 'real' court.

> ### Covenant of the League of Nations
> **Article 14**
> The Council shall formulate and submit to the Members of the League for adoption plans for the establishment of a Permanent Court of International Justice. The Court shall be competent to hear and determine any dispute of an international character which the parties thereto submit to it. The Court may also give an advisory opinion upon any dispute or question referred to it by the Council or by the Assembly.

Whereas parties to a dispute could choose the law applicable when using the PCA, the PCIJ adhered to a single legal system: the rules and principles of international law. In addition, its decisions, published in yearly records, became

---

18   James Scott, The Project of a Permanent Court of International Justice and Resolutions of the Advisory Committee of Jurists, 1920 (1920, reprint. 2013), at 2–3.

14 CHAPTER 1

part-and-parcel of the corpus of international law. Judges came to consider their rulings not only in relation to the circumstances of the cases at hand, but also in terms of their influence on the development of international law more generally. Max Huber, a Judge and former President of the PCIJ, compared the court's rulings "to ships which are intended to be launched on the high seas of international criticism."[19] The publication of PCIJ decisions contributed to the development of international law beyond the decisions themselves.

Importantly, the PCIJ was not established as a formal part of the League but rather a separate entity. The Statute of the PCIJ was approved in 1921 as an independent treaty, separate from the Covenant of the League of Nations and external to the League, although intertwined.

The PCIJ was the first truly permanent international judicial forum serving all nations – even non-Members of the League. It had, in effect, the imprimatur of openness and inclusivity. A State that was not party to the Statute could still appear before the PCIJ in certain circumstances. In the *S.S. Wimbledon* case, Britain brought Germany before the PCIJ under the Treaty of Versailles, even though Germany was neither a member of the League of Nations nor a party to the Statute of the PCIJ at the time.[20] Germany did not object to jurisdiction so the PCIJ did not address its jurisdiction over Germany and proceeded to hear the case.[21]

At the time the PCIJ was established, the main issue was whether or not to grant the court compulsory jurisdiction. As previously noted, the idea had been discussed but rejected at the 1899 and 1907 Hague Conferences. Granting the court compulsory jurisdiction meant obligating states to accept its jurisdiction in all cases. In other words, consent would not be necessary to establish jurisdiction – at least for certain types of disputes. The League's Council nominated an Advisory Committee to examine this issue. The committee's report ultimately recommended compulsory jurisdiction. The Council, however, was not willing to go this far and the principle of consent remained firmly enshrined as the *only* basis for the exercise of jurisdiction by the PCIJ. As a matter of compromise, the committee's proposal to add an optional mechanism was approved, which allowed states to voluntarily confer automatic jurisdiction to the PCIJ at the time of signing or at a later date. States could, for the first

---

19   Ole Spiermann, International Legal Argument in the Permanent Court of International Justice (2005), at 275.

20   S.S. Wimbledon (Gr. Brit., Fr., Ital., Jap., Pol. v. Ger.), 1923 PCIJ (ser. A) No. 1.

21   Sienho Yee, Towards an International Law of Co-Progressiveness (2004).

time, express support for compulsory jurisdiction *ahead of the emergence of a dispute* by signing the "Protocol of Signature" adjoined to the court's statute or submitting a declaration to that effect.[22] Following the ratification of the protocol of signature by the majority of the members of the League of Nations, the Statute of the PCIJ entered into force in 1921.

> **Statute of the Permanent Court of International Justice**
> **Article 36**
> The jurisdiction of the Court comprises all cases which the parties refer to it and all matters specially provided for in treaties and conventions in force. The Members of the League of Nations and the States mentioned in the Annex to the Covenant may, either when signing or ratifying the Protocol to which the present Statute is adjoined, or at a later moment, declare that they recognize as compulsory ipso facto and without special agreement, in relation to any other Member or State accepting the same obligation, the jurisdiction of the Court in all or any of the classes of legal disputes concerning:
> (a)   the interpretation of a treaty;
> (b)   any question of international law;
> (c)   the existence of any fact which, if established, would constitute a breach of an international obligation;
> (d)   the nature or extent of the reparation to be made for the breach of an international obligation.
> The declaration referred to above may be made unconditionally or on condition of reciprocity on the part of several or certain Members or States, or for a certain time. In the event of a dispute as to whether the Court has jurisdiction, the matter shall be settled by the decision of the Court.

This commitment, whether expressed in the protocol or a declaration, applied only between nations that opted to make such a declaration. Reciprocity was critical; jurisdiction could only be established when all parties made unilateral declarations and only if the declarations did not harbor reservations about the issue at hand. For example, under this mechanism, if Norway's declaration was unconditional and France's declaration excluded financial issues, France could not bring a dispute with Norway over an unpaid debt. This is because the commitment to financial issues was not mutual. The content and form of each

---

22   Statute of the Permanent Court of International Justice, Article 36, Dec. 16, 1920, 6 U.N.T.S. 391.

declaration was determined by the state and each state enjoyed full discretion to devise its own criteria for the disputes that qualified for PCIJ jurisdiction.

It was a major innovation in international practice, but time was required for states to adjust. The use of the 'optional clause' mechanism was slow and, when states began submitting declarations, they often did so halfheartedly by including many reservations and safeguards. Nevertheless, by the end of 1939, more than 40 states had accepted the PCIJ's compulsory jurisdiction – a very high percentage of the members of the League of Nations at the time.[23]

As per Article 36 of its statute, the PCIJ could settle four types of disputes: (1) disputes as to the interpretation of a treaty; (2) disputes as to any question of international law; (3) disputes as to the existence of any fact which, if established, would constitute a breach of any international obligation; and (4) disputes as to the extent and nature of the reparation to be made for any such breach. The four categories, taken together, were broad enough to cover every international *dispute*, but still sufficiently particular to exclude instances of benign *tension*. This formula proved fruitful and was later transcribed with little to no changes into the Statute of the International Court of Justice (henceforth ICJ Statute).[24]

States' long-standing yearning for an international body capable of resolving legal disputes materialized under the League of Nations' roof and protection. Though the PCIJ was not an official part of the League, in practice the two bodies were guided by the same desire to establish "a broad legal – some would say legalistic – basis for the maintenance of international peace and security."[25] The PCIJ stood in a special, and to some extent distanced, position from the League's political organs. Notwithstanding, it was "a necessary part of the machinery" and possibly "the strongest."[26]

4   The PCIJ's Achievements

As the first court and institution of its kind, the PCIJ achieved much more than its creators expected. Thanks to the permanence of the institution and the accumulation of practice, the PCIJ made tremendous advances in international judicial procedure. Building on the experience of international arbitration and domestic principles of procedure within states, international adjudication acquired a much-needed autonomy.

---

23   Shabtai Rosenne, *The Permanent Court of International Justice*, Max Planck Encyclopedia of Public International Law (2006).

24   Statute of the International Court of Justice, 26 June 1945, 33 U.N.T.S. 993.

25   Shabtai Rosenne, *Codification Revisited after 50 Years*, 2 Max Planck Y.B.U.N.L. 1 (1998).

26   David Hunter Miller, The Drafting of the Covenant, vol. 1 (1928), at 13.

Ole Spiermann, *International Legal Argument in the Permanent Court of International Justice*[27]

Simply because the Permanent Court was first, it formulated some often-quoted statements regarding international adjudication, which, as remarked by Sir Robert Jennings, make for the draftsman an easy initial run. For example, in the *Mavrommatis* case, the Permanent Court defined a dispute as 'a disagreement on a point of law or fact, a conflict of legal views or of interests between two persons'; in the *Eastern Carelia* opinion, it held that '[t]he Court, being a Court of Justice, cannot, even in giving advisory opinions, depart from the essential rules guiding their activity as a Court'; in the *Free Zones* case, it stated that 'the judicial settlement of international disputes, with a view to which the Court has been established, is simply an alternative to the direct and friendly settlement of such disputes between the Parties'; and, in the *Electricity Company* case, it pronounced that 'the parties to a case must abstain from any measure capable of exercising a prejudicial effect in regard to the execution of the decision to be given and, in general, not allow any step of any kind to be taken which might aggravate or extend the dispute'.

The Permanent Court put international law into practice, and it did so within a novel context. No permanent international court preceded the Permanent Court, while a number of international courts have taken over and carried on other projects of international justice. (...)

In erecting this new edifice, the judges had to care about the disputes to come as well as the past and the actual dispute before them. There is no doubt that the eleven men who met in the Peace Palace in 1922 saw themselves as being in an unprecedented situation. Whereas subsequent international courts have been able to draw on an ever-expanding repository of judicial precedent, the Permanent Court was often left without any such guidance (and thus also without any such means of rationalising or embellishing its decisions). Indeed, parts of the International Court's work cannot be properly appreciated without thorough knowledge of the Permanent Court, while the opposite does not apply.

---

27 See *supra* note 19, at 20–21 (references omitted).

18   CHAPTER 1

In less than twenty years, the PCIJ delivered thirty-two judgments and twenty-seven advisory opinions, amounting to an average of nearly three major judicial pronouncements per year. A closer look shows that the numbers would have been higher were it not for the outbreak of World War II. Over two thirds of the cases were filed between 1922 and 1932, in the heyday of the League of Nations, until the prospect of war permeated the political atmosphere. After the Nazis came to power only sixteen new cases were filed over seven years. This sharp decline in caseload indicates that resort to litigation is influenced not only by the institution itself, but also by global geopolitical changes. The PCIJ's influence and authority was severely weakened and eventually crippled by the hostile and tense climate that clouded Europe after Hitler came to power. In the years leading up to World War II, the activity of the PCIJ sharply diminished, eventually reaching a standstill not long after the official commencement of the war in September 1939. Even though the PCIJ was not able to prevent World War II, it kept some form of control and stability during the volatile years before the war erupted.

> **Compulsory Jurisdiction and Defiance in the World Court: A Comparison of the PCIJ and the ICJ[28]**
>
> Up a certain point, we can see great similarities in state behavior toward third party adjudication between the PCIJ and the ICJ. Both Courts saw their busiest periods in the decade or decade and one-half after their creation. At this point, both Courts began to experience a decline in the number of cases presented to them. The reasons for the decline in the numbers of cases for the two Courts seem to be similar, and both seem to be related to the perceived instability of the international system at the time. With the PCIJ, the decline in business is coincident with, and seems dependent upon, the uncertainties generated by the major international financial crisis begun in 1929 and the rise of National Socialist Germany after 1933.

All that said, the 'real' measure of its worth is not found in the number of cases decided by the PCIJ (though that is not to be belittled) or in its contribution to the development of the law (a by-product of the activity of all courts in all

---

28   Gary L. Scott and Karen D. Csajko, *Compulsory Jurisdiction and Defiance in the World Court: A Comparison of the PCIJ and the ICJ*, 16 Denv. J. Int'l L. & Pol'y 377 (1988), at 387.

legal systems), but in the widely-held satisfaction at its performance. When the League of Nations was dismantled and the United Nations took its place, it was never suggested that the PCIJ outlived its usefulness and should be disbanded. On the contrary, states wished to increase the effectiveness of the PCIJ and strengthen its ties with the new international organization.[29] They wanted judicial activities to resume where they tapered off in 1939. It was never seriously proposed that the PCIJ be replaced, that it failed its primary mission, or that its structure was fundamentally faulty.

•••

Questions

1. How was the PCIJ different from the PCA? Consider these institutions' composition, role, and legacy.[30]

2. Would you qualify the PCIJ's non-compulsory jurisdiction as a strength or a weakness? Why would a state want to submit to compulsory jurisdiction? Would your answer differ if given in 1945?

3. How can the experience of the PCIJ be of value today in understanding the potential and limits of the international judicial function? Specifically, what does the PCIJ teach us about the relationship between justice, peace, and politics?

4. "The PCIJ's influence and authority was severely weakened and eventually crippled by the hostile and tensed climate that beclouded Europe after Hitler came to power." What does this mean regarding the function of a "world" court? Can/should its role be affected by events taking place internationally?

5. In 1988, Scott and Csajko wrote that "[b]oth Courts saw their busiest periods in the decade or decade and one-half after their creation" and that, "[a]t this point, both Courts began to experience a decline in the number of cases presented to them." Consider the activity of the ICJ as broken down in the table below. Do you agree with the authors' statements as it relates to the ICJ?

---

29   The Statute of the International Court of Justice: A Commentary (Andreas Zimmermann, Christian Tomuschat, eds., (3rd ed., 2019)), Introduction (Sir Robert Jennings, Dame Rosalyn Higgins, and Peter Tomka), at 5.

30   *See Id.* at 95.

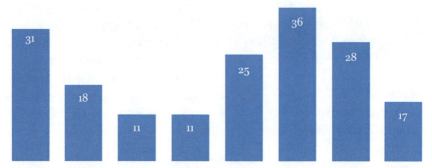

FIGURE 1.2   ICJ activity by decade (contentious cases – including discontinued cases, and advisory opinions). (Note that for 1996–2005, the total number includes 11 cases brought simultaneously by Serbia.)

Further Reading

Russell D. Greene, *The Progress of the Permanent Court of International Justice*, 6 St. John's L. Rev. 226 (1932).

United Nations: Report of the Informal Inter-Allied Committee on the Future of the Permanent Court of International Justice, 39 Am. J. Int'l L. 1 (1945).

Ruth C. Lawson, *The Problem of the Compulsory Jurisdiction of the World Court*, 46 Am. J. Int'l L. 219 (1952).

Ole Spiermann, *A Permanent Court of International Justice*, 72 Nordic J. Int'l L. 399 (2003).

Shabtai Rosenne, *The Permanent Court of International Justice*, Max Planck Encyclopedia of International Law (2006).

W.C. van der Wolf and C. Tofan, The Permanent Court of International Justice: Its History and Landmark Cases (2011).

Legacies of the Permanent Court of International Justice (Malgosia Fitzmaurice and Christian Tams eds., 2013).

B   Legal Underpinnings

1   *The Establishment of the United Nations*

In the midst of World War II, the British government invited a group of international legal experts to discuss the future of the PCIJ. The twelve members of the Informal Inter-Allied Committee on the Future of the Permanent Court of International Justice met nine times in one year, and submitted their report in February 1944. The committee's review of the PCIJ's work was positive, as

THE INTERNATIONAL COURT OF JUSTICE AND ITS PREDECESSOR

was its assessment of the Statute. However, the question of whether the PCIJ should resume its operations was left unanswered: the committee thought it was a political rather than legal matter and, therefore, beyond its competence. The committee did note that any future activity of the court required a new international agreement since the League of Nations was unlikely to reconvene in its original form following the war.

> ### Report of the Informal Inter-Allied Committee on the Future of the Permanent Court of International Justice[31]
>
> We accordingly recommend that the organic connection which has existed between the Permanent Court of International Justice and the League should not be continued. This does not mean, however, that there should be no connection between the Court and the General International Organization at all. In our view, the Court should be regarded as part of the machinery at the disposal of the Organization, and this would appear to be consistent with such proposals as have been made in connection with the Organization, which, so far as our knowledge goes, all seem to contemplate the existence of an International Court as part of its machinery. Once the Court has been established, it would be open to the International Organization to make such use of it as it thought fit; it could, for instance, provide in its own constitution the conditions in which its members would be bound to submit disputes of a justiciable character to the Court, and it might similarly prescribe any measures which it thought appropriate for ensuring that the decisions of the Court were effectively complied with.

Meanwhile, at Dumbarton Oaks, a group of nations gathered to discuss the future of international relations. China, Great Britain, the Soviet Union, and the United States agreed on a blueprint for a new international organization – the United Nations (UN) – to replace the League of Nations, and on the creation of a court within this organization. This international court would be the principal judicial organ of the new international organization and all members of that organization would automatically be parties to its Statute.

---

31 Report of the Informal Inter-Allied Committee on the Future of the Permanent Court of International Justice, 39 American Journal of International Law (S1) 1(1945).

> *Proposals for the Establishment of a General International Organization*[32]
>
> **Chapter 2: Principles**
>
> (...)
>
> All members of the Organization shall settle their disputes by peaceful means in such a manner that international peace and security are not endangered.
>
> **Chapter 7: An International Court of Justice**
>
> 1. There should be an international court of justice which should constitute the principal judicial organ of the Organization.
>
> 2. The court should be constituted and should function in accordance with a statute which should be annexed to and be a part of the Charter of the Organization.
>
> 3. The statute of the court of international justice should be either (a) the Statute of the Permanent Court of International Justice, continued in force with such modifications as may be desirable or (b) a new statute in the preparation of which the Statute of the Permanent Court of International Justice should be used as a basis.
>
> 4. All members of the Organization should *ipso facto* be parties to the statute of the international court of justice.
>
> 5. Conditions under which states not members of the Organization may become parties to the statute of the international court of justice should be determined in each case by the General Assembly upon recommendation of the Security Council.

After further work and negotiations, the Charter of the United Nations and the ICJ Statute were finalized at the San Francisco Conference in 1945. Fifty states participated, more than 3,500 delegates and staff members took part in the conference, and at least 2,500 journalists covered the event.[33] At last, the efforts of the four Allied Powers came to fruition and the Charter of the United Nations as well as the ICJ Statute were unanimously adopted on June 25, 1945.[34]

---

32 Dumbarton Oaks, Proposals for the Establishment of a General International Organization, Ch. 2 and 7, Oct. 7, 1944, available at http://www.ibiblio.org/pha/policy/1944/441007a .html.

33 *1945: The San Francisco Conference*, United Nations, available at http://www.un.org/en /sections/history-united-nations-charter/1945-san-francisco-conference/index.html.

34 *See A Great Day*, UN Radio Classics, available at https://www.un.org/en/sections/history -united-nations-charter/1945-san-francisco-conference/index.html; *Founding of the UN-San Francisco Conference*, available at https://www.flickr.com/photos/un_photo/sets

THE INTERNATIONAL COURT OF JUSTICE AND ITS PREDECESSOR

• • •

Questions

1. Why was it so important for states to include an adjudication body in the new organization and make member states of the organization automatically party to the Statute of the new International Court of Justice? What does it say about the legacy of the PCIJ?

2. Why did states decide to create a new court rather than reinvigorate the existing PCIJ?

Further Reading

Grayson Kirk and Lawrence H. Chamberlain, *The Organization of the San Francisco Conference*, 60 Pol. Sci. Q. 321 (1945).

Shabtai Rosenne, *The Court and the Judicial Process*, 19 Int'l Org. 518 (1965).

Edward Gordon, *The ICJ: On Its Own*, 40 Denv. J. Intl'l L. & Pol'y 74 (2012).

2   The UN Charter and the ICJ Statute

The PCIJ met in October 1945 for the last time to discuss the transfer of its archives. The judges resigned a few months later and the PCIJ was officially dissolved when the League of Nations voted itself out of existence in April 1946. On the same day, the new International Court of Justice held its inaugural meeting in The Hague. The elected President was Judge José Gustavo Guerrero – the last president of the PCIJ.

The ICJ is composed of fifteen judges, including a President and a Vice-President. Judges *ad hoc* may be appointed when a party to a contentious case does not have a judge of its nationality on the bench.[35]

The Registrar plays a key role in ensuring the proper functioning of the Court and managing communications between the Court and the UN on one hand, and the Court and states, on the other hand. Mr. Philippe Couvreur, pictured in his office below, served as Registrar for more than nineteen years.

/72157616945763028 (collection of historic photos chronicling the founding of the UN and the adoption of the ICJ Statute).

35   For more information on judges *ad hoc*, see Rosalyn Higgins, Philippa Webb, Dapo Akande, Sandesh Sivakumaran, and James Sloan, OPPENHEIM'S INTERNATIONAL LAW: UNITED NATIONS (2017), at 1143–1157.

FIGURE 1.3   Judges
SOURCE: JEROEN BOUMAN, PHOTOGRAPHER

ICJ Statute

Article 21
1. The Court shall elect its President and Vice-President for three years; they may be re-elected.
2. The Court shall appoint its Registrar and may provide for the appointment of such other officers as may be necessary.

Articles 1(2) and (3) of the Rules of the Court

For the purposes of a particular case, the Court may also include upon the Bench one or more persons chosen under Article 31 of the Statute to sit as judges *ad hoc*.

In the following Rules, the term "Member of the Court" denotes any elected judge; the term "judge" denotes any Member of the Court, and any judge *ad hoc*.

FIGURE 1.4 Office of the President, picturing President Dame Rosalyn Higgins (the first woman appointed as a Judge to the ICJ, and who also served as President between 2006 and 2009) (credit: Jeroen Bouman)

Besides a few minimal modifications, the ICJ Statute is by and large a faithful reproduction of the Statute of the Permanent Court of International Justice. The Charter of the United Nations, on the other hand, was created practically *ex nihilo* and borrowed little from the Covenant of the League of Nations. The ICJ Statute was annexed to the Charter of the United Nations and, accordingly, forms an indispensable part of the organization's constitutive document.[36] The two documents should be read as one instrument.[37] Most remarkably, as a principal organ of the United Nations, the new court stands on equal footing with other key organs of the United Nations.[38]

---

36   *See* The Statute of the International Court of Justice: A Commentary, *supra* note 28, at 96.
37   This is evident among other things in the fact that the revision of the Statute is accomplished in the same manner as the revision of the Charter. *See also* Shabtai Rosenne, The Law and Practice Of The International Court, vol. 1, 1920–2005 (5th ed., 2016, edited by Malcolm Shaw), para. 23; *Ambatielos Case* (Greece v. UK), 1952 I.C.J. 40, Judgment (McNair, J. dissenting) (asking not to place much emphasis on the word 'annex' itself but on the intention of the contracting parties to incorporate the statute into the Charter).
38   *See Main Organs*, United Nations, available at http://www.un.org/en/sections/about-un/main-organs/.

FIGURE 1.5   Office of the Registrar

Charter of the United Nations
Article 7
1. There are established as principal organs of the United Nations: a General Assembly, a Security Council, an Economic and Social Council, a Trusteeship Council, an International Court of Justice and a Secretariat.
2. Such subsidiary organs as may be found necessary may be established in accordance with the present Charter.

Article 92
The International Court of Justice shall be the principal judicial organ of the United Nations. It shall function in accordance with the annexed Statute, which is based upon the Statute of the Permanent Court of International Justice and forms an integral part of the present Charter.

ICJ Statute
Article 1
The International Court of Justice established by the Charter of the United Nations as the principal judicial organ of the United Nations shall be constituted and shall function in accordance with the provisions of the present Statute.

THE INTERNATIONAL COURT OF JUSTICE AND ITS PREDECESSOR

The decision to establish the ICJ as an integral organ of the UN was a conceptual breakthrough. The international community realized that an effective international court could not operate as an independent institution and needed "to be closely geared to the requirements of the political community which it is designed to serve."[39]

The implications of this institutional constellation on the ICJ are profound. As an organ of the UN, the ICJ operates within the framework of the general purposes and principles of the UN as set out in the Charter. Judge Philadelpho Azevedo said that the Court, "which had been raised to the status of a principal organ, and thus more closely geared into the mechanism" of the UN, "must do its utmost to co-operate with the other organs with a view to attaining the aims and principles that have been set forth."[40]

The Statute ensures judicial continuity with the PCIJ in two important ways. First, the precedents created by the PCIJ remain valid contributions to international law; second, treaties and conventions conferring jurisdiction on the PCIJ are interpreted as giving jurisdiction to the ICJ.[41]

> **ICJ Statute**
>
> **Article 37**
> Whenever a treaty or convention in force provides for reference of a matter to a tribunal to have been instituted by the League of Nations, or to the Permanent Court of International Justice, the matter shall, as between the parties to the present Statute, be referred to the International Court of Justice.

Once again, during the creation of the ICJ, questions arose as to whether to grant the new court compulsory jurisdiction. The majority of small countries participating in the San Francisco Conference were in favor of the proposal. However, larger states, especially the Soviet Union and the United States, opposed any radical change. Eventually, all proposals to entrust the Court with automatic jurisdiction over certain disputes were rejected, and consensual

---

39   Shabtai Rosenne, The Law and Practice of The International Court, 1920–2005 (5th ed. 2016, edited by Malcolm Shaw), at 161.

40   *Interpretation of Peace Treaties with Bulgaria, Hungary and Romania* (First Phase), Advisory Opinion, Sep. Op. Azevedo, I.C.J. Reports 1950, p. 79, para. 8. See also, *infra* Chapter 3.

41   *See also* The Statute of the International Court of Justice: A Commentary, *supra* note 28, at 799.

jurisdiction similar to the PCIJ was retained.[42] Membership in the United Nations, therefore, does not automatically confer jurisdiction on the Court, unless express consent is given to that effect, as explained further in Chapter 2.

●●●

Questions

1. In the ICJ's design, what features point to the Court's intimate relationship with the UN and what features point to its independence from the UN?[43]
2. From the standpoint of international adjudication, does the establishment of the ICJ mean rupture or continuity? Why?

Further Reading

Manley O. Hudson, *The Succession of the International Court of Justice to the Permanent Court of International Justice*, 51 Am. J. Int'l L. 569 (1957).

Robert Kolb, The International Court of Justice (2013).

Cosette Creamer and Zuzanna Godzimirska, *The Job Market for Justice: Screening and Selecting Candidates for the International Court of Justice*, 30 Leiden Journal of International Law 947 (2017).

Conclusion

International adjudication certainly witnessed significant changes, evolving from an *ad hoc* mechanism to a permanent, well-settled court. The continued existence of an international judicial mechanism over the past century suggests a basic agreement by states on the need for an international court capable of resolving disputes, creating case law, and opining on international legal matters. The ICJ is far from perfect; it suffers from enforcement limitations, it cannot solve all legal issues arising in the international arena absent

---

42   For the Dumbarton Oaks Proposals, *see Documents of the United Nations Conference on International Organization* (hereafter UNCIO), vol. III. For the records of the Washington Committee of Jurists, in session between 9–20 April 1945, *see* UNCIO Docs., vol. XIV. A selection of documents illustrating the work of this Committee is contained in *The International Court of Justice, Selected Documents relating to the Drafting of the Statute*, Dep't of State, Pub. 2491, Ser. 84 (1946). For the records of Committee IV, *see* UNCIO Docs., vol. XIII. *See also The United Nations Conference on International Organization*, selected documents, Department of State, Publication 2490, Conference Series 83 (1946). For a comprehensive index to the proceedings of the San Francisco Conference, *see* UNCIO Docs. vol. XXI.

43   *See* The Statute of the International Court of Justice: A Commentary, *supra* note 28, at 5.

FIGURE 1.6 The Peace Palace, in The Hague, is the home of the ICJ
SOURCE: JEROEN BOUMAN, PHOTOGRAPHER

consensual jurisdiction, and it remains a state-centric institution. This last point, in particular, raises questions about the Court's future in a world where non-state actors play a growing role and are likely to be increasingly embroiled or affected by international legal issues.

The creation of a multitude of additional international judicial institutions alongside the ICJ only reinforces these concerns. The Court has adapted to the changing landscape of international law by asserting the value of its precedents and reminding the international community of its unique features. The Court has even added a sentence to its press releases to distinguish itself from other institutions – many of which also have their seat in The Hague.[44]

Despite the deep changes that have impacted the fabric of the international community since the Court's establishment, its has succeeded in portraying itself as a pillar of stability within and beyond the United Nations. Its activity and prestige have not suffered as a result of, for example, the incremental increase in UN membership over the years. The community of states has almost quadrupled since the Court's establishment – yet the Court continues to serve this growing constituency unabated.

---

44 See, *infra* Chapter 4 (I).

CHAPTER 2

The International Court of Justice and States

The International Court of Justice was created by states and for states. States mainly use the Court as a mechanism for the peaceful settlement of disputes. In such situations the ICJ serves as a court of law of first and last resort: the adjudicatory process culminates with a final and binding solution the parties must comply with. This type of interaction, known as contentious jurisdiction, forms the crux of this chapter.

Additional opportunities for states to interact with the Court arise when the Court is asked to provide legal advice to states and UN organs on international legal issues in the exercise of its advisory jurisdiction (those are addressed in Chapter 3).

Neither the Court nor states are monolithic and homogeneous entities; endless factors bear on decisions taken by the Court and by states. The relationship between states and the Court is therefore a complex one. As noted above, this chapter focuses on the main type of interaction between states and the Court: the peaceful settlement of international disputes, namely the exercise of the Court's contentious jurisdiction.

The UN Charter enjoins its member states to settle disputes peacefully, allowing states to choose the method of dispute settlement.[1] The ICJ is only one of many methods of peaceful dispute settlement available to states, alongside an array of international and regional fora that produce both binding and non-binding outcomes. This wide range of options means that the decision to submit a dispute to the ICJ not only symbolizes the parties' willingness to resolve their dispute peacefully but also entails a vote of confidence in the Court itself.

> *Joan E. Donoghue, The Role of the World Court Today*[2]
> The ICJ must be seen as one component of a larger international legal system, one that is loosely integrated, complex, and sometimes bewildering and that differs markedly from national legal systems. In many situations, the role of the ICJ in settling specific disputes is best understood

---

1   UN Charter, Article 33.
2   Joan E. Donoghue, *The Role of the World Court Today*, 47 Georgia L. Rev. 181 (2012), at 192. *See also Diplomatic Protection and the International Court of Justice*, Sibley Lecture Ser. (2012), available at http://digitalcommons.law.uga.edu/sibley_lectures/1/.

© KONINKLIJKE BRILL NV, LEIDEN, 2020 | DOI:10.1163/9789004226968_004

THE INTERNATIONAL COURT OF JUSTICE AND STATES   31

> when the Court is seen as one actor within a set of nested and overlapping institutions comprising the international legal system. After all, the UN Charter not only established a principal judicial organ, but it also set up other UN organs, including the Security Council and the General Assembly. (...) [M]any new institutions have blossomed in the intervening decades – both inside and outside of the UN system. Some have been comprised of governments, while others have been independent of them. National courts can also play an important role in addressing some disputes arising under international law.

The Court has shown awareness of its role among the other available diplomatic, judicial, and quasi-judicial channels otherwise available to states:

> ### Passage through the Great Belt Case[3]
> the judicial settlement of international disputes, with a view to which the Court has been established, is simply an alternative to the direct and friendly settlement of such disputes between the Parties; consequently it is for the Court to facilitate, so far as is compatible with its Statute, such direct and friendly settlement, and any negotiation between the parties with a view to achieving a direct and friendly settlement is to be welcomed.[3]

Its adjudicative function undoubtedly offers the Court ample opportunity to interact with states.

A   Access to the Court: States Only

Only states may appear as parties before the Court.[4] This rule is axiomatic.[5] It remains true even though non-state actors play a significant role in the international scene and have been granted rights and obligations under

---

3   *Passage through the Great Belt Case* (Finland v. Denmark), Provisional Measures, Order of 29 July 1991, I.C.J. Reports 1991, p. 12, para. 35.
4   ICJ Statute, Article 34.
5   This strict limitation has its roots in dispute settlement itself, often resolving disagreements as to the interpretation and validity of treaties to which non State actors cannot be parties. In addition, the Permanent Court of Arbitration – which did allow the adjudication of claims between states and nonstate actors – was already in existence at the time of the

32   CHAPTER 2

international law.[6] Accordingly, the Court's contentious jurisdiction can only be set in motion by states; its judgments, endowed with the authority of the *res judicata*, are only formally binding upon states.

All states may have access to the Court, including those that are not members of the UN. A State that is not a member of the UN may become a party to the Statute of the Court, based on a Security Council recommendation to the General Assembly, as provided in Article 93(2) of the UN Charter. Five states became party to the ICJ Statute before they were members of the United Nations: Japan, Liechtenstein, San Marino, Switzerland, and Nauru.[7] Even a state that is not a party to the Statute may access the Court if it accepts the conditions laid down by Security Council Resolution 9 of 1946.[8] The resolution places those states, for the purposes of the case at hand, on equal footing with the state parties to the Statute, including the obligation to comply with the Court's decision.

> **Security Council Resolution 9 (1946)**
>
> The International Court of Justice shall be open to a State which is not a party to the Statute of the International Court of Justice, upon the following condition, namely, that such State shall previously have deposited with the Registrar of the Court a declaration by which it accepts jurisdiction of the Court, in accordance with the Charter of the United Nations and with the terms and subject to the conditions of the Statute and Rules of the Court, and undertakes to comply in good faith with the decision or decisions of the Court and to accept all the obligations of a Member of the United Nations under Article 94 of the Charter.

Though access to the Court is reserved exclusively to states, the interests of an individual could form the subject-matter of a dispute before the ICJ. This happens when a state espouses the claim of one of its nationals in the exercise of the right to diplomatic protection. The litigation proceeds exclusively between

---

   creation of the PCIJ, as explained in Chapter 1. I am indebted to Christopher Borgen for these points.

6 For a discussion of how non-state actors have been granted greater access to the Court in advisory proceedings, *see infra* Chapter 4.

7 They were parties to the Statute of the Court from 2 April 1954 to 18 December 1956, from 29 March 1950 to 18 September 1990, from 18 February 1954 to 2 March 1992, from 28 July 1948 to 10 September 2002, and from 29 January 1988 to 14 September 1999, respectively. These states are now all members of the UN.

8 *See also*, Article 35(2) of the UN Charter and Article 41 of the Rules.

THE INTERNATIONAL COURT OF JUSTICE AND STATES 33

the two governments concerned, as one state seeks to uphold the rights of its nationals and obtain a remedy for the wrongful act allegedly caused by the other state:

> By taking up the case of one of its subjects and by resorting to diplomatic protection or international judicial proceedings on his behalf, a State is in reality asserting its own rights – its right to ensure, in the person of its subjects, respect for the rules of international law.[9]

The ICJ has heard claims based on diplomatic protection on repeated occasions.[10] In 1962, Belgium filed an application against the Spanish government alleging that actions of the Spanish government violated international law and the rights of Belgian nationals who were shareholders in a Spanish company.[11] Similarly, Mexico filed suit against the United States alleging that the United States violated its international legal obligations when it sentenced fifty-four Mexican nationals to the death penalty.[12] Mexico espoused the claims of its nationals and alleged, on their behalf, that their rights were violated by the United States.

The Court's contentious jurisdiction remains out of reach to international organizations and other non-state actors.[13] In one notable exception, the 1986 Vienna Convention on the Law of Treaties between States and International Organizations or between International Organizations envisages the settlement of a dispute between a state (or states) and an international organization

---

9   *Mavrommatis Palestine Concessions* (Greece v. U.K.), Judgment, 1924 PCIJ (ser. A) No. 2 (Aug. 30).

10   *See Ambatielos* (Greece v. U.K.), Judgment, Preliminary Objection, I.C.J. Reports 1952, p. 28; *Anglo-Iranian Oil Co.* (U.K. v. Iran), Preliminary Objection, I.C.J. Reports 1952, p. 112 (Liechtenstein v. Guatemala), I.C.J. Reports 1955, p. 4; *Norwegian Loans* (France v. Norway), I.C.J. Reports 1957, p. 9; *Interhandel* (Switz. v. US), I.C.J. Reports 1959, p.6; *Case concerning the Application of the Convention of 1902 governing the Guardianship of Infants* (Netherlands v. Sweden), I.C.J. Reports 1958, p. 55; *Elettronica Sicula S.P.A.* (*ELSI*) (US v. Italy), I.C.J. Reports 1989, p. 15; *Breard* (Paraguay v. US), I.C.J. Reports 1998, p. 99; *La Grand* (Germany v. US), I.C.J. Reports 2001, p. 466; *Certain Property* (Liechtenstein v. Germany), I.C.J. Reports 2005, p. 19; *Ahmadou Sadio Diallo* (Rep. of Guinea v. Dem. Rep. of Congo), I.C.J. Reports 2010. p. 639. This practice contrasts with that of the European Court of Human Rights. *See* Shabtai Rosenne, An International Law Miscellany (1993), at 111.

11   *Case Concerning Barcelona Traction, Light & Power Company, Ltd.* (Belgium v. Spain), Judgment, I.C.J. Reports 1964, p. 6, at 2–3.

12   *Case Concerning Avena and Other Mexican Nationals* (Mexico v. United States), I.C.J. Reports 2004, p. 12.

13   As explained *infra* in Chapter 3, advisory jurisdiction offers greater avenue for non-state participation.

(or between organizations) by the ICJ.[14] Importantly, however, that treaty has not yet entered into force.

> **The Vienna Convention on the Law of Treaties between States and International Organizations or between International Organizations**
> **Article 66**
> If, under paragraph 3 of Article 65, no solution has been reached within a period of twelve months following the date on which the objection was raised, the procedures specified in the following paragraphs shall be followed.
>
> (...)
>
> (a) If a state is a party to the dispute with one or more states, it may, by a written application, submit the dispute to the International Court of Justice for a decision;
>
> (b) If a state is a party to the dispute to which one or more international organizations are parties, the State may, through a Member State of the United Nations if necessary, request the General Assembly or the Security Council or, where appropriate, the competent organ of an international organization which is a party to the dispute and is authorized in accordance with Article 96 of the Charter of the United Nations, to request an advisory opinion of the International Court of Justice in accordance with Article 65 of the Statute of the Court.
>
> (...)
>
> (e) The advisory opinion given pursuant to sub-paragraph (b), (c) or (d) shall be accepted as decisive by all the parties to the dispute concerned.

Another noteworthy development took place in 2018, when Palestine initiated proceedings against the United States for relocating the United States embassy to Jerusalem.[15] Since 2012, Palestine has been designated by the UN General Assembly as a non-member observer state within the organization – a status that falls short of full UN membership but does enable Palestine to

---

14 UN Doc. A/CONF.129/15, *in* 25 I.L.M. 543 (1986). *See* Shabtai Rosenne, Developments in the Law of Treaties 1945–1956 (1989), at 317–324.

15 *See Application Instituting Proceedings* (Palestine v. United States) (Sept. 28, 2018), available at https://www.icj-cij.org/files/case-related/176/176-20180928-APP-01-00-EN.pdf. *See also, infra* Chapter 4.

sign and ratify international treaties.[16] This case will certainly influence the future relationship of the Court with non-state actors, aspirant states, and states-in-the-making.

As states created the Court to serve their own needs, any appearance or involvement of a non-state actor in the Court's business is fortuitous in contentious cases. The ICJ exists because states want it to exist and the Court will intervene in the settlement of a dispute only if states agree to its intervention.

•••

Question
Given the expansion of international law to new actors and new areas since the Court was created in 1946, should non-state actors get access to the Court and, if so, which ones and why? Consider multi-national corporations, individuals, and international organizations

B   The Principle of Consent

The Court can hear disputes on any international legal question. This broad jurisdiction distinguishes the ICJ from other international courts and tribunals whose jurisdiction is often limited to specific subject-matters. For example, the International Tribunal for the Law of the Sea only settles disputes arising out of the UN Convention on the Law of the Sea.

> **ICJ Statute**
>
> **Article 36(1)**
> The jurisdiction of the Court comprises all cases which the parties refer to it and all matters specially provided for in the Charter of the United Nations or in treaties or conventions in force.

The cases heard by the ICJ in the past decade illustrate the breadth of its competence. The Court has addressed international legal issues as varied as territorial delimitation (*Temple of Preah Vihear* (Cambodia v. Thailand)),

---

16   UNGA A/RES/67/19 (Dec. 4, 2012).

maritime delimitation (*Maritime Delimitation in the Black Sea* (Romania v. Ukraine)), the distribution of natural resources (*Construction of a Road in Costa Rica along the San Juan River* (Nicaragua v. Costa Rica)), racial discrimination (*Application of the International Convention on the Elimination of All Forms of Racial Discrimination* (Georgia v. Russian Federation)), consular activities (*Case Concerning Avena and other Mexican Nationals* (Mexico v. United States of America)), universal jurisdiction (*Certain Criminal Proceedings in France* (Republic of Congo v. France)), and political asylum (*Asylum Case* (Colombia v. Peru)).

> **The Lotus Case (France v. Turkey)[17]**
> International law governs relations between independent States. The rules of law binding upon States therefore emanate from their own free will as expressed in conventions or by usages generally accepted as express-ing principles of law and established in order to regulate the relations between these co-existing independent communities or with a view to the achievement of common aims. Restrictions upon the independence of States cannot therefore be presumed.

Though not limited in scope, the International Court of Justice's authority to settle a dispute is conditioned upon the consent of the parties. Neither the Charter of the United Nations, nor any general rule of international law obligates states to refer their legal disputes to the Court (or even settle their disputes, for that matter!). This is because the Court's jurisdiction is premised on the sacrosanct principle of consent; only when consent is given can the Court examine a case. Like many other aspects of international law, the prin-ciple of consent seeks to protect state sovereignty.

According to Article 36(1) states are obligated to refer a dispute to the ICJ if they committed to doing so in (1) a treaty whose subject-matter relates to the dispute at hand, or (2) an optional clause declaration. States may also decide to turn to the ICJ following the emergence of a dispute, even if they had not agreed to submit the dispute to the Court in earlier instruments.

When the UN Charter and the Statute of the Court were adopted, states rejected proposals entrusting the Court with automatic jurisdiction over cer-tain disputes. Even though all members of the UN Charter are automatically party to the ICJ Statute, there was still an interest in limiting the reach of the Court.

---

17   *Lotus Case* (Fra. v. Turk.), 1927 P.C.I.J. (ser. A) No. 10.

THE INTERNATIONAL COURT OF JUSTICE AND STATES

Once consent is given, resort to the Court is mandatory and its decision is final and binding, with no opportunity for appeal.[18] The Court must therefore establish its jurisdiction over each case before it can examine the substance of the case. Even if the subject-matter of the dispute is extremely grave or far-reaching, the Court is only competent to adjudicate when both the Applicant and the Respondent agree to have *this specific dispute* adjudicated by the Court.

Given the importance of establishing the Court's jurisdiction prior to adjudication, contentious cases before the Court often consist of two phases: (1) a jurisdictional phase during which the Court establishes its jurisdiction, followed by (2) a merits phase during which the Court decides the substance of the dispute. This explains why the Court sometimes renders two judgements in a given case (for example in *Case Concerning Military and Paramilitary Activities in and Against Nicaragua*[19] and in *Case Concerning Oil Platforms*[20]). About half of the Court's judgments were rendered in such fashion, with a pronouncement on jurisdiction preceding a pronouncement on the merits.

Whether the Court deals with jurisdiction as part of its decisions on the merits or in a separate judgment, it has competence to delineate the contours of its own competence (a principle typically known as *competence-competence*). Article 36(6) of the Statute provides that "[i]n the event of a dispute as to whether the Court has jurisdiction, the matter shall be settled by the decision of the Court." At times, the Court might consider that a state has consented to jurisdiction even though that state may argue otherwise, as discussed further below.

---

18   *See* UN Charter, Article 94, and ICJ Statute, Articles 59 and 60.

19   The United States contested Nicaragua's Application by asserting that the ICJ lacked jurisdiction to resolve the dispute. In the Court's Order on May 10, 1984, the Court rejected the United States' request to remove the case from the Court's docket but indicated that the question of jurisdiction would be decided first, in separate proceedings. *Case Concerning Military and Paramilitary Activities in and Against Nicaragua* (Nicaragua v. US), Jurisdiction and Admissibility, Judgment, I.C.J. Reports 1984, p. 392, paras. 3–4. Following the Court's decision on jurisdiction, proceedings on the merits continued and a judgment was issued in 1986. *Case Concerning Military and Paramilitary Activities in and Against Nicaragua* (Nicaragua v. US), Merits, Judgment, I.C.J. Reports 1986, p. 14, paras. 3–4.

20   The United States contested the ICJ's jurisdiction under the 1995 Treaty of Amity, Economic Relations and Consular Rights between the United States and Iran. However, the Court rejected the United States' argument, noting the Court's jurisdiction to entertain the dispute fell under the compromissory clause of the 1995 Treaty. *Case Concerning Oil Platforms* (Iran v. US), Preliminary Objection, Judgment, I.C.J. Reports 1996, p. 161. Subsequently, proceedings on the merits were held and a judgment was issued in 2003. *Case Concerning Oil Platforms* (Iran v. US), Merits, Judgment, I.C.J. Reports 2003, p. 161.

The Court has reiterated the importance of the principle of consent on numerous occasions. In *Armed Activities on the Territory of the Congo* – filed by the Democratic Republic of the Congo (DRC) against Uganda, Burundi, and Rwanda – the Court held that it had no jurisdiction to settle the dispute between the DRC and Rwanda.

> **Armed Activities on the Territory of the Congo (*New Application:* 2002) (Democratic Republic of the Congo v. Uganda)[21]**
>
> The Court recalls its jurisprudence, as well as that of its predecessor, the Permanent Court of International Justice, regarding the forms which the parties' expression of their consent to its jurisdiction may take. According to that jurisprudence, "neither the Statute nor the Rules require that this consent should be expressed in any particular form", and "there is nothing to prevent the acceptance of jurisdiction (...) from being effected by two separate and successive acts, instead of jointly and beforehand by a special agreement". The attitude of the Respondent State must, however, be capable of being regarded as "an unequivocal indication" of the desire of that State to accept the Court's jurisdiction in a "voluntary and indisputable" manner.
>
> In the present case the Court will confine itself to noting that Rwanda has expressly and repeatedly objected to its jurisdiction at every stage of the proceedings. Rwanda's attitude therefore cannot be regarded as "an unequivocal indication" of its desire to accept the jurisdiction of the Court in a "voluntary and indisputable" manner. The fact, as the DRC has pointed out, that Rwanda has "fully and properly participated in the different procedures in this case, without having itself represented or failing to appear", and that "it has not refused to appear before the Court or make submissions", cannot be interpreted as consent to the Court's jurisdiction over the merits, inasmuch as the very purpose of this participation was to challenge that jurisdiction. (...)
>
> The Court observes, however, as it has already had occasion to emphasize, that "the erga omnes character of a norm and the rule of consent to jurisdiction are two different things", and that the mere fact that rights and obligations erga omnes may be at issue in a dispute would not give the Court jurisdiction to entertain that dispute. The same applies to the relationship between peremptory norms of general international law (*jus*

---

21   *Armed Activities on the Territory of the Congo (New Application:* 2002) (Dem. Rep. Congo v. Rwanda), Jurisdiction and Admissibility, Judgment, I.C.J. Reports 2006, p. 6, paras. 21–22 (references omitted).

THE INTERNATIONAL COURT OF JUSTICE AND STATES

cogens) and the establishment of the Court's jurisdiction: the fact that a dispute relates to compliance with a norm having such a character, which is assuredly the case with regard to the prohibition of genocide, cannot of itself provide a basis for the jurisdiction of the Court to entertain that dispute. Under the Court's Statute that jurisdiction is always based on the consent of the parties. (...)

When a compromissory clause in a treaty provides for the Court's jurisdiction, that jurisdiction exists only in respect of the parties to the treaty who are bound by that clause and within the limits set out therein.[22]

The important nature of the legal issues and norms at hand (related to the prohibition of genocide) had no incidence on this finding. Although the Court held that it had no jurisdiction to hear the DRC's claims against Rwanda, it granted provisional measures to stop all military activity in the DRC. This decision was criticized by Judge Buergenthal, who insisted on the importance of upholding the principle of consent even in the face of a grave subject-matter.

Armed Activities on the Territory of the Congo (*New Application:* 2002) (Democratic Republic of the Congo v. Rwanda), Provisional Measures, Order of 10 July 2002, Declaration of Judge Buergenthal[23]
The Court's function is to pronounce itself on matters within its jurisdiction and not to voice personal sentiments or to make comments, general or specific, which, despite their admittedly "feel-good" qualities, have no legitimate place in this Order.

Who, for example, would not be "deeply concerned by the deplorable human tragedy, loss of life, and enormous suffering in the east of the Democratic Republic of the Congo resulting from the continued fighting there"? But the expression of this concern in a formal Order of the Court presupposes that the Court has the requisite jurisdiction to deal with that subject-matter. Having determined that it lacks that jurisdiction, it should not pronounce itself with regard to that subject-matter.

---

22 A compromissory clause refers to a provision in a treaty identifying a forum where future disputes, if any, will be adjudicated. Jurisdiction can be given to the ICJ via a compromissory clause, as explained further in Section C(2) below.

23 *Armed Activities on the Territory of the Congo* (*New Application:* 2002) (Democratic Republic of the Congo v. Rwanda), Provisional Measures, Order of 10 July 2002, Decl. Buergenthal, ICJ Reports 2002, p. 257. Separate Opinion of Judges Higgins, Kooijmans, Elaraby, Owada, and Simma.

40

CHAPTER 2

Taking a different position, Judges Higgins, Kooijmans, Elaraby, Owada, and Simma expressed doubt as to the absolute validity of the principle of consent in all situations.

> **_Armed Activities on the Territory of the Congo_ (_New Application:_ 2002)**
> **(Democratic Republic of the Congo v. Rwanda), Joint Separate Opinion**
> **of Judges Higgins, Kooijmans, Elaraby, Owada, and Simma[24]**
>
> It is a matter for serious concern that at the beginning of the twenty-first century it is still for States to choose whether they consent to the Court adjudicating claims that they have committed genocide. It must be regarded as a very grave matter that a State should be in a position to shield from international judicial scrutiny any claim that might be made against it concerning genocide. A State so doing shows the world scant confidence that it would never, ever, commit genocide, one of the greatest crimes known.

Despite the diversity of opinions expressed in _Armed Activities_, the ICJ's own view on this matter has been fairly consistent. It has recognized the importance of certain international norms (which it qualifies as _erga omnes_, i.e., obligations weighing on the international community as a whole), yet such character cannot, in itself, overcome the necessity of consent and afford jurisdiction to the Court to settle a dispute.

In understanding the scope and limits of consensual jurisdiction, it is helpful to contrast the Court's position in _Armed Activities on the Territory of the Congo_ with that of the Court in _Oil Platforms_. The basis of the Court's jurisdiction in _Oil Platforms_ was a Treaty of Amity entered into between Iran and the United States

---

24   _Armed Activities on the Territory of the Congo_ (_New Application:_ 2002) (Democratic Republic of the Congo v. Rwanda), Jurisdiction and Admissibility, Joint Separate Opinion of Judges Higgins, Kooijmans, Elaraby, Owada, and Simma, ICJ Reports 2006, p. 65. Joint Separate Opinion of Judges Higgins, Kooijmans, Elaraby, Owada and Simma (ICJ Reports 2006), at 65.

> **Treaty of Amity, Economic Relations, and Consular Rights between the United States of America and Iran**[25]
>
> The United States of America and Iran, desirous of emphasizing the friendly relations which have long prevailed between their peoples, of reaffirming the high principles in the regulation of human affairs to which they are committed, of encouraging mutually beneficial trade and investments and closer economic intercourse generally between their peoples, and of regulating consular relations, have resolved to conclude, on the basis of reciprocal equality of treatment, a Treaty of Amity, Economic Relations, and Consular Rights.
>
> **Article I**
>
> There shall be firm and enduring peace and sincere friendship between the United States of America and Iran.
>
> **Article x**
>
> 1. Between the territories of the two High Contracting Parties there shall be freedom of commerce and navigation.
>
> (...)
>
> **Article xx**
>
> 1. The present Treaty shall not preclude the application of measures:
>
> (...)
>
> (d)   necessary to fulfill the obligations of a High Contracting Party for the maintenance or restoration of international peace and security, or necessary to protect its essential security interests
>
> **Article xxi(2)**
>
> Any dispute between the High Contracting Parties as to the interpretation or application of the present Treaty, not satisfactorily adjusted by diplomacy, shall be submitted to the International Court of Justice, unless the High Contracting Parties agree to settlement by some other pacific means.

Based on Article xxi(2) of the Treaty of Amity, Iran brought the case against the United States, asking the Court to declare, inter alia, "that in attacking and destroying the oil platforms referred to in the Application on 19 October 1987 and 18 April 1988, the United States breached its obligations to the Islamic Republic, inter alia, under Articles I and x(1) of the Treaty of Amity and

---

25   Treaty of Amity, Economic Relations, and Consular Rights between the United States of America and Iran, Aug. 15, 1955.

international law."[26] The United States objected to jurisdiction for a number of reasons, including on the ground that the dispute concerned the right of self-defense – a subject-matter not covered by the bilateral treaty upon which the Court's jurisdiction was based. In its assessment of its own competence, the Court relied on Article 31(3) of the Vienna Convention on the Law of Treaties (VCLT) and rejected the view of the United States.

Vienna Convention on the Law of Treaties

Article 31

1. A treaty shall be interpreted in good faith in accordance with the ordinary meaning to be given to the terms of the treaty in their context and in the light of its object and purpose.

2. The context for the purpose of the interpretation of a treaty shall comprise, in addition to the text, including its preamble and annexes: (a) any agreement relating to the treaty which was made between all the parties in connection with the conclusion of the treaty; (b) any instrument which was made by one or more parties in connection with the conclusion of the treaty and accepted by the other parties as an instrument related to the treaty.

3. There shall be taken into account, together with the context: (a) any subsequent agreement between the parties regarding the interpretation of the treaty or the application of its provisions; (b) any subsequent practice in the application of the treaty which establishes the agreement of the parties regarding its interpretation; (c) any relevant rules of international law applicable in the relations between the parties.

4. A special meaning shall be given to a term if it is established that the parties so intended.

The Court interpreted the term "context" broadly and determined that "[t]he application of the relevant rules of international law relating to [an unlawful use of force] thus forms an integral part of the task of interpretation entrusted to the Court." Accordingly, Article XX of the Treaty of Amity – permitting both parties to protect essential security interests – was interpreted in light of international norms governing the use of force. The Court considered that questions pertaining to self-defense and the use of force could be read into

---

26   *Application of the Islamic Republic of Iran to the International Court of Justice* (Nov. 2, 1992), available at https://www.icj-cij.org/public/files/case-related/90/7211.pdf.

text of the treaty, extending the bounds of jurisdiction beyond what the US claimed to have consented to.

> ### Enzo Cannizzaro and Beatrice Bonafe, Fragmenting International Law through Compromissory Clauses? Some Remarks on the Decision of the ICJ in the Oil Platforms Case[27]
>
> Not infrequently, however, the Court, having jurisdiction under a compromissory clause, must settle disputes over conduct which is governed at the same time by the treaty and by other international rules applicable to the relationship between the parties. In such case, the Court must preliminarily ascertain if the dispute falls within the scope of the jurisdictional clause, and then ultimately identify the rules under which the differing views of the parties must be settled.
>
> This latter question has been considered by the Court in its interesting decision in the Oil Platforms case. The case concerned the legality of certain forcible measures adopted by the United States towards Iran in the context of the Gulf War between Iran and Iraq at the end the 1980s. The jurisdiction of the Court was limited to disputes on the interpretation and application of the 1955 [Friendship, Commerce and Navigation] Treaty in force between the parties; therefore, the question arose as to whether the Court could determine the legality of the forcible measures on the basis of the Treaty provisions alone, or whether it could do so on the basis of international customary law on the use of force. That is, the Court had the choice between a narrow approach, focusing on the Treaty provisions as the only law applicable to the dispute, and a broader approach, which would admit that the dispute could be settled according to a wider range of international law rules applying to both of the parties.

Judge Higgins argued against the Court's broad interpretation of word "context" in Article 31 of the VCLT. According to Higgins, the majority ruling construed "context" to refer to any applicable rules of international law, whereas the article sets the specific context of the said treaty as the relevant benchmark.

---

27   Enzo Cannizzaro and Beatrice Bonafé, *Fragmenting International Law through Compromissory Clauses? Some Remarks on the Decision of the ICJ in the Oil Platforms Case,* 16 Eur. J. Int'l L. 481 (2005).

> **Oil Platforms (Islamic Republic of Iran v. United States of America), Separate Opinion of Judge Higgins[28]**
>
> The Court reads this provision as incorporating the totality of the substantive international law (which in paragraph 42 of the Judgment is defined as comprising Charter law) on the use of force. But this is to ignore that Article 31, paragraph 3, requires "the context" to be taken into account: and "the context" is clearly that of an economic and commercial treaty. What is envisaged by Article 31, paragraph 3 (c), is that a provision that requires interpretation in Article xx, paragraph 1 (d), will be illuminated by recalling what type of a treaty this is and any other "relevant rules" governing Iran-United States relations. It is not a provision that on the face of it envisages incorporating the entire substance of international law on a topic not mentioned in the clause – at least not without more explanation than the Court provides.

As *Armed Activities on the Territory of the Congo* and *Oil Platforms* illustrate, the principle of consensual jurisdiction plays a significant role in shaping the relationship between states and the Court. Automatic jurisdiction was never favored over consensual jurisdiction, affording states more flexibility in deciding whether to give jurisdiction to the Court. The principle of consent is therefore here to stay, at least formally. As with all other procedural and substantive matters, the Court retains some discretion as to how to interpret the principle – stringently or not – on a case-by-case basis. This, too, is unlikely to change.

$$\bullet \bullet \bullet$$

Questions

1. Should the Court be entitled to circumvent the principle of consent in cases of grave violations of international law?

2. In deciding the subject-matter of a treaty and its own competence to adjudicate a case, does the ICJ in effect overrule the consent of a State? Should it be able to do so?

3. In the *Armed Activities on the Territory of the Congo* debate, do you agree with Judge Buergenthal or with Judges Higgins, Kooijmans, Elaraby, and Owada? Why or why not?

---

28   *See Case Concerning Oil Platforms* (Iran v. US), Judgment, I.C.J. Reports 2003, Sep. Op. Higgins, p. 225, 237.

THE INTERNATIONAL COURT OF JUSTICE AND STATES

4. The Court has at times doubted its own jurisdiction, even when both parties to the dispute had consented to it! In *Monetary Gold*, the Court decided that the principle of consent required it to abstain from deciding the case because the legal interests of a non-consenting third state formed "the very subject matter" of the case.[29] Does this strengthen or weaken the principle of consent and state sovereignty? Would the *Monetary Gold* principle apply if the third state party was an international organization?

5. Beyond the extreme cases discussed above, do you think the ICJ should *generally* exercise less stringency when establishing its jurisdiction?

Further Reading

Stanimir Alexandrov, *The Compulsory Jurisdiction of the International Court of Justice: How Compulsory Is It?*, 5 Chinese J. Int'l L. 29 (2006).

Dan Hammer, *Allowing Genocide?, An Analysis of Armed Activities on the Territory of the Congo, Jurisdictional Reservations, and the Legitimacy of the International Court of Justice*, 16 Minn. J. Int'l L. 495 (2007).

C   Admissibility and Jurisdiction

Given the centrality of the principle of consent, the rules governing admissibility and jurisdiction play a significant role in determining which cases will come before the Court. First, the Court may only hear *legal disputes*. Behind this expression hide two important criteria: that there exists a *dispute* between the parties; and that the subject-matter of this dispute be of a *legal* nature (this requirement is typically interpreted loosely by the Court).

1   *Legal Disputes*

Under Article 36(2) of the ICJ Statute, the Court has competence to resolve "legal disputes." However, the dividing line that separates "disputes" from other interactions, and the difference between legal and non-legal disputes is not easily identified. Disputes are rarely publicly announced as such; today, even armed conflicts are no longer initiated by dramatic national addresses or formal declarations of war. There must be a disagreement, of course, yet not every disagreement qualifies as a dispute.

---

29   *Case of the Monetary Gold Removed from Rome in 1942* (Italy v. France), Judgment, I.C.J. Reports 1954, p. 19.

A disagreement turns into a dispute only after "it reaches a certain threshold,"[30] but what exactly does this mean?

A disagreement can be considered a dispute by one side, and a temporary disagreement by the other, especially in its earlier stages. If a question arises over whether or not a dispute exists, the Court must find more objective ways of making a determination (for example, by analyzing the parties' correspondence). In situations where the Court's jurisdiction is limited to a specific time frame, for example, the question of *when* the dispute started may be crucial in determining whether or not the Court has competence to hear the case.

> ### *Gerhard Hafner, The Physiognomy of Disputes and the Appropriate Means to Resolve Them*[31]
>
> The traditional definition of the term "dispute" as found in the jurisprudence of the Permanent Court of International Justice or the International Court of Justice is too wide and too narrow at the same time. It is too wide in so far as, according to international judicial practice, a mere divergence of views or interests as such, without any likelihood of follow-up action by States, is not viewed as sufficient to be submitted to international proceedings. It is too narrow in so far as it is no longer possible to confine international disputes only to those between two or more States disagreeing among themselves. Consequently, international disputes have to be understood as conflicting and, from the point of view of international law, irreconcilable attitudes of international actors, i.e., subjects of international law, where the actors involved are unable to pursue their intended line of action as expressed in concrete claims without confrontation.

In addition, it has proved difficult to distinguish between legal and political disputes. Neither the ICJ nor the disputes and advisory requests that come before it can be hermetically separated from the political context in which they arise. As the Court itself made clear in *United States Diplomatic and Consular Staff in*

---

30 *Certain Property* (Liechtenstein v. Germany), Preliminary Objections, Judgment, I.C.J. Reports 2005, p. 6, para. 23.

31 Gerhard Hafner, *The Physiognomy of Disputes and the Appropriate Means to Resolve Them, in* International Law as a Language for International Relations. Proceedings of the United Nations Congress on Public International Law 559 (1995).

THE INTERNATIONAL COURT OF JUSTICE AND STATES 47

Tehran, it cannot categorically refuse to exercise jurisdiction whenever political considerations are at stake.

> **United States Diplomatic and Consular Staff in Tehran**
> **(United States of America v. Iran), Judgment[32]**
> Nor has [Iran] made any attempt to explain, still less define, what connection, legal or factual, there may be between the "overall problem" of its general grievances against the United States and the particular events that gave rise to the United States' claims in the present case which, in its view, precludes the separate examination of those claims by the Court (...) [L]egal disputes between sovereign States by their very nature are likely to occur in political contexts, and often form only one element in a wider and long-standing political dispute between the States concerned (...) if the Court were, contrary to its settled jurisprudence, to adopt such a view, it would impose a far-reaching and unwarranted restriction upon the role of the Court in the peaceful solution of international disputes.

• • •

Questions

1. What do you think about Gerhard Hafner's definition of a "legal dispute"?
2. Respondents often argue that the case is inadmissible, i.e., that there is no "legal dispute," to demonstrate that the Court does not have jurisdiction in the case at hand. How seriously do you think these claims should be taken by the Court? Are they merely an attempt at delaying proceedings pending before the Court?

2   *Conferring Jurisdiction on the Court*

States can confer jurisdiction on the Court in three main ways: (1) by treaty, whether multilateral or bilateral; (2) by making a unilateral declaration to that effect; or (3) by *forum prorogatum*. When filing an application before the Court, a state may initially invoke more than one title of jurisdiction. The Court will choose the title of jurisdiction, if any, that gives it competence to proceed with the case. Once a case is filed with the Court, the defendant can object to the Court's jurisdiction by filing preliminary objections, as explained further below.

---

32 *United States Diplomatic and Consular Staff in Tehran* (US v. Iran), Judgment, I.C.J. Reports (1980), p. 3, at para. 37.

a   Jurisdiction Conferred by Treaty

Many international agreements contain "compromissory clauses" that identify a forum where future disputes, if any, will be adjudicated. Compromissory clauses conferring jurisdiction on the ICJ need not comply with any formal requirements. In order to facilitate recourse to the Court, the process is deliberately flexible. However, the Court needs to be convinced that the parties indeed agreed to confer jurisdiction, regardless of how this agreement was formulated. Jurisdiction can be conferred by treaty at two different stages of the dispute – before or after a dispute arises.

(i)   *Jurisdiction Conferred by Treaty before a Dispute Arises*

States can choose to include a "compromissory clause" that confers jurisdiction on the Court in any bilateral or multilateral agreement. The clause can be integrated into the treaty or included in an ancillary document. In such situations, the scope of the disputes falling within the Court's competence is defined in advance, typically in reference to the treaty, and may cover any dispute regarding the interpretation or application of the treaty. A large number of cases have been brought before the Court using this mechanism. Take, for example, the *Oil Platforms* case analyzed above: Iran initiated the case against the United States on the basis of the compromissory clause included in Article XXI(2) of the bilateral Treaty of Amity between Iran and the United States (reproduced above).

Compromissory clauses conferring jurisdiction on the ICJ can also be incorporated into multilateral treaties, as in the Convention on the Prevention and Punishment of the Crime of Genocide.

> **Convention on the Prevention and Punishment of the Crime of Genocide (1948)**
>
> **Article IX**
>
> Disputes between the Contracting Parties relating to the interpretation, application or fulfilment of the present Convention, including those relating to the responsibility of a State for genocide or for any of the other acts enumerated in Article III, shall be submitted to the International Court of Justice at the request of any of the parties to the dispute.

Generally speaking, states are divided on the value of compromissory clauses. A provision conferring jurisdiction on the ICJ may cause certain states *not* to become party to that treaty. To avoid this problem, states occasionally enter

THE INTERNATIONAL COURT OF JUSTICE AND STATES 49

supplementary agreements providing for dispute settlement by the Court, which states party to the main treaty can then choose to ratify. Optional protocols of the sort were adopted alongside the Vienna Conventions on Diplomatic and Consular Relations of 1961 and 1963. This accounts for the fact that certain states may be unwilling to commit to the ICJ's involvement in undefined disputes. It also reflects the sentiment that judicial settlement leading to a final, binding decision is not always the only or even the best means to settle a dispute.

Though treaties, whether bilateral or multilateral in nature, are an important source of business for the Court, the Court has at times declined to hear cases brought under compromissory clauses.[33] This happens when allegations that have little or no relationship to the subject matter of the treaty. Therefore, a distinction should be made between cases brought on the basis of a genuine disagreement over the interpretation or breach of a given treaty, and cases involving allegations of illegal conduct which have little or no relationship to the subject-matter of the treaty.

Jurisdiction may also be conferred to the Court by a treaty that deals specifically with the settlement of disputes. In such cases, the peaceful settlement of international disputes forms the very substance of the treaty. The practice evolved from arbitration practices in the nineteenth century and was encouraged by the League of Nations and the Permanent Court of International Justice. In 1928, states adopted the General Act for the Pacific Settlement of Disputes under the League of Nations' umbrella.[34] Similar regional agreements were concluded in South America (by members of the Organization of American States)[35] and in Europe (resulting in the European Convention for the Peaceful Settlement of Disputes).[36]

• • •

---

33 In *Democratic Republic of Congo v. Rwanda*, the Court rejected eight treaties as a basis for jurisdiction. *See Work of the Court in 2008–2009*, 63 Int'l Ct. Justice Y.B. 226, 383 (2009).

34 General Act for the Pacific Settlement of Disputes (Sept. 26, 1928), 93 L.N.T.S. 2123.

35 Examples of cases brought on the basis of such treaties include *Alleged Violations of Sovereign Rights and Maritime Spaces in the Caribbean Sea* – brought by Nicaragua against Colombia on the basis of Article XXXI of the American Treaty on Pacific Settlement (also known as the Pact of Bogota).

36 *Certain Property* (Liechtenstein v. Germany), Preliminary Objections, I.C.J. Reports (2005), p. 6. 19 (submitted on the basis of the European Convention for the Peaceful Settlement of Disputes).

Questions

1. Do you agree, as noted earlier in this section, that "a distinction should be made between cases brought on the basis of a genuine disagreement over the interpretation or breach of a given treaty, and cases involving allegations of illegal conduct which have little or no relationship to the subject-matter of the treaty"? Does it really matter so long as jurisdiction has been established?

2. What are arguments in favor and against the inclusion of a compromissory clause in a treaty? Do the considerations vary between bilateral and multilateral treaties?

(ii) *Jurisdiction Conferred by Treaty after a Dispute Arises*

After a dispute arises, two or more states may conclude an agreement – also known as a compromis or special agreement – *to refer the dispute to the Court*. In such a situation, there can be no "Applicant" or "Respondent" as the parties jointly make the decision to have the Court settle their dispute. The practice in such cases has been for the parties to file memorials simultaneously to avoid having a party castigated as "Applicant" and the other as "Respondent". This practice, however, has been discouraged by the Court, which has urged states to reach an agreement on the number and order of the pleadings.[37]

Although the PCIJ's docket included a fair share of cases brought via this mechanism, only three such cases were brought before the ICJ in its first two decades of existence.[38] This period of decline did not pick up since then: cases brought "jointly" before the Court on the basis of special agreements only make up approximately ten percent of the Court's docket. This is quite unfortunate, as special agreements offer an opportunity for states to use the Court's services in a particularly friendly atmosphere. That said, it should be noted that a number of states have demonstrated a clear preference for submitting their disputes to the Court via special agreement. Burkina Faso and Niger, for example, were party to two jointly submitted cases to the Court; and yet they were never Applicant to the Court (see Figure 2.1).

---

37 Practice Direction I (2001), available at https://www.ICJ-cij.org/en/practice-directions. *See also* The Statute of the International Court of Justice: A Commentary (Andreas Zimmermann, Christian J. Tams, Karin Oellers-Frahm & Christian Tomuschat, eds. (3rd ed, 2019)), at 1237–38, 1261 (noting that in oral proceedings, the states will take the stage either in the order in which they submitted their written pleadings, in alphabetical order, or by lottery).

38 *Corfu Channel* (U.K. v. Albania), Merits, I.C.J. Reports (1949), p. 4; *Minquiers and Ecrehos* (U.K./France), I.C.J. Reports (1953), p. 47. Case Concerning *Sovereignty over Certain Frontier Land* (Belgium/Netherlands) I.C.J. Reports (1959), p. 209.

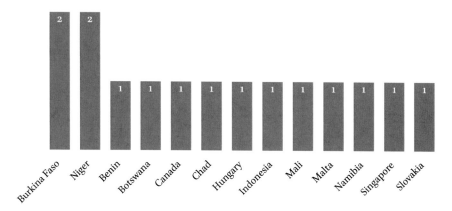

FIGURE 2.1 States that appeared in cases brought jointly but never as Applicant

When diplomatic considerations hinder states' ability to define the dispute in a compromis, they may enter into a framework agreement instead. By doing so, the parties recognize they are in a state of disagreement, whose nature or scope they are unable to define clearly. Whereas the common procedure in compromis agreements is for states to jointly "seize" the Court, a framework agreement allows a party to later unilaterally request the Court settle the dispute while limiting the unfriendly connotation of such a move.[39] The ICJ will not necessarily settle the dispute; the agreement may only authorize the Court to articulate the legal positions of the different sides. The parties may prefer such a course of action, which may or may not lead them back to the ICJ: "The creation of this form of agreement to refer a case to the Court and its proven adaptability to different diplomatic and political currents and requirements is a welcome addition to the machinery of international adjudication as one of the means for the peaceful settlement of international disputes."[40] Because framework agreements do not fully define the substance of the dispute,

---

39   See, for example, *Framework Agreement on the Peaceful Settlement of the Territorial Dispute between the Great Socialist People's Libyan Arab Jamahiriya and the Republic of Chad* (Sep. 1990), available at https://www.icj-cij.org/public/files/case-related/83/6687.pdf. In the agreement the parties, *inter alia*, "undertake to settle first their territorial dispute by all political means, including conciliation, within a period of approximately one year, unless the Heads of State otherwise decide" and "submit the dispute to the International Court of Justice" in the absence of political settlement of their territorial dispute.
40   Shabtai Rosenne, Essays on International Law and Practice (2007), at 170.

52   CHAPTER 2

however, they often make it difficult for the Court to delineate the precise contours of the dispute over which it has jurisdiction.[41]

b   Jurisdiction Conferred by Optional Clause Declaration

As explained in Chapter 1, the "optional clause" embodied one of the most noteworthy innovations of the Statute of the PCIJ.[42] At the time, it was a compromise between those who favored giving the Permanent Court of International Justice compulsory jurisdiction over all legal disputes, as proposed by the Committee of Jurists who prepared the draft Statute of the PCIJ, and those who wanted to retain the exclusively consensual basis of the jurisdiction. Eventually consensual jurisdiction was adopted, allowing states to make individual declarations accepting the jurisdiction of the PCIJ on their own terms. Almost all members of the League of Nations ended up making declarations accepting the jurisdiction of the PCIJ, and many cases came before the PCIJ on these grounds.[43] Overall, the mechanism was viewed positively and was therefore adopted, virtually unchanged (save some technical details), in the Statute of the ICJ in 1945.

> ### ICJ Statute
>
> **Article 36(2)**
>
> The states parties to the present Statute may at any time declare that they recognize as compulsory *ipso facto* and without special agreement, in relation to any other state accepting the same obligation, the jurisdiction of the Court in all legal disputes concerning:
>
> a. the interpretation of a treaty;
> b. any question of international law;
> c. the existence of any fact which, if established, would constitute a breach of an international obligation;
> d. the nature or extent of the reparation to be made for the breach of an international obligation.

As its name indicates, this is an *optional* mechanism available to states. As of July 2020, seventy-four states had deposited a declaration recognizing the

---

41   *See Request for Interpretation of the Judgment of November 20, 1950 in the Asylum Case,* I.C.J. Reports (1950), p. 395.

42   *See supra,* Chapter 1, Section A(3).

43   Manley O. Hudson, The Permanent Court of International Justice: 1920–1942 (1943), at 473.

THE INTERNATIONAL COURT OF JUSTICE AND STATES

jurisdiction of the International Court of Justice as compulsory.[44] Reciprocity is inherent in the system, and where two declarations operate under different terms, jurisdiction exists only to the extent that the terms coincide. The Court must determine the categories of disputes to which each declaration is applicable and then inquire whether the dispute in question falls within these categories of disputes. The dispute must be covered by both declarations in order for the Court to establish its jurisdiction. To put it differently, the Court determines the extent of its jurisdiction by delineating the common denominator between the two declarations. The Court will have jurisdiction if the dispute in question falls within this common denominator.

As with other methods of granting jurisdiction to the Court, no formal criteria applies to optional clause declarations, save the requirement that the declaration be deposited with the Secretary-General of the United Nations. A declaration conferring jurisdiction on the Court enters into force when it is deposited, unless stated otherwise.

Declarations can be conditional and include temporal, personal, or material limitations.[45] Temporal reservations limit the application of the declaration to a certain time frame. Personal reservations may exclude disputes involving specific states. Material reservations are conditions pertaining to other dispute settlement mechanisms. For example, optional clause declarations may provide that the Court will be competent only when other means of dispute settlement have failed. Finally, reservations can be made as to the subject-matter of the dispute itself.

Estonia's Declaration

I, Arnold Ruutel, Chairman of the Supreme Council of the Republic of Estonia, declare on behalf of the Republic of Estonia and in accordance with the Resolution of September 26, 1991 of the Supreme Council of the Republic of Estonia, that the Republic of Estonia recognizes as compulsory ipso facto and without special agreement, in relation to any other State accepting the same obligation, on condition of reciprocity, the jurisdiction of the International Court of Justice, in conformity with paragraph 2 of Article 36 of the Statute of the Court, provided that this declaration shall not apply to disputes, the solution of which the parties shall entrust to other tribunals by virtue of agreements already in existence or which may be concluded in the future.

---

44   See *Declarations Recognizing the Jurisdiction of the Court as Compulsory*, available at http://www.ICJ-cij.org/en/declarations.

45   Robert Kolb, The Elgar Companion to the International Court of Justice (2014), at 191.

Greece's Declaration

I declare, on behalf of the Greek Government, that I recognize as compulsory ipso facto and without special agreement, on condition of reciprocity, in relation to any other State accepting the same obligation, the jurisdiction of the International Court of Justice in all legal disputes referred to in Article 36, paragraph 2, of the Statute of the Court. However, the Greek Government excludes from the competence of the Court any dispute relating to defensive military action taken by the Hellenic Republic for reasons of national defense.

This declaration shall remain in force for a period of five years. Upon the expiry of that period, it shall continue to have effect until notice of its termination is given.

United Kingdom's Declaration

1. The Government of the United Kingdom of Great Britain and Northern Ireland accept as compulsory ipso facto and without special convention, on condition of reciprocity, the jurisdiction of the International Court of Justice, in conformity with paragraph 2 of Article 36 of the Statute of the Court, until such time as notice may be given to terminate the acceptance, over all disputes arising after 1 January 1974, with regard to situations or facts subsequent to the same date, other than:

(i) any dispute which the United Kingdom has agreed with the other Party or Parties thereto to settle by some other method of peaceful settlement;

(ii) any dispute with the government of any other country which is or has been a Member of the Commonwealth;

(iii) any dispute in respect of which any other Party to the dispute has accepted the compulsory jurisdiction of the International Court of Justice only in relation to or for the purpose of the dispute; or where the acceptance of the Court's compulsory jurisdiction on behalf of any other Party to the dispute was deposited or ratified less than twelve months prior to the filing of the application bringing the dispute before the Court.

2. The Government of the United Kingdom also reserve the right at any time, by means of a notification addressed to the Secretary-General of the United Nations, and with effect as from the moment of such notification, either to add to, amend or withdraw any of the foregoing reservations, or any that may hereafter be added.

THE INTERNATIONAL COURT OF JUSTICE AND STATES

•••

Questions

1. How do the declarations of Estonia, the UK and Greece differ? What type of reservations do they include?
2. Assuming that a dispute arises between Estonia and Greece about environmental damage caused during an armed conflict, would the Court be competent to settle the dispute? What if the same dispute arises between Greece and the United Kingdom?
3. What type of limitations can states place on the Court's jurisdiction? Should there be any limit to the conditions states can pose to the Court's jurisdiction?
4. Why do states choose to limit the Court's jurisdiction to certain types of disputes?

As the Court's jurisdiction rests on the principle of consensual jurisdiction, declarations made under Article 36(2) may be modified or withdrawn at any time. Some states even formulate a specific denunciation clause. Germany, for example, stipulated that its declaration is in force "until such time as notice may be given to the Secretary General of the United Nations withdrawing the declaration and with effect as from the moment of such notification."

There is, however, one important restriction to states' right of withdrawal: a state may not withdraw its declaration after proceedings have started. In the days leading to *Case Concerning Military and Paramilitary Activities in and Against Nicaragua* in 1984, the United States withdrew its optional clause declaration before Nicaragua filed its application. The withdrawal notice preceded Nicaragua's application by three days, but the Court refused to give it legal effect:

> Although the United States retained the right to modify the contents of the 1946 Declaration or to terminate it, a power which is inherent in any unilateral act of a State, it has nevertheless assumed an inescapable obligation towards other States accepting the Optional Clause, by stating formally and solemnly that any such change should take effect only after six months have elapsed as from the date of notice.[46]

By its own terms, the US optional clause declaration provided that it would "remain in force for a period of five years and thereafter until the expiration

---

46   *Case Concerning Military and Paramilitary Activities in and Against Nicaragua, supra* note 23, para. 61.

of six months after notice may be given to terminate this declaration."[47] Accordingly, the withdrawal could not take effect immediately.

Other states terminated their acceptance of compulsory jurisdiction following litigation to which they did not consent. Thailand terminated its declaration following the Court's judgment in *Temple of Preah Vihear*. South Africa terminated its declaration in 1967, following a series of advisory opinions and judgments concerning its administration of South West Africa (Namibia). France terminated its acceptance of the Court's compulsory jurisdiction following the *Nuclear Tests* cases. Other states terminated or circumscribed their acceptance of compulsory jurisdiction when it appeared likely that proceedings would be instituted against them, or when developments in the law or the Court's practice required them to reconsider their national policy in this regard. The United States is the only state that withdrew its optional clause while serving as Respondent in a case pending before the Court.

In the end, the relatively limited use of the optional clause (only about a third of UN member states have deposited such a declaration) and the reservations included therein suggest that certain states are still apprehensive toward compulsory jurisdiction.

> *Cesare P.R. Romano, From the Consensual to the Compulsory Paradigm*[48]
> The "optional clause" introduced first by the PCIJ and inherited by the ICJ has not met the expectations of its inventors. States have not rushed to make optional declarations. Even worse, the number of declarations relative to the number of states has steadily decreased to its current level of about one-third of all UN members. Second, as reciprocity is the underlying principle of the optional clause mechanism, jurisdiction is scaled down to the lowest common denominator of the declarations of the two parties. States can, and very often do, restrict the scope of declarations with reservations and "interpretative declarations," thus greatly reducing the area of overlap. Although treaties in force worldwide number in the thousands, the ICJ currently reports only 268 treaties, both bilateral and multilateral, containing clauses granting jurisdiction to the Court in contentious proceedings. Finally, despite the fact that the number of entities

---

47 *Id.*, para. 13.

48 Cesare P.R. Romano, *Shift from the Consensual to the Compulsory Paradigm in International Adjudication: Elements for a Theory of Consent*, 39 N.Y.U. J. Int'l L. & Pol. 791, 872 (2007).

THE INTERNATIONAL COURT OF JUSTICE AND STATES 57

able to litigate before the Court is very limited (i.e., only sovereign states) and that only a minority is willing to accept the jurisdiction of the Court ex ante, only one out of seven cases put on the ICJ docket in sixty years of existence has been submitted by way of agreement between the parties. Thus, it should be no wonder that preliminary objections to jurisdiction are extremely frequent.

Nevertheless, the Court rarely finds against its own jurisdiction. Unless jurisdiction is manifestly lacking, it tends to err in favor of the Applicant and against the objections of the Respondent, proceeding to the merits rather than dismissing the case. In those cases in which jurisdiction is not clearly lacking, it has often been fiercely debated both in and outside the courtroom.

The significance of the optional clause mechanism cannot be measured solely by the number of states that have accepted it or the number of cases that have been brought on the basis of such clauses. In the early years of international adjudication, it was a useful instrument for disseminating the idea that the judicial settlement of international disputes was both possible and desirable. Today the act of depositing or, for that matter, withdrawing an optional clause declaration does not seem to provide the best indicator of how states will interact with the Court in the future. As explained in Chapter 5, states that have chosen not to confer jurisdiction on the Court *ex ante* via an optional clause declaration, nevertheless bring cases to the Court. [49]

•••

Questions

1. What are the strengths and weaknesses of the optional clause mechanism?
2. Why would a state ever accept the Court's jurisdiction in an optional clause declaration if it could just accept the Court's jurisdiction after a dispute arises?
3. On the ICJ's website, take a look at the list of states that have deposited optional clause declarations.[50] Can you discern any pattern as to size, geography, or any other attribute of those states?
4. Are optional clause declarations more or less important in facilitating international adjudication than compromissory clauses included in treaties? Would you expect states to have a preference for the former or the latter?

---

49 *See, infra* Chapter 5.
50 *See Declarations Recognizing the Jurisdiction of the Court as Compulsory, supra* note 49.

FIGURE 2.2   View of the Great Hall of Justice

5. Mexico has excluded disputes covered under domestic law from the scope of its optional clause declaration. Can you reconcile Mexico's optional clause declaration (below) with Article 2(7) of the Charter, which prohibits the UN from intervening "in matters which are essentially within the domestic jurisdiction of any state," and Article 36(6) of the Court's Statute?[51]

> **Mexico's Declaration**[52]
> In regard to any legal dispute that may in the future arise between the United States of Mexico and any other State out of event subsequent to the date of this Declaration, the Mexican Government recognizes as compulsory ipso fact, and without any special agreement being required therefore, the jurisdiction of the International Court of Justice in accordance with Article 36, paragraph 2, of the Statute of the said Court, in relation to any other State accepting the same obligation, that is, on

---

51   For more information, *see Norwegian Loans*, Judgment, Sep. Op. Lauterpacht, I.C.J. Reports (1957), p. 34, and *Interhandel Case* (Switzerland v. United States), I.C.J. Reports (1959), p. 6.

52   *See* Declarations Recognizing the Jurisdiction of the Court as Compulsory, *supra* note 49 (emphasis added).

> condition of strict reciprocity. This Declaration, which *does not apply to disputes arising from matters that, in the opinion of the Mexican Government, are within the domestic jurisdiction of the United States of Mexico,* shall be binding for a period of five years as of 1 March 1947 and after that date shall continue in force until six months after the Mexican Government gives notice of denunciation.

Further Reading

Gary Scott, *The ICJ and Compulsory Jurisdiction: The Case for Closing the Clause,* 81 Am. J. Int'l L. 57 (1987).

Maria Vogiatzi, *The Historical Evolution of the Optional Clause,* 2 Non-State Actors & Int'l L. 41 (2002).

Cesare P.R. Romano, *The Shift from the Consensual to the Compulsory Paradigm in International Adjudication: Elements for a Theory of Consent,* 39 N.Y.U. J. Int'l L. & Pol. 791, 872 (2007).

c   *Forum Prorogatum*

Under the *forum prorogatum* doctrine, a state can bring a case to the ICJ even if no basis for jurisdiction exists at the outset. Via the filing of an application, a state may invite another state to grant jurisdiction to the ICJ for the purpose of settling an ongoing dispute. The Applicant's consent is implicit in the act of submitting the application. The Respondent may then consent and take part in the proceedings.[53] Unlike special agreements, here the parties do not enter into a formal arrangement before using the Court's services. The principle of consent is by no means compromised under the doctrine of *forum prorogatum* as both parties separately manifest their consent to the Court's jurisdiction. There are no strict rules governing how and when the Respondent expresses such consent. The Respondent can do so expressly, or the ICJ can infer acceptance by conduct – this is why *forum prorogatum* is often referred to as implied consent. If the Respondent sends a written statement in response to the application (also known as a "memorial") without formally accepting the Court's jurisdiction, the Court can consider consent as tacitly given.

In *Certain Questions of Mutual Assistance in Criminal Matters,* Djibouti invited France to settle a dispute before the Court – an invitation that France accepted. In January 2006, the Republic of Djibouti filed in the Registry of the

---

53   A state is only considered a Respondent when it has accepted the jurisdiction of the ICJ, but we use the term Respondent here for the clarity of the presentation.

60   CHAPTER 2

Court an application against the French Republic regarding a dispute concerning refusal by the French governmental and judicial authorities to transfer criminal records to the judicial authorities in Djibouti in violation of, inter alia, the 1977 Treaty of Friendship and Co-operation between the two countries and the 1986 Convention on Mutual Assistance in Criminal Matters between France and Djibouti.

Djibouti indicated in its Application that it "was confident that the French Republic will agree to submit to the jurisdiction of the Court to settle the present dispute." Indeed, by a letter dated July 25, 2006, the French Minister for Foreign Affairs informed the Court that France "consents to the Court's jurisdiction to entertain the Application pursuant to, and solely on the basis of ... Article 38, paragraph 5," of the Rules of Court,[54] while specifying that this consent was "valid only for the purposes of the case, within the meaning of Article 38, paragraph 5, i.e., in respect of the dispute forming the subject of the Application and strictly within the limits of the claims formulated therein" by Djibouti.

Later, some disagreement arose as to the specific scope of France's acceptance of the Court's jurisdiction. After examining France's letter of acceptance, the Court declared that France's consent was not limited to the "subject of the dispute" as described in paragraph 2 of Djibouti's Application. The Court found that when France, which had full knowledge of the claims formulated by Djibouti in its Application, sent its letter to the Court, it did not seek to exclude certain aspects of the dispute forming the subject of the Application from its jurisdiction.

The Court, examining the mutual consent of the parties, consequently held that "the claims concerning both subject-matters referred to in Djibouti's Application, namely, France's refusal to comply with Djibouti's letter rogatory and the summonses to appear sent by the French judiciary, on the one hand to the President of Djibouti dated 17 May 2005, and on the other hand to two senior Djiboutian officials dated 3 and 4 November 2004 and 17 June 2005, are within the Court's jurisdiction."[55] However, the Court also noted that "[w]here jurisdiction is based on *forum prorogatum*, great care must be taken regarding

---

54   Article 38(5) of the Rules of the Court provides as follows: "When the Applicant State proposes to found the jurisdiction of the Court upon a consent thereto yet to be given or manifested by the State against which such application is made, the application shall be transmitted to that State. It shall not however be entered in the General List, nor any action be taken in the proceedings, unless and until the State against which such application is made consents to the Court's jurisdiction for the purposes of the case."

55   *Certain Questions of Mutual Assistance in Criminal Matters* (Djibouti v. France), I.C.J. Reports (2008), p. 177, para. 84.

THE INTERNATIONAL COURT OF JUSTICE AND STATES 61

the scope of the consent as circumscribed by the Respondent State. The arrest warrants against the two senior Djiboutian officials, having been issued after the date the Application was filed, are nowhere mentioned therein."[56] Accordingly, the Court concluded that the claims relating to these arrest warrants were outside the scope of its jurisdiction.[57]

•••

Questions

1. Does the doctrine of *forum prorogatum* prevent any jurisdictional questions from arising before the Court?
2. From the parties' perspective, what are the advantages of *forum prorogatum* over other methods of granting jurisdiction to the Court?

Further Reading

Sienho Yee, *Forum Prorogatum and the Advisory Proceedings of the International Court*, 95 Am. J. Int'l L. 381 (2001).

D   Arguing before the Court

When appearing before the Court, parties should recall certain principles and values inherent in how the Court operates. The principle of equality ensures that all parties to a case receive equal opportunities to present their case before the Court. The value of legal precedents is also important in that it determines how much the Court is bound its previous decisions, and the impact of its decisions on subsequent findings and overall international law.

1   The Principle of Equality

The principle of equality between the parties is a fundamental principle of judicial proceedings, whose reach goes much beyond that of the ICJ. It protects the parties and seeks to guarantee a fair trial. At the ICJ, it finds expression, first and foremost, in ensuring that party to the dispute consents to its adjudication by the Court. The principle is so fundamental that even states that are

---

56   *Id.*, para. 87.
57   *Id.*, para. 88.

not party to the ICJ Statute are guaranteed equality with other parties before the Court.[58]

In addition, in the course of the proceedings, the Court ensures that both parties are subject to similar procedural rights and obligations, including time limits for the submission of their memorials and speaking allowances during oral proceedings.[59]

The Court has affirmed on multiple occasions that the principle of equality is indispensable to the proper administration of justice.[60] The Statute of the Court and the Rules of the Court have built in mechanisms to uphold these principles, and the Court's jurisprudence has further anchored the principle of equality into its practice. At time when formal requirements might afford one party an unfair advantage over the other, the Court may interpret the rule to preserve the essential equality between the parties.[61]

In the same vein, the Statute empowers the Court to award costs, if it so decides, even though it is standard practice for each party to bear its own costs in international litigation.[62] This further ensures that parties are not prejudiced by financial limitations. The United Nations set up the Secretary-General's Trust Fund to Assist States in the Settlement of Disputes through the International Court of Justice to provide financial support to parties that seek financial assistance, ensuring equality for both parties involved.[63]

Importantly, the Court has adhered to the principle of equality even when confronted to a non-appearing Respondent. In such circumstances, the Court and all other parties continue to proceed according to established practices;

---

58   *See* ICJ Statute, Article 35(2) ("[I]n no case shall such conditions place the parties in a position of inequality before the Court.").

59   *See Pulp Mills on the River Uruguay* (Argentina v. Uruguay), Order for Provisional Measures, I.C.J. Reports 2006, p. 113, 120 (assessing Argentina's claim that documents presented by Uruguay during a public hearing were filed late and, therefore, incompatible with the equality of the parties).

60   *See*, for example, *Complaints made Against UNESCO*, para. 77, 86. *See also, Judgment No. 2867 of the Administrative Tribunal of the International Labour Organization upon a Complaint Filed against the International Fund for Agricultural Development*, Separate Opinion of Judge Cançado Trinidade (2012).

61   *See Case Concerning Barcelona Traction, Light & Power Company, Ltd.* (Belgium v. Spain), Preliminary Objection, I.C.J. Reports 1964, at 6, 25.

62   ICJ Statute, Article 64 ("Unless otherwise decided by the Court, each party shall bear its own costs.").

63   Press Release, *Secretary-General Awards $700,000 from Trust Fund to Assist States in Settlement of Disputes through International Court of Justice*, June 4, 2004, UN Doc. SG/2087-L/3070.

the Court determines whether it possesses jurisdiction, organizes written and oral hearings, and delivers its judgment.[64]

> *Military and Paramilitary Activities in and against Nicaragua*, **Merits (1986), para. 31**[65]
>
> The provisions of the Statute and Rules of Court concerning the presentation of pleadings and evidence are designed to secure a proper administration of justice, and a fair and equal opportunity for each party to comment on its opponent's contentions. The treatment to be given by the Court to communications or material emanating from the absent party must be determined by the weight to be given to these different considerations, and is not susceptible of rigid definition in the form of a precise general rule. The vigilance which the Court can exercise when aided by the presence of both parties to the proceedings has a counterpart in the special care it has to devote to the proper administration of justice in a case in which only one party is present.

In accordance with the principle of equality, the non-participating Respondent continues to be considered a party to the proceedings, and remains obligated to comply with the Court's decision.[66]

2   The Value of Legal Precedents

The importance of consent also transpires from how the Court conceives of its *res judicata*. Article 38 of the ICJ Statute, which sets out the sources of law upon which decisions should be based, is surprisingly vague on the normative weight of ICJ decisions. Whereas it does note that "judicial decisions" constitute "subsidiary means for the determination of rules of law," it does not specify whether this applies to the Court's own decisions. It is unclear if "judicial decisions" refers to ICJ decisions, the decisions of domestic courts, or the decisions of other international and regional tribunals.

---

64   *See* ICJ Statute, Article 53; and The International Court of Justice Handbook (2014), at 62. *See also* discussion *infra*, Chapter 5.

65   *Case Concerning Military and Paramilitary Activities in and Against Nicaragua, supra* note 23.

66   ICJ Statute, Article 59, UN Charter, Article 94.

> **ICJ Statute**
>
> **Article 38**
>
> The Court, whose function is to decide in accordance with international law such disputes as are submitted to it, shall apply:
>
> a. international conventions, whether general or particular, establishing rules expressly recognized by the contesting states;
> b. international custom, as evidence of a general practice accepted as law;
> c. the general principles of law recognized by civilized nations;
> d. subject to the provisions of Article 59, judicial decisions and the teachings of the most highly qualified publicists of the various nations, as subsidiary means for the determination of rules of law.

That decisions of the Court have binding effect is instead provided for in Article 59 of the Statute. Formally speaking, the Court's decisions only bind the parties to the dispute in question.

> **ICJ Statute**[67]
>
> **Article 59**
>
> The decision of the Court has no binding force except between the parties and in respect of that particular case.

This is not to say, however, that the Court's decisions do not impact other states. A judgment rendered in case A may certainly influence how the Court will decide in case B. This does not result from a formal obligation but, rather, from the Court's perception of its role and the preservation of its legitimacy. Though "there is no room for rigid veneration of precedent" in the international sphere, the Court does not lightly make radical shifts in how it interprets the law.[68] Maintaining general consistency within its case law contributes to the creation of "good" international law and reinforces the Court's legitimacy as the premier international adjudicative organ. Predictability and stability also play a role in this context. Respect for precedents allow parties to plan

---

67   *See also* ICJ Statute, Article 60; UN Charter, Article 94.

68   *See* Hersch Lauterpacht, The Development of International Law by the International Court of Justice (1982), at 19.

THE INTERNATIONAL COURT OF JUSTICE AND STATES 65

their legal strategies based on previous rulings, and naturally, states can take previous decisions into account when making their arguments. The Court's case law ought to provide states with an indication of the possible outcome for future decisions on similar points of law.[69] The legal reasons grounding the Court's decision in each case – what it considers the correct legal position *and why* – enters into the general storehouse of public international law. As such, the Court's decisions are an important tool for the development of international law. The case law of the Court and the way it is invoked as a source of authority leave little doubt as to the standing of the Court's decisions.

> ### *Hersch Lauterpacht, The Development of International Law by the International Court of Justice*[70]
>
> The Court follows its own decisions for the same reasons for which all courts – whether bound by the doctrine of precedent or not – do so, namely, because uch decisions are a repository of legal experience to which it is convenient to adhere; because they embody what the Court has considered in the past to be good law; because respect for decisions given in the past makes for certainty and stability, which are of the essence of the orderly administration of justice; and (a minor and not invariably accurate consideration) because judges are naturally reluctant, in the absence of compelling reasons to the contrary, to admit that they were previously in the wrong (...) Moreover, the Court relies on its own decisions for the reason which, more than anything else, has caused the establishment of the formal doctrine of precedent in the countries of the common law (...), namely, the absence of a code or of a generally recognized system of law (...) Above all, for reasons which – once more – are even more compelling in the international sphere than within the state, reliance on precedent is not only in keeping with the ever-present requirement of certainty in the administration of justice, but with the necessity of avoiding the appearance of any excess of judicial discretion.

---

69   *See also* Hugh Thirlway, The Law and Procedure of the International Court of Justice (2013).

70   *See* Lauterpacht, *supra* note 73, at 14.

> *Armin von Bogdandy and Ingo Venzke, On the Functions of International Courts: An Appraisal in Light of Their Burgeoning Public Authority*[71]
>
> The development of normative expectations is (...) a core function of international courts. This dimension of judicial practice can best be understood as generating new legal normativity or simply as lawmaking. The lawmaking effect of judicial decisions, in particular in their general and abstract dimension that goes beyond the individual case, does not only depend on the *voluntas* but also on its *ratio*. But international decisions enjoy an exceptional standing in semantic disputes about what the law means and thus contribute to its making. Courts regularly use precedents in their legal argumentation and at times engage in detailed reasoning on how earlier decisions are relevant or not. Judicial precedents thus redistribute argumentative burdens in legal discourse. Overlooking or even negating this lawmaking function means missing out on an important aspect of the dynamics of the international legal order. Accordingly, the respective procedural law of international courts should be interpreted and developed in a way that also responds to this function.

• • •

Questions

1. Can you think of additional ways in which the Court, in its practice, ensures the equality of the parties?
2. Why does Article 38 not provide more information as to the normative weight of the Court's very own judicial decisions? Do you agree with Armin von Bogdandy that the development of "normative expectations" is "a core function" of the International Court of Justice?

E   How a Case is Tried

This section is supplemented with interactive material, available at DOI: 10.6084/m9.figshare.15093243

A few procedural events can occur over the course of contentious proceedings before the ICJ. The Respondent State can, first and foremost, object to the

---

71   Armin von Bogdandy and Ingo Venzke, *On the Functions of International Courts: An Appraisal in Light of Their Burgeoning Public Authority*, 26 Leiden J. Int'l L. 49, 55–56 (2003).

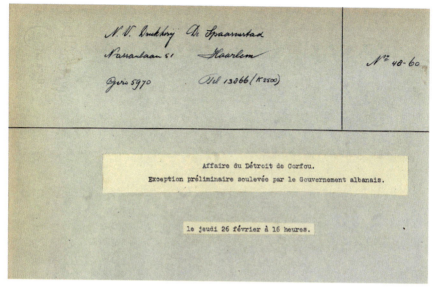

FIGURE 2.3   A preliminary objection file

Court's jurisdiction. In such a case, the Court will first hear these "preliminary objections," meaning that it will postpone its consideration of the substance of the case (also known as the "merits") until it assesses the arguments of the parties on jurisdiction. In addition, at any time during the proceedings (which typically last many years), the Court may order provisional measures to prevent the situation between the two states from deteriorating. Neither of these procedural incidents ought to affect the decision of the Court on the merits of the case – at least in theory.

a   Preliminary Objections

Once an Applicant seizes the Court, the Respondent may challenge the Court's jurisdiction by submitting preliminary objections.[72] Preliminary objections must be filed *before* the pleadings on the merits,[73] and must be of an

---

72 Though normally the objection is made by the Respondent, under certain conditions it may be submitted by a third party. A preliminary objection may also be raised on the Court's own initiative.

73 Of course, it will almost always be the Respondent that disputes the Court's jurisdiction. However, in very exceptional circumstances the Applicant may raise a preliminary objection. If a preliminary objection is raised, the proceedings on the merits are suspended until the matter is decided. If the Court finds it cannot entertain a case or part of a case

68   CHAPTER 2

"exclusively preliminary character" in the sense that they must not require an examination of the merits of the case.[74]

> **Rules of the International Court of Justice**
>
> **Article 79**
>
> 1. Any objection by the Respondent to the jurisdiction of the Court or to the admissibility of the application, or other objection the decision upon which is requested before any further proceedings on the merits, shall be made in writing as soon as possible, and not later than three months after the delivery of the Memorial.[75] Any such objection made by a party other than the Respondent shall be filed within the time-limit fixed for the delivery of that party's first pleading.
>
> 2. Notwithstanding paragraph 1 above, following the submission of the application and after the President has met and consulted with the parties, the Court may decide that any questions of jurisdiction and admissibility shall be determined separately (...)
>
> 5. Upon receipt by the Registry of a preliminary objection, the proceedings on the merits shall be suspended and the Court, or the President if the Court is not sitting, shall fix the time-limit within which the other party may present a written statement of its observations and submissions; documents in support shall be attached and evidence which it is proposed to produce shall be mentioned (...)9. After hearing the parties, the Court shall give its decision in the form of a judgment, by which it shall either uphold the objection, reject it, or declare that the objection does not possess, in the circumstances of the case, an exclusively preliminary character. If the Court rejects the objection or declares that it does not possess an exclusively preliminary character, it shall fix time-limits for the further proceedings.

Though prior to 2001, preliminary objections were required to be submitted "as soon as possible, and not later than three months after the delivery of the Memorial,"[76] today preliminary objections can be submitted much later in the process ("within the time-limit fixed for the delivery of the

---

     due to lack of jurisdiction or inadmissibility, the proceedings, or at least part of the proceedings, will be brought to an end.

74   Originally adopted on April 14, 1978, Article 79 was amended on February 1, 2001.

75   This is the result of an amendment of the Rules of Court of December 5, 2000 in order to expedite the conduct of the proceedings.

76   Rules of the Court, Article 79, Apr. 14, 1978, available at http://www.ICJ-cij.org/en/rules.

THE INTERNATIONAL COURT OF JUSTICE AND STATES   69

Counter-Memorial").[77] In most cases, the filing of preliminary objections will delay the proceedings and postpone a judgment on the merits.

As part of its preliminary objections, the Respondent may argue that (1) the Court was not properly seized, (2) it was properly seized but lacks jurisdiction on the merits, or (3) the case is inadmissible.

The first type of objection refers to the instrument invoked by the Applicant as granting jurisdiction to the Court. For example, when jurisdiction is conferred by a treaty, the Respondent could claim that the treaty is no longer in force, that it does not exist, or that the Respondent is not part of the agreement. This kind of objection does not require an analysis of the merits.

The second type of objection focuses on the jurisdiction of the Court or, more accurately, the lack thereof. In such a situation, the Respondent argues that the instrument invoked by the Applicant as conferring jurisdiction on the Court does not actually do so. For instance, if jurisdiction is accepted only for disputes arising after a certain date, the Respondent could argue that the dispute arose before that date. When faced with this type of objection, the Court analyzes the conformity of the issue or topic of the claim to the instrument but avoids ruling on the merits themselves.

Finally, the Respondent can argue that the case is inadmissible and cannot be heard before the Court. This includes objections related to judicial policy, abuse of process, the existence of prior negotiations, or the involvement of third parties. Although jurisdiction is not technically contested here, this type of preliminary objection is treated in the same manner at the procedural level.

The Court, by virtue of its Statute, is competent to address preliminary objections and ascertain the scope of its own jurisdiction. It may (1) accept the preliminary objection and terminate the proceedings; (2) accept objections that limit, but do not negate, its jurisdiction (the proceedings then move forward to discuss the merits, but on the basis of a narrower scope of jurisdiction); (3) conclude that the objections do not possess an exclusively preliminary character and defer them to the merits stage (this happens when the objection involves both preliminary aspects and aspects relating to the merits of the case); or (4) reject all objections and proceed to discuss the merits.[78]

As in the first scenario, the Court accepted the preliminary objection raised by the Russian Federation in *Application of the International Convention on the*

---

77   Rules of the Court, Article 79 (amended), Feb. 1, 2001, available at http://www.ICJ-cij.org/en/rules.

78   There are minor variations to these possibilities: the Respondent can also withdraw its objections at any point or contest the Court's competence to rule on the merits without formally raising a preliminary objection.

Elimination of All Forms of Racial Discrimination. In its application to the Court, Georgia claimed that the Russian Federation had breached the International Convention on the Elimination of All Forms of Racial Discrimination (CERD). The Russian Federation raised two preliminary objections to jurisdiction. Russia's first preliminary objection questioned the existence of a dispute – and was dismissed by the Court. Russia's second preliminary objection questioned the ability of the Court to take on the case given that the conditions laid down by Article 22 of the CERD had not been met. Under Article 22, the CERD imposed an obligation on the parties to negotiate prior to having recourse to the International Court of Justice. Georgia maintained that the parties had negotiated; the Russian Federation argued that they had not. The Court found that the parties had not engaged in negotiations prior to Georgia's application to the Court – essentially barring the Court from exercising jurisdiction over the case. The case, therefore, never proceeded to the merits phase.

> **Application of the International Convention on the Elimination of All Forms of Racial Discrimination (Georgia v. Russian Federation)[79]**
>
> Considering (...) that under Article 22 of CERD, negotiations and the procedures expressly provided for in CERD constitute preconditions to the exercise of its jurisdiction, and considering the factual finding that neither of these two modes of dispute settlement was attempted by Georgia, the Court does not need to examine whether the two preconditions are cumulative or alternative (...) The Court accordingly concludes that neither requirement contained in Article 22 has been satisfied. Article 22 of CERD thus cannot serve to found the Court's jurisdiction in the present case. The second preliminary objection of the Russian Federation is therefore upheld.

The Russian Federation's preliminary objection pertaining to Article 22 of the CERD was clearly of a preliminary character; it did not require any examination of the merits of the case.

---

79   *Case Concerning Application of the International Convention on the Elimination of All Forms of Racial Discrimination* (Georgia v. Russian Federation), Preliminary Objections, Judgment, I.C.J. Reports (2011), p. 70, paras. 181–84.

THE INTERNATIONAL COURT OF JUSTICE AND STATES 71

In some situations, however, the Court can find it difficult to establish whether the objection is of a preliminary character, i.e., whether it challenges the Court's jurisdiction or the Applicant's claims on the substance of the dispute.[80] If the preliminary objections relate to the existence and character of the dispute, for example, the Court might need to interpret a treaty allegedly breached by the Respondent.

The preliminary objections in *South West Africa* illustrate the difficulty in keeping jurisdiction and merits distinct at the preliminary objection stage.[81] Ethiopia and Liberia, the Applicants, requested the Court declare that South West Africa was "a Territory under the Mandate (...) and that the Mandate is a treaty in force within the meaning of Article 37 of the Statute." In one of its preliminary objections, South Africa argued that the Mandate in general, and its Article 7 in particular (which conferred jurisdiction on the ICJ), was no longer in force within the meaning of Article 37. The Court ruled only on the validity of Article 7 of the Mandate, in order to avoid going into the merits of the case

> **South West Africa Cases (Ethiopia v. Liberia)**
> **(Liberia v. South Africa)[82]**
> The Court concludes that Article 7 of the Mandate is a treaty or convention still in force within the meaning of Article 37 of the Statute of the Court and that the dispute is one which is envisaged in the said Article 7 and cannot be settled by negotiation. Consequently the Court is competent to hear the dispute on the merits.

In reality, not all objections qualify exclusively as preliminary or merits-based in nature; determining where they fall often requires getting deeper into the merits. During the preliminary hearing, the Court is presented with only a very broad view of the case and may find it impossible to formulate a decision without considering the arguments and evidence on the merits.

In its early days, when the Court encountered ambiguous claims that were not clearly preliminary, it had the option to join these claims with the

---

80 Shabtai Rosenne, The Law and Practice of the International Court (vol. 2, 1997), at 881 para. 231.

81 *South West Africa* (Ethiopia v. South Africa & Liberia v. South Africa), Preliminary Objections, I.C.J. Reports 1962, p. 319, at 347.

82 *Id.,* at 347.

72   CHAPTER 2

discussions on the merits. Since 1972, and the revision of the Rules of the
Court, this option is no longer available. Today, whenever a party raises preliminary objections, the Court separates the jurisdiction phase and the merits
phase, and renders two distinct judgments as required under Article 79(9) of
the Rules of the Court, reproduced above.

> **Shabtai Rosenne, Controlling Interlocutory Aspects of Proceedings in the International Court of Justice[83]**
>
> The Permanent Court first adopted its Rules of Court in 1922. They were
> amended slightly in 1926, 1927, and 1931, and revised after thorough review
> in 1936. The International Court adopted those Rules with minor adapta-
> tions and amendments in 1946, and they remained unchanged until 1972.
> In 1972 the Court made a few amendments to the Rules, the most important
> (as far as concerns litigation techniques) relating to preliminary objec-
> tions. The former well-established and well-understood practice of joining
> objections (especially to the admissibility) to the merits was abolished. In
> its place the Court introduced as a possible decision, a declaration that a
> specific objection "does not possess, in the circumstances, an exclusively
> preliminary character." This change has severely confused modern litiga-
> tion without any appreciable benefits either for the Court or for states,
> and has complicated the organization of coherent litigation strategy. In
> 1978 the Court promulgated a more thorough revision, which comprises
> the Rules currently in force. Comparison of the Rules of 1978 with those of
> 1922 will quickly show that they are all cast in the same mold, the mold of
> the diplomacy of the 1920s. The changes that have been made do not touch
> fundamentals. The only difference between litigation today and litigation
> in the 1920s, is that today the proceedings are much more drawn out, the
> written and oral pleadings are much longer, and the individual opinions
> of judges more frequent and also more extensive. This suggests that the
> time is ripe for a fundamental review of the Court's procedure than has yet
> been undertaken.

The Court's consideration of preliminary objections has become part-and-
parcel of its judicial function. Decisions declining jurisdiction on the basis
of preliminary objections can contribute to the settlement of a dispute. The

---

83   Shabtai Rosenne, *Controlling Interlocutory Aspects of Proceedings in the International
      Court of Justice*, Essays on International Law and Practice (2007).

THE INTERNATIONAL COURT OF JUSTICE AND STATES 73

Court can use such decisions to ease tensions and assist the parties in negotiating a solution. Like most aspects of the ICJ's work, preliminary objections serve both a political and a legal function.

•••

Questions

1. Should another international body or institution have authority to determine whether or not the ICJ has jurisdiction in a given case instead of the ICJ itself?

2. In many instances, if the ICJ does not have jurisdiction, then no other court or tribunal will. Should this affect how the judges assess preliminary objections?

3. Note that Georgia may not have had the ability to get Russia to come to the negotiating table in *Application of the International Convention on the Elimination of All Forms of Racial Discrimination.* In your view, should this political reality have affected the Court's decision on jurisdiction?

4. Impatience is often expressed at the increasingly common practice of raising successive preliminary objections and subsequently delaying judgments on the merits (by as much as a decade in some cases). What is your view of Article 79? Does it achieve the right balance in protecting the rights of the Respondents, on one hand, and creating the conditions for the administration of justice, on the other?

5. Every state is arguably entitled to intimate, through whatever procedure it deems appropriate and compatible with the Statute of the Court, that it is not willing to be implicated in a dispute before the Court. The state's subjective willingness is something quite different from its objective legal obligation to submit to the Court's jurisdiction. Would the situation be any different were the Court to operate under the principle of compulsory jurisdiction (as opposed to consensual jurisdiction)?

b   Provisional Measures

Under Article 41 of its Statute, the Court may issue certain measures before it makes a final decision on the merits of the case. These measures are known as "provisional" or "interim" measures of protection, and are designed to preserve the rights of the parties and avoid irreparable damage from being caused to the rights which are at the heart of the dispute. Via provisional measures the Court may request a state to immediately refrain from the use of violence or stay the execution of a death penalty sentence, for example.

> **ICJ Statute**
>
> Article 41
>
> 1. The Court shall have the power to indicate, if it considers that circumstances so require, any provisional measures which ought to be taken to preserve the respective rights of either party.
> 2. Pending the final decision, notice of the measures suggested shall forthwith be given to the parties and to the Security Council.

In determining whether to indicate provisional measures the Court will seek to satisfy itself of their urgency and of its *prima facie* jurisdiction over the dispute (meaning the existence of a possible basis on which the Court's jurisdiction might be founded, without prejudice to the decision of the Court's on the merits). It will also highlight the risk of irreparable damage (for example if there is a danger that economic assets that form the object of the dispute may be lost).

Requests for the indication of provisional measures have priority over all other cases – even over a pending hearing. When approving a request, the Court does not have to endorse the requested measures and enjoys full discretion to order whatever measures it sees fit, provided the measures comply with Article 41. The Court then gives notice of measures to the parties and the Security Council. The measures remain in force while the case is pending, unless they are ordered with a fixed time limit or are revoked or amended.

A request for provisional measures may be made by a party at any time in the course of the proceedings. The Court may also order such measures *proprio motu,* in the absence of a request by one of the parties.[84] Interim measures of protections are often requested in the early stages of a case, but this does not preclude one or both parties from making additional requests later. In *Pulp Mills on the River Uruguay*, the Court denied Argentina's request for provisional measures to limit construction along the river, but made clear that "[t]he decision also leaves unaffected the right of Argentina to submit in the future a fresh request for the indication of provisional measures under Article 75, paragraph 3 of the Rules of Court based on new facts."[85]

---

84 Rules of the Court, Article 75.

85 *Pulp Mills on the River Uruguay* (Argentina v. Uruguay), Provisional Measures, Order of 14 July 2006, I.C.J. Reports 2006, p. 113, para. 86.

The Court ordered provisional measures in *US Diplomatic and Consular Staff in Tehran* and *Military and Paramilitary Activities in and against Nicaragua*. In both instances, the Court ordered the parties to cease the use of force and refrain from violence.[86] The Court also ordered provisional measures in the *Breard* and *LaGrand* cases. In these cases, the Applicant petitioned for provisional measures to prevent the United States from carrying out death sentences against nationals of the Applicant States, pending the outcome of the proceedings. The Court granted the requests, but the executions were performed nonetheless. Following one execution, Germany, in the *LaGrand* case, claimed that the United States' failure to comply with the provisional measures constituted a breach of the Court's Statute. As a result, the Court had to determine whether provisional measures are binding upon the parties. This was a matter of longstanding controversy, and the Court ultimately brought some clarity when it held that an order granting provisional measures produces binding legal effects.[87]

By contrast, in the *Arrest Warrant* case, the Court rejected Congo's request to withdraw an arrest warrant issued by a Belgian judge against its (former) Foreign Minister, due to a lack of urgency. Belgium's request for provisional measures in *Questions Relating to the Obligation to Prosecute or Extradite* was rejected for similar reasons.

---

86 See *United States Diplomatic and Consular Staff in Tehran* (US v. Iran), Order, Request for the Indication of Provisional Measures (Dec. 15, 1979), I.C.J. Reports (1980), p. 3 (the United States requested provisional measures intended to secure the release of diplomatic hostages by Iran. The Court, ultimately, issued provisional measures for Iran to adhere to its diplomatic and consular obligations under the 1995 Treaty of Amity and required the parties not taking any action to "aggravate the tension between the two countries." Iran ignored the order calling for the release of the diplomatic hostages, leading the United States to attempt an abortive military rescue of its diplomatic personnel in Iran in 1980.); and *Case Concerning Military and Paramilitary Activities in and against Nicaragua. Case Concerning Military and Paramilitary Activities in and Against Nicaragua* (Nicaragua v. US), Order, Request for the Indication of Provisional Measures (May 10, 1984), I.C.J. Reports (1989), p. 169.

87 *LaGrand* (Germany v. US), Judgment, I.C.J. Reports (2001), p. 466, para. 102. Similarly, the ICJ indicated provisional measures in *Avena* in relation to four of the accused Mexican nationals on death row. *Case Concerning Avena and Other Mexican Nationals* (Mexico v. US), I.C.J. Reports (2004, p. 12.

> ### *Shigeru Oda, Provisional Measures the Practice of the International Court of Justice*[88]
>
> In the Nicaragua/US case (No. 15), the Court indicated provisional measures in 1984 which stated, inter alia, that the US should immediately cease and refrain from any action blocking access to or from Nicaraguan ports and the laying of mines, and that the right of Nicaragua to sovereignty and to political independence should be fully respected and should not in any way be jeopardized by any military and paramilitary activities which were prohibited by the principles of international law. In fact, the situation in Nicaragua remained unchanged even after the indication of these provisional measures. In the Burkina Faso/Mali Frontier Dispute case (No. 14), presented to a Chamber by a special agreement of the parties in dispute on boundary issues, the Chamber responded, in 1986, in favor of the requests for provisional measures submitted separately by both states and ordered that no action that might affect the delimitation of boundaries and cease-fire agreements should be taken. The Court's Order is believed in this case of joint submission to have been observed by both parties.

A long-standing territorial dispute concerning the Preah Vihear Temple brought Thailand and Cambodia before the Court on two occasions – in 1962 and again in 2011 (the latter as part of a request for interpretation of the 1962 judgment). In 1962, the Court decided in favor of Cambodia. In 2008, Cambodia had the Temple nominated as a UNESCO World Heritage site – but the decision was made without the agreement of Thailand, which had sovereignty over some of the land surrounding the temple. The unilateral Cambodian move sparked political tensions, which escalated to military confrontation and the deployment of 1,500 Thai and Cambodian soldiers to the border. Military clashes lasted from 2008 until 2011, resulting in casualties and displaced residents. As part of its request for interpretation of the 1962 judgment, Cambodia asked the Court to indicate provisional measures. The Court ordered both parties to refrain from taking any action that would aggravate the dispute while the case was pending before it.

---

88   Shigeru Oda, *Provisional Measures: The Practice of the International Court of Justice, in* Fifty Years of the International Court of Justice (V. Lowe and M. Fitzmaurice eds., 1996), at 541.

THE INTERNATIONAL COURT OF JUSTICE AND STATES

> **Request for Interpretation, Temple of Preah Vihear**
> **(Cambodia v. Thailand)[89]**
>
> Both Parties shall immediately withdraw their military personnel currently present in the provisional demilitarized zone, as defined in paragraph 62 of the present Order, and refrain from any military presence within that zone and from any armed activity directed at that zone; (...)
>
> Thailand shall not obstruct Cambodia's free access to the Temple of Preah Vihear or Cambodia's provision of fresh supplies to its nonmilitary personnel in the Temple; (...)
>
> Both Parties shall continue the co-operation which they have entered into within ASEAN and, in particular, allow the observers appointed by that organization to have access to the provisional demilitarized zone;
>
> Both Parties shall refrain from any action which might aggravate or extend the dispute before the Court or make it more difficult to resolve (...).

Requests for provisional measures have steadily increased over the years. Only requested in two cases in the first twenty years of the Court's existence, they were requested in 17 cases between 1990 and 2010. This tends to burden the Court's workload, as provisional measures take priority over all pending cases. Though at times these delays are justified by a genuine want to maintain international peace and security, at others it is used by states to delay proceedings, achieve a strategic advantage, or compensate for the inability to obtain relief from the Security Council.

• • •

Questions

1. Based on the examples above, what factors influence the Court in accepting or rejecting requests for provisional measures? Recall that the Court does not have direct responsibility for the maintenance of international peace (the Security Council has primary responsibility for maintaining international peace and security under Article 2(4) of the Charter). How do you think this plays out in the context of provisional measures? Can any of the requests for provisional

---

[89] *Case Concerning the Temple of Preah Vihear* (Cambodia v. Thailand), Provisional Measures, I.C.J. Reports 2011, p. 537. For more on this case, *see also infra*, Chapter 4.

measures be interpreted as attempts to influence or replace the Security Council in this task, particularly when the Court may not have jurisdiction to hear the case?

2. How does the Court's power to order provisional measures fit within the over-arching principle of consent?

3. Could/should the ICJ order provisional measures even though there is no request to do so on the part of the parties?

Further Reading

Giorgio Gaja, *Requesting the ICJ to Revoke or Modify Provisional Measures*, 14 L. & Prac. Int'l Cts. & Tribunals 1 (2015).

Lando, M., *Compliance with Provisional Measures Indicated by the International Court of Justice*, 8 JIDS 22 (2017).

Merrills, J.G., *Interim Measures of Protection in the Recent Jurisdiction of the International Court of Justice*, 44 ICLQ 90 (1995).

Miles, C.A., *Provisional Measures before International Courts and Tribunals* (2017).

Conclusion

Like the PCIJ before it, the ICJ's main role lies in resolving disputes between states in order to prevent escalation and, ultimately, the use of military force. Though states championed the existence of a permanent court of international adjudication, they carefully crafted the scope of their commitment to the ICJ as an institution. The principle of consent remains fundamental to the relationship between states and the ICJ; verifying that consent to its jurisdiction forms a significant part of the Court's work. It can take years for a determination, and it often requires the issuance of a separate judgment devoted exclusively to matters of jurisdiction.

Notwithstanding these limitations, there is nothing trivial about sovereign states subjecting themselves to the jurisdiction of the Court. The data analyzed in Chapter 5 suggests that certain states are indeed reluctant to make such a far-reaching decision ahead of time, before a dispute arises, when the subject-matter of the dispute and the identity of the opposing state are still unknown. Yet the vast majority of states does so regularly by entering into bilateral and multi-lateral treaties conferring jurisdiction on the Court. The more parties to the treaty, the greater the unknown, and consequently, the greater the vote of confidence in favor of the Court. Each state makes its own decision as to how much or how little support it wishes to express – or, to put it differently, on what terms it wishes to interact with the Court.

Ultimately, the ICJ directly interacts with states more than it interacts with any other actor (without undermining the impact of such other interactions, which will be analyzed in the remainder of this book). States embody the Court's main constituency. The Court even reports to states when it submits its yearly report to the UN General Assembly.

Chapter 5 delves deeper into the relationship between states and the ICJ, using novel tools to analyze how individual states choose to interact with the Court. Patterns of deference and defiance are identified, and states' preferences – including those of the P5 – are investigated. This groundbreaking research shows that most UN member states have interacted with the Court in the contentious *or* advisory context (150 states out of 193). The Charter, the Court's Statute and its Rules make it possible for states to do so in a variety of ways, and states have taken advantage of this flexibility by interacting with the Court in a way that best suits their needs.

FIGURE 2.4 Sealed judgment in *Barcelona Traction*
SOURCE: JEROEN BOUMAN, PHOTOGRAPHER

CHAPTER 3

The International Court of Justice and the United Nations

Article 1 of the Statute of the Court explicitly recognizes that the ICJ is "established by the Charter of the United Nations as the principal judicial organ of the United Nations." The Court serves as one of its principal organs alongside the General Assembly, the Security Council, the Economic and Social Council, the Secretariat and the now-defunct Trusteeship Council. To understand the ICJ, it is therefore essential to examine its relationship with other UN organs and the role it plays within the UN system as a whole.

The ICJ interacts with UN organs primarily via the exercise of advisory jurisdiction. Advisory jurisdiction enables the Court to provide legal advice at the request of a UN body. Advisory jurisdiction constitutes the ICJ's second type of jurisdiction, alongside contentious jurisdiction (discussed in Chapter 2).

In the exercise of its advisory function, the Court is not acting as a traditional judicial body. Via advisory jurisdiction, the Court facilitates UN activity and ensures that UN organs and sub-organs adhere to their respective mandates and functions. The Court also enhances cooperation between various branches of the organization. Finally, the ICJ's advisory "hat" provides additional opportunities for the ICJ to contribute to the development of international law.

Advisory jurisdiction therefore holds significant potential for the United Nations and for the Court. The extent to which the ICJ is invited to contribute, and the extent to which it seizes opportunities to contribute, very much depend on how the Court views its role within the organization. This chapter examines the unique features of advisory jurisdiction, the difficulty of distinguishing between "questions" and "disputes", and the relationship between the ICJ and other principal UN organs.

A Advising the UN as an Organization

1 *Nature and Scope of the Advisory Function*
The Court inherited its advisory function from its predecessor, the Permanent Court of International Justice (PCIJ). Whereas the PCIJ delivered twenty-seven

© KONINKLIJKE BRILL NV, LEIDEN, 2020 | DOI:10.1163/9789004226968_005

advisory opinions in seventeen years, the ICJ delivered twenty-seven advisory opinions between 1948 and 2018, i.e., in 70 years.[1] Overall, advisory opinions only account for about a fifth of the ICJ's overall activity.

Although used substantially less, the scope of the ICJ's advisory jurisdiction is broader than the PCIJ's. The competence of the General Assembly and the Security Council to request advisory opinions was extended in 1945 to "[o]ther organs of the United Nations and specialized agencies." Specialized agencies of the UN authorized to seek advisory opinions from the ICJ are listed on the Court's website.[2]

The Security Council and the General Assembly may request opinions on *any* legal question. Other bodies may only ask for opinions on legal questions arising within the scope of their respective activities; their ability to request advisory opinions is thus more limited.[3] For instance, the Court held that a request by the World Health Organization (WHO) for an advisory opinion on the legality of nuclear weapons was inadmissible on the ground that the question did not fall within the scope of the WHO's activities.[4] The request was later re-submitted by the General Assembly, and answered by the Court.[5]

A request for an advisory opinion comes in the form of a decision adopted by the requesting organ. The advisory procedure encourages multilateralism, since the request must come in the form of a collegial decision adopted by the Security Council, the General Assembly, or other duly authorized bodies. Individual states cannot request an advisory opinion from the Court. They must garner the support of other states in order to constitute a majority at one of the UN bodies. The decision is subject to an internal vote: states must vote in favor

---

1 The International Court of Justice Handbook (2014), at 84.

2 *See also* Robert Kolb, The International Court of Justice (2013), at 1047. List of organs and agencies authorized to request advisory opinions available at https://www.icj-cij.org/en/organs-agencies-authorized.

3 In some rare instances, an organ may be obligated to refer a question to the Court. For example, Article VIII, Section 30 of the Convention on Privileges and Immunities of the United Nations provides as follows: "All differences arising out of the interpretation or application of the present convention shall be referred to the International Court of Justice, unless in any case it is agreed by the parties to have recourse to another mode of settlement. If a difference arises between the United Nations on the one hand and a Member on the other hand, a request shall be made for an advisory opinion on any legal question involved in accordance with Article 96 of the Charter and Article 65 of the Statute of the Court. The opinion given by the Court shall be accepted as decisive by the parties."

4 *Legality of the Use by a State of Nuclear Weapons in Armed Conflict*, Advisory Opinion, I.C.J. Reports 1996, p. 68.

5 *Request for an Advisory Opinion from the ICJ on the Legality of the Threat or Use of Nuclear Weapons*, G.A. Res. 49/75K, UN GAOR (1997).

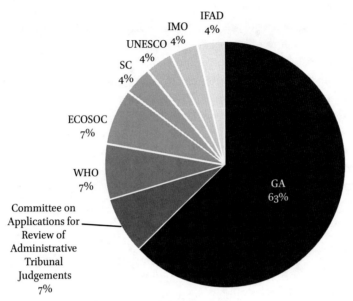

FIGURE 3.1   Bodies requesting advisory opinions

of or against the referral of the question to the ICJ. At the General Assembly, the decision to request an advisory opinion must be adopted by a majority of states present and voting. At the Security Council, a majority of nine members (subject to the veto power of the five permanent members) is required. Most requests for advisory opinions emanate from the General Assembly; only once did the Security Council seek an advisory opinion.[6]

Please note that a table of advisory opinions and the corresponding requesting organs may be found at the end of this chapter (Table 3.2).

The ICJ's advisory jurisdiction is an optional mechanism at the disposal of the UN and its approved organs. Article 96 of the UN Charter provides that the relevant organs "may" request advisory opinions, thus even when legal questions do arise, UN bodies have no obligation to refer them to the ICJ.[7] Similarly, Article 65 of the Statute of the Court provides that the ICJ "may" give an advisory opinion. The Court can therefore decline a request for an advisory opinion.

---

6   *Legal Consequences for States of the Continued Presence of South Africa in Namibia (South West Africa) notwithstanding Security Council Resolution 276*, Request for Advisory Opinion, Aug. 5, 1970. See Kolb, *supra* note 2, at 1044.

7   Kolb, *supra* note 2, at 1022.

When a request for an advisory opinion lands on the Court's desk, the Court first establishes whether it has jurisdiction to take on the request. The Court must make sure that the UN organ requesting the opinion meets the required criteria. For example, if the request emanates from an organ other than the General Assembly or the Security Council, the Court must ascertain whether the question falls within the scope of that organ's activities. Assuming the Court has jurisdiction to hear the request, the Court must then decide whether it wishes to answer the question asked. This second stage is known as *propriety*, i.e., the Court decides whether it is appropriate for it to answer the request. Here, the Court weighs a wide array of considerations – from involvement in an ongoing political process to a potential violation of the principle of consent or, more generally, the compatibility of the request with the Court's judicial character.

The inherent flexibility of the advisory function also manifests itself in the conduct of advisory proceedings.

ICJ Statute

Article 66

1. The Registrar shall forthwith give notice of the request for an advisory opinion to all states entitled to appear before the Court.

2. The Registrar shall also, by means of a special and direct communication, notify any state entitled to appear before the Court or international organization considered by the Court, or, should it not be sitting, by the President, as likely to be able to furnish information on the question, that the Court will be prepared to receive, within a time-limit to be fixed by the President, written statements, or to hear, at a public sitting to be held for the purpose, oral statements relating to the question.

3. Should any such state entitled to appear before the Court have failed to receive the special communication referred to in paragraph 2 of this Article, such state may express a desire to submit a written statement or to be heard; and the Court will decide.

4. States and organizations having presented written or oral statements or both shall be permitted to comment on the statements made by other states or organizations in the form, to the extent, and within the time-limits which the Court, or, should it not be sitting, the President, shall decide in each particular case. Accordingly, the Registrar shall in due time communicate any such written statements to states and organizations having submitted similar statements.

84 CHAPTER 3

In advisory proceedings, access to the Court is not restricted to states – an important difference with contentious proceedings. Broad access to the Court allows the ICJ to collect as much information as possible on the legal question asked. The Court may invite states that are not members of the UN, as well as international organizations, to take part in advisory proceedings. It has also invited individuals in exceptional circumstances.[8]

In 2003, the Court invited Palestine to take part in advisory proceedings on account of Palestine's special status within the UN and its sponsorship of the request for an advisory opinion.

> **Legal Consequences of the Construction of a Wall in the Occupied Palestinian Territory[9]**
>
> Decides further that, in light of General Assembly resolution A/RES/ES-10/14 and the report of the Secretary-General transmitted to the Court with the request, and taking into account the fact that the General Assembly has granted Palestine a special status of observer and that the latter is co-sponsor of the draft resolution requesting the advisory opinion, Palestine may also submit to the Court a written statement on the question within the above time-limit.

Finally, in yet another display of informality, advisory opinions rendered by the Court are not binding; the requesting organ is not obligated to implement the Court's opinion. Only rarely will the Court stipulate that an opinion is binding (usually with regard to administrative UN questions),[10] although states may agree ahead of time that an advisory opinion will be binding. For example, when the Economic and Social Council requested an advisory opinion on the immunity of Dato Param Cumaraswamy, then Special Rapporteur of the Commission on Human Rights on the Independence of Judges and Lawyers, the resolution specified that the opinion "should be accepted as decisive by the parties."[11]

---

8   *See* Hugh Thirlway, *The International Court of Justice 1989–2009: At the Heart of the Dispute Settlement System*, 57 Netherlands Int'l L. Rev. 347, 389 (2010). *See also, infra*, Chapter 4.

9   *Legal Consequences of the Construction of a Wall in the Occupied Palestinian Territory*, Order of 19 December 2003, I.C.J. Reports 2003, p. 428, para. 2.

10 The International Court of Justice Handbook, *supra* note 1 at 90.

11 *Request for an Advisory Opinion from the International Court of Justice*, UN ECOSOC 1998/297 (Aug. 5, 1998).

THE INTERNATIONAL COURT OF JUSTICE AND THE UNITED NATIONS   85

Although advisory opinions are not formally legally binding, ICJ authority and legitimacy attach to such opinions: "they are judicial pronouncement and not only legal advice in the ordinary sense."[12] Opinions tend to be taken seriously by the requesting organ, since it expects guidance from the Court. States with a stake in the question asked to the Court – particularly if they voted against the request for an advisory opinion – may be less inclined to implement the Court's advisory opinion. Finally, advisory opinions can contribute to the development of customary international law depending on how states, scholars, and practitioners react to the opinion. Criticism of advisory opinions can at times affect the opinion's legal standing.

To conclude, advisory jurisdiction stands out by its flexibility and the specificity of its features – particularly when compared to contentious jurisdiction: non-states may be invited to take part in the proceedings, states are under no obligation to participate, consent need not be expressed and advisory opinions do not possess the *res judicata*. Much like contentious jurisdiction, however, advisory jurisdiction fulfills multiple functions, from enhancing cooperation within the UN to providing legal advice, and safeguarding the UN system.

• • •

Questions

1. What is the normative value of an advisory opinion? As legal opinions delivered by a court of law, do you think that advisory opinions should have binding legal force?

2. According to Judge John Bassett Moore, "to impose upon a court of justice the duty of giving advice, which those requesting it were wholly at liberty to reject, would reduce the court to a position inferior to that of a tribunal of conciliation."[13] Does the ability to provide non-binding legal advice enhance or weaken the ICJ's authority and legitimacy? Do you think the advisory function adds to the Court's prestige as the "World Court"?

3. Since the opinions delivered by the Court are not binding, why limit the bodies authorized to request advisory opinions? Should states be permitted to request opinions on an individual basis? Why?

---

12   Armin von Bogdandy, International Judicial Lawmaking (2012), at 87.
13   Publications of the PCIJ, Series D, Acts and Documents Concerning Organisation of the Court, No. 2, Annex 58A, 383.

4. Why do you think it is necessary for the Court to fulfill an advisory role for the United Nations, in addition to deciding contentious cases?

5. What procedural and structural measures, if any, could enhance the Court's advisory jurisdiction? Consider Judge Higgins's view (below) in this regard. Do you agree?

6. It has been suggested that the ability to request advisory opinions be extended to the Secretary-General.[14] In 1992, then Secretary-General Dr. Boutros Boutros-Ghali encouraged UN agencies to rely more often on the advisory function of the Court and recommended that the Secretary-General be authorized to request advisory opinions.[15] The Security Council and the General Assembly, however, did not take any action. What could be the arguments for and against granting the Secretary-General authority to request the Court for an advisory opinion? Consider Judge Higgins' view (below) in this regard. Do you agree?

> ### Rosalyn Higgins, A Comment on the Current Health of Advisory Opinions[16]
>
> The Advisory Opinion will surely continue to serve a useful judicial function. The relatively infrequent contemporary recourse to Advisory Opinions is not necessarily a matter to be regretted. Its use most naturally occurs at certain moments in the institutional life of an international organization (in the early years), and from time to time when unforeseeable problems arise for the working of UN organs or agencies. Little purpose is served by artificially inventing new business for the Advisory Opinion, whether in the context of interstate disputes settlement or through new powers to be afforded to the Secretary-General. Recourse to the Court must work with the seams of political and institutional realities and not against the grain.

7. Should the Security Council be authorized to implement advisory opinions under Chapter VII of the United Nations Charter (as is the case with the Court's judgments)?

---

14   Stephen M. Schwebel, *Widening the Advisory Jurisdiction of the International Court of Justice without Amending Its Statute*, 33 Catholic U.L. Rev. 355, 360 (1984).

15   *Preventive diplomacy, peacemaking and peace-keeping, Report of the Secretary-General pursuant to the statement adopted by the Summit Meeting of the Security Council on 31 January 1992* (June 12,1992), para. 38.

16   Rosalyn Higgins, *A Comment on the Current Health of Advisory Opinions, in* Fifty Years of the International Court of Justice: Essays in Honor of Sir Robert Jennings (Vaughan Lowe and Malgosia Fitzmaurice eds., 2007), at 580–81.

2 *Facilitating UN Activity and Cooperation*

By preventing individual states from requesting advisory opinions, the UN Charter and the ICJ Statute have given the procedure a resolutely collegial undertone. The right to request advisory opinions is meant to be exercised internally, i.e., within the organization itself. The objective goes beyond the settlement of disputes: the Court has the responsibility to ensure the proper functioning of the international organization. In its own words, it "guides the United Nations in respect of its own action."[17]

UN bodies and specialized agencies can turn to the Court if and when they encounter legal issues. By providing legal advice, the Court thereby facilitates UN activity and promotes the objectives of the organization.

> **Interpretation of Peace Treaties with Bulgaria, Hungary and Romania**[18]
> The Court's opinion is given not to the States, but to the organ which is entitled to request it; the reply of the Court, itself an 'organ of the United Nations,' represents its participation in the activities of the Organisation, and, in principle, should not be refused.

The Court has taken this responsibility seriously, often referred to as a "duty to cooperate."[19] The ICJ has never refused to give an advisory opinion when asked to do so by another UN organ – even though states have objected at times.[20] According to the Court, there must be "compelling reasons" *not* to give an advisory opinion.[21]

---

17   *Reservations to the Convention on Prevention and Punishment of Crime of Genocide*, I.C.J. Reports 1951, p. 15, at 19.

18   *Interpretation of Peace Treaties with Bulgaria, Hungary and Romania*, Advisory Opinion, I.C.J. Reports 1950, p. 65, at, 71.

19   Shabtai Rosenne, Law and Practice of the International Court of Justice, 5th ed. (2017), vol. II, para 248.

20   While the ICJ has never refused to give an advisory opinion, the PCIJ refused to provide one in *Status of Eastern Carelia*. In doing so, the Permanent Court of International Justice placed great emphasis on the fact that the Soviet Union, which had direct stakes in the legal question asked to the court, was not a party to the Covenant of the League of Nations. See *Eastern Carelia*, Series B., No. 5 (1923).

21   *Certain Expenses of the United Nations, Art. 17, para. 2 of the Charter*, Advisory Opinion, I.C.J. Reports 1962, p. 155.

88 CHAPTER 3

3 Developing International Law

Advisory opinions provide opportunities for the Court to interpret and develop international law. Interestingly, the Court has not adopted a consistent position regarding its level of involvement in international legal matters. It has, at times, adopted advisory opinions with far-reaching legal repercussions. At others, it has shied away from clarifying contested points of international law in advisory opinions.

> **Karin Oellers-Frahm, Lawmaking through Advisory Opinions?[22]**
>
> In the *Reparation for Injuries* opinion, the Court ruled in favor of the capacity of an international organization to bring a claim against a state, a decision that was standard-setting on the issue of the international personality of an international organization; on the basis of this opinion the United Nations' claim for recovery of pecuniary reparation from Israel was successful. In the *Certain Expenses* opinion, the Court had to decide on the budgetary powers of the General Assembly; it found that expenses authorized by the General Assembly in relation to two peacekeeping forces were expenses in the meaning of Art. 17(2) UNC and thus had to be borne by the member states. The significance of the three advisory opinions delivered in the context of the *South Africa* cases, in particular the *Namibia* opinion, concerning the international responsibility of a state resulting from physical control, not from sovereignty, over a particular territory, is undisputed. In particular, the findings concerning the consequences for UN member states as well as non-member states flowing from the illegal presence of South Africa in Namibia had far reaching repercussions, although the South Africa Government maintained its original position and did not cooperate with the General Assembly in its efforts to "implement" the opinion.

The Court took a similarly bold approach in *Legal Consequences of the Separation of the Chagos Archipelago from Mauritius in 1965*, following a request from the General Assembly concerning the decolonization of Mauritius and

---

22   Karin Oellers-Frahm, *Lawmaking Through Advisory Opinions?*, International Judicial Lawmaking (Armin von Bogdandy ed., 2012), at 81–82.

THE INTERNATIONAL COURT OF JUSTICE AND THE UNITED NATIONS   89

the United Kingdom's responsibilities.[23] A number of participating states asserted that the Court should decline to exercise its jurisdiction as a matter of discretion, in light of the complexity of the factual issues, the inability of the Court to assist the General Assembly, the prior examination of the question by an arbitral tribunal, and the absence of consent to the Court's jurisdiction by interested states. The Court found no basis to decline the request, ultimately determining that the process of decolonization had not been lawfully completed and declaring the United Kingdom's continued administration of the Chagos Archipelago an internationally wrongful act.

In contrast to *Reparations for Injuries, Certain Expenses of the United Nations*, or *Legal Consequences of the Separation of the Chagos Archipelago from Mauritius in 1965*, the Court took a much more prudent approach in *Accordance with International Law of the Unilateral Declaration of Independence in Respect of Kosovo*. The General Assembly requested that opinion in 2008, in the wake of Kosovo's unilateral declaration of independence. It provided an opportunity for the Court to clarify the role played by recognition in acceding to statehood, and the contours of the rights to secession. Yet the Court said very little.[24]

The different paths taken by the Court in the exercise of its advisory jurisdiction suggest that something else might be at play – beyond the development of international law. Political and legal stakes likely affect the Court's willingness to contribute new insight, leading it to prioritize its role as an appeaser of international tensions. For instance, in *Kosovo*, the Court acted more as a peacemaker than as a legal adviser (arguably to prevent an escalation of the tensions between Kosovo and Serbia, and potential instability in states vulnerable to secessionist movements).[25] In other situations, the Court finds it more appropriate to act as a "trusted advisor" or a judicial body.

---

23   *Legal Consequences of the Separation of the Chagos Archipelago from Mauritius in 1965*, Advisory Opinion, I.C.J. Reports 2019, p. 95.

24   See, for example, Daphné Richemond-Barak, *The International Court of Justice on Kosovo: Missed Opportunity or Dispute 'Settlement'?*, 23 Hague Y.B. Int'l L. 1 (2010).

25   *Id.*

> ### *Sir Franklin Berman, The Uses and Abuses of Advisory Opinions*[26]
>
> A court asked to play an advisory role is (...) faced with a choice. It may decide that the role requires it to bring to bear its collective judicial experience and wisdom, to be sure, but nevertheless not to act as a court; so it may conceive its function as analogous instead to that of a trusted advisor, like a family lawyer or the legal counsel of a government department or international organization. It may, on the contrary, decide that the advisory role is a judicial one, requiring it still to function as a court.

Ultimately, the Court's reasons for seizing (or not) an opportunity to develop international law by way of advisory opinions often remain a matter of speculation.

4   *Safeguarding the System*

Advisory jurisdiction enables the ICJ to fulfill yet another function – protecting the UN system. By maintaining obedience to the law, the ICJ promotes good governance in the organization.[27] Neither the UN Security Council nor the General Assembly possesses formal constitutional powers, creating an opportunity for the ICJ to fill this gap. Via advisory proceedings, which are by nature more flexible and open than contentious proceedings, the Court can provide guidance on the inner workings of the organization and the functioning of UN organs.

States long resisted the exercise of the Court's advisory function on *"questions of a constitutional or a juridical character arising within the scope of their activities."*[28] A Subcommittee at the San Francisco Conference advised against giving the Court's explicit competence to interpret the Charter. As a result, the Court was not endowed with a formal, explicit constitutional function.[29]

A mere two years later, however, the General Assembly re-opened the debate. In 1947, by 46 votes to 6, it declared that it is "of paramount importance that

---

26   Sir Franklin Berman, *The Uses and Abuses of Advisory Opinions,* Judge Shigeru Oda: Liber Amicorum (Nisuke Ando, Edward McWhinney and Rudger Wolfrum eds., 2002), at 809, 818–19.

27   Kolb, *supra* note 2, at 1020.

28   Dapo Akande, *The Competence of International Organizations and the Advisory Jurisdiction of the International Court of Justice,* 9 EJIL 437, 455 (1998).

29   Bernd Martenczuk, *The Security Council, the International Court and Judicial Review: What Lessons from Lockerbie?,* 10 EJIL 517, 526 (1999).

THE INTERNATIONAL COURT OF JUSTICE AND THE UNITED NATIONS 91

the Court should be utilized to the greatest practicable extent in the progressive development of international law, both in regard to legal issues between States and in regard to constitutional interpretation."[30]

The Court's own pronouncements on the matter echo these hesitations.[31] In *Conditions of Admission of a State to Membership in the United Nations*, the Court expressed the view the interpretation of the UN Charter forms part-and-parcel of its judicial function.

> ### Conditions of Admission of a State to Membership in the United Nations[32]
>
> Lastly, it has also been maintained that the Court cannot reply to the question put because it involves an interpretation of the Charter. Nowhere is any provision to be found forbidding the Court, "the principal judicial organ of the United Nations", to exercise in regard to Article 4 of the Charter, a multilateral treaty, an interpretative function which falls within the normal exercise of its judicial powers.

At the time, the Court recognized both the importance of consistency in the interpretation and application of the Charter – and its role in ensuring such consistency.

Later opinions take a more muted approach. In *Certain Expenses*, the Court noted that the responsibility to delineate the competence of UN organs lies first within such organs.

---

30   *Need for a Greater Use by the United Nations and its Organs of the International Court of Justice*, A/Res/171(ii) (Nov. 14, 1947). The vote was unrecorded so there is no information regarding the six states that voted no.

31   For more on this, and a slightly different view, see Mohamed Sameh M. Amr, The Role of the International Court of Justice as Principal Judicial Organ of the UN (2003), at 127–29.

32   *Conditions of Admission of a State to Membership in the United Nations*, Advisory Opinion, I.C.J. Reports 1947, p. 57, at 61.

> **Certain Expenses of the United Nations[33]**
> In the legal systems of States, there is often some procedure for determining the validity of even a legislative or governmental act, but no analogous procedure is to be found in the structure of the United Nations. Proposals made during the drafting of the Charter to place the ultimate authority to interpret the Charter in the International Court of Justice were not accepted (...) As anticipated in 1945, therefore, each organ must, in the first place at least, determine its own jurisdiction.

The Court reiterated this view in the *Namibia* case, asserting that it has no competence to engage in judicial review (namely that it does not have competence to determine the validity of acts or decisions adopted by other UN organs).

> **Legal Consequences for States of the Continued Presence of South Africa in Namibia[34]**
> Undoubtedly, the Court does not possess powers of judicial review or appeal in respect of the decisions taken by the United Nations organs concerned (...) However, in the exercise of its judicial function and since objections have been advanced the Court, in the course of its reasoning, will consider these objections before determining any legal consequences arising from these resolutions.

In the absence of a centralized body endowed with such competence, the potential of having the Court fulfill a constitutional role cannot be underestimated. Whether the Court chooses to make use of its advisory function in this way is another matter.

•••

---

33 *Certain Expenses of the United Nations, Art. 17, para. 2 of the Charter*, Advisory Opinion, I.C.J. Reports 1962, p. 168.

34 *Legal Consequences for States of the Continued Presence of South Africa in Namibia (South West Africa) Notwithstanding Security Council Resolution 276*, Advisory Opinion, 1971 I.C.J. Reports (1971), p. 16.

Questions

1. Though the ICJ did in fact play a constitutional role in *Conditions of Admission of a State to Membership in the United Nations* (setting out the conditions for the admission of new states into United Nations) and in *Certain Expenses* (regarding the legal status of UN peacekeeping operations), it emphasized that it was merely interpreting "a multi-lateral treaty" (i.e., the UN Charter), and that its interpretation was of a non-binding nature. What does this mean as to the ICJ's view of its own role within the UN system? Why would the ICJ *not* want to act and portray itself as the constitutional court of the United Nations?

2. Can the Court, via the exercise of advisory jurisdiction, simultaneously provide legal advice, facilitate cooperation within the UN, and/or safeguard the United Nations as an institution? Which of these functions is most important in the exercise of the Court's advisory competence? Is it reasonable to expect the Court to fulfill them all?

3. Building on *Kosovo*, does advisory jurisdiction have a role to play in the peaceful settlement of disputes?

4. Do you agree with former ICJ Judge Thomas Burgenthal that the advisory process has the advantage "of making it politically easier for a government to comply with advisory opinions: by their very nature, they do not stigmatize the state as a lawbreaker and permit a delinquent government to make its compliance appear to be a voluntary act"?[35]

Further Reading

Manley O. Hudson, *Advisory Opinions of National and International Courts*, 37 Harv. L. Rev. (1924).

Stephen M. Schwebel, *Widening the Advisory Jurisdiction of the International Court of Justice without Amending Its Statute*, 33 Catholic U.L. Rev. 355 (1984).

Roberto Ago, *"Binding" Advisory Opinions of the International Court of Justice*, 85 Am. J. Int'l L. 439 (1991).

Michla Pomerance, *The Advisory Role of the International Court of Justice and its "Judicial" Character: Past and Future Prisms*, in The International Court of Justice: Its Future Role After Fifty Years (Muller et al. eds., 1996).

David Schweigman, The Authority of the Security Council Under Chapter VII of the UN Charter: Legal Limits and the Role of the International Court of Justice (2001).

---

35 Thomas Buergenthal, *The Advisory Practice of the Inter-American Human Rights Court*, 79 AJIL 1, 26 (1985).

94 CHAPTER 3

Charles Brower and Pieter Becker, *Understanding "Binding" Advisory Opinions of the International Court of Justice, in* Judge Shigeru Oda: Liber Amicorum (N. Ando et al. eds., 2002).

B Advising on Disputes

Although the ICJ inherited its advisory competence from the PCIJ, the ICJ's advisory jurisdiction is more circumscribed. Under Article 14 of the League's Covenant, the PCIJ could give an advisory opinion on "any dispute or question."

> ### Covenant of the League of Nations[36]
> **Article 14**
> The Council shall formulate and submit to the Members of the League for adoption plans for the establishment of a Permanent Court of International Justice. The Court shall be competent to hear and determine any dispute of an inter-national character which the parties thereto submit to it. The Court may also give an advisory opinion upon any *dispute or question* referred to it by the Council or by the Assembly.

This double formulation – dispute or question – implied that the PCIJ could be consulted by referral from the Assembly or the Council of the League about a state-to-state dispute. The committee in charge of drafting the ICJ Statute objected to importing this idea into the ICJ's Statute, considering that it would amount to circumventing the principle of consent if the interested states had not given their consent.[37] The reference to disputes was rejected, and the ICJ was entrusted with the competence to provide advisory opinions exclusively on legal *questions*.

> ### Charter of the United Nations[38]
> **Article 96**
> The General Assembly or the Security Council may request the International Court of Justice to give an advisory opinion on any legal *question*.

---

36 Emphasis added.
37 Edvard Hambro, *The Authority of the Advisory Opinions of the International Court of Justice*, 3 Int'l & Comp. L.Q. 2 (1954); Advisory Committee of Jurists, Procès-Verbaux of the Proceedings of the Committee, June 16–July 24 1920, with Annexes (1920), at 731.
38 Emphasis added.

THE INTERNATIONAL COURT OF JUSTICE AND THE UNITED NATIONS 95

Designed to fulfill a different function, advisory proceedings differ in many ways from contentious proceedings: there are no parties, advisory opinions are not binding, states may not submit a question to the Court unilaterally, and – at least theoretically – there is no dispute.[39] Yet in practice, contentious jurisdiction has strongly influenced the way the Court exercises its advisory prerogatives. Inadvertently or not, the Court has struggled to keep the two procedures entirely distinct, and has found it difficult to refrain from getting involved in disputes via advisory jurisdiction.

States, however, have remained consistent in restricting the Court from offering advisory opinions on disputes. Since the Court's early days, states have repeatedly resisted the exercise of advisory jurisdiction in situations that would amount to the resolution of a bilateral dispute. Consider, for example, the arguments put forward by Spain regarding the request for an advisory opinion on the legal status of Western Sahara.

Western Sahara[40]

Spain considers that the subject of the dispute which Morocco invited it to submit jointly to the Court for decision in contentious proceedings, and the subject of the questions on which the advisory opinion is requested, are substantially identical; thus the advisory procedure is said to have been used as an alternative after the failure of an attempt to make use of the contentious jurisdiction with regard to the same question. Consequently, to give a reply would, according to Spain, be to allow the advisory procedure to be used as a means of bypassing the consent of a State, which constitutes the basis of the Court's jurisdiction. If the Court were to countenance such a use of its advisory jurisdiction, the outcome would be to obliterate the distinction between the two spheres of the Court's jurisdiction, and the fundamental principle of the independence of States would be affected, for States would find their disputes with other States being submitted to the Court, by this indirect means, without their consent; this might result in compulsory jurisdiction being achieved by majority vote in a political organ. Such circumvention of the well-established principle of consent for the exercise of international jurisdiction would constitute, according to this view, a compelling reason for declining to answer the request.

---

39   *See*, for example, Achilles Skordas, Epilogemena *to a Silence: Nuclear Weapons, Terrorism, and the Moment of Concern*, 6 J. Conflict & Sec. L. 191 (2001).

40   *Western Sahara*, Advisory Opinion, I.C.J. Reports 1975, p. 12, para. 27.

States voice similar objections virtually every time an advisory opinion is requested from the Court.

> ### Statement by British Ambassador Matthew Rycroft[41]
> If the draft resolution were passed, the Court would, of course, have to decide whether it could properly respond to the request. Our view is that it could not do so, as it concerns a bilateral dispute between two member states. The United Kingdom has always been and continues to be a strong upholder of international law. We are not opposing this Resolution because we have changed our principles, nor because we believe the rule of law does not apply in this case, rather we oppose this resolution because referring a bilateral dispute to the ICJ in not the appropriate course of action.

The reluctance to see the Court get involved in a bilateral dispute often has its roots in the principle of consent.[42] As explained in Chapter 2, the Court can only settle disputes when states explicitly confer jurisdiction on the Court. No consent means no involvement of the Court, regardless of the gravity of the issues at stake. Given that no such requirement exists in advisory proceedings, the latter can arguably provide an avenue of recourse to the Court – albeit an objectionable one – when the Court cannot otherwise resolve a dispute for lack of consent.

In such circumstances, the ICJ may decline to answer a request for an advisory opinion by the terms of Article 65 of its Statute.

> ### ICJ Statute
> **Article 65**
> The Court may give an advisory opinion on any legal question at the request of whatever body may be authorized by or in accordance with the Charter of the United Nation to make such a request.

---

41 Permanent Representative to the UN, at the General Assembly meeting to discuss request for an advisory opinion of the ICJ on the Legal consequences of the separation of the Chagos Archipelgo from Mauritius in 1965, adopted 22 June 2017.

42 *See supra* Chapter 2, Section B.

The Court has acknowledged its right to decline requests for advisory opinions in the past. Yet, in practice, it has always brushed aside objections related to lack of consent. When faced with a request for an advisory opinion closely related to a dispute, the Court has typically emphasized that the opinion was needed by the requesting organ to perform its duties, and that the legal question was not merely of concern to the two interested states.[43]

Western Sahara[44]

[The l]ack of consent might constitute a ground for declining to give the opinion requested if, in the circumstances of a given case, considerations of judicial propriety should oblige the Court to refuse an opinion. In short, the consent of an interested State continues to be relevant, not for the Court's competence, but for the appreciation of the propriety of giving an opinion.

Interpretation of Peace Treaties with Bulgaria, Hungary and Romania[45]

Another argument that has been invoked against the power of the Court to answer the Questions put to it in this case is based on the opposition of the Governments of Bulgaria, Hungary and Romania to the advisory procedure. The Court cannot, it is said, give the Advisory Opinion requested without violating the well-established principle of international law according to which no judicial proceedings relating to a legal question pending between States can take place without their consent.

This objection reveals a confusion between the principles governing contentious procedure and those which are applicable to Advisory Opinions.

---

43   Dapo Akande and Antonios Tzanakopoulos, *Can the International Court of Justice Decide on the Chagos Islands Advisory Proceedings without the UK's Consent?*, EJIL Talk! (June 27, 2017).

44   *Western Sahara, supra* note 40, para. 33.

45   *Interpretation of Peace Treaties with Bulgaria, Hungary and Romania*, Advisory Opinion, I.C.J. Reports 1950, p. 10.

> The consent of States, parties to a dispute, is the basis of the Court's jurisdiction in contentious cases. The situation is different in regard to advisory proceedings even where the Request for an Opinion relates to a legal question actually pending between States.

Legal Consequences of the Construction of a Wall in the Occupied Palestinian Territory[46]

The object of the request before the Court is to obtain from the Court an opinion which the General Assembly deems of assistance to it for the proper exercise of its functions. The opinion is requested on a question which is of particularly acute concern to the United Nations, and one which is located in a much broader frame of reference than a bilateral dispute. In the circumstances, the Court does not consider that to give an opinion would have the effect of circumventing the principle of consent to judicial settlement, and the Court accordingly cannot, in the exercise of its discretion, decline to give an opinion on that ground.

The Court accordingly enjoys a level of flexibility in deciding whether to answer a request for an advisory opinion. This flexibility permeates all aspects of advisory proceedings – from the participatory nature of the process to its non-binding outcome, and even the possibility of borrowing from contentious jurisdiction.[47] With respect to the latter, Article 68 of the Statute provides that "[i]n the exercise of its advisory functions the Court shall further be guided by the provisions of the present Statute which apply in contentious cases to the extent to which it recognizes them to be applicable." The Statute therefore leaves it to the Court to decide the extent to which advisory proceedings resemble contentious proceedings.[48]

---

46 *Legal Consequences of the Construction of a Wall in the Occupied Palestinian Territories,* Advisory Opinion, I.C.J. Reports 2004, p. 136, para. 50.

47 Article 102 of the Rules of the Court provides as follows: "When an advisory opinion is requested upon a legal question actually pending between two or more States, Article 31 of the Statute shall apply, as also the provisions of these Rules concerning the application of that Article." The ICJ appointed a judge ad hoc in advisory proceedings only once, on behalf of Morocco in Western Sahara.

48 Jean-Pierre Cot and Stephan Wittich, The Statute of the International Court of Justice: A Commentary (Andreas Zimmermann, Christian Tomuschat, eds., (3rd ed., 2019)), at 1843.

THE INTERNATIONAL COURT OF JUSTICE AND THE UNITED NATIONS 99

...

Questions

1. Should the Court be entitled or precluded from opining on *disputes* as opposed to *questions*?

2. Parties to the UN charter and the ICJ Statute are regarded as having automatically consented to the Court's advisory jurisdiction, but not to contentious jurisdiction. In the words of Hugh Thirlway: "[s]ince there is no consent requirement in advisory proceedings, the consent aspect is reduced to the consent of states as expressed in the terms of the Charter to which they have become parties."[49] In your view, how much consent should be required in advisory proceedings, if any? Is it acceptable to require two different levels of consent in contentious and advisory proceedings? What significance does consent hold in non-binding procedures?

3. Requests for advisory opinions inevitably address, directly or not, matters of significance to states. When states have direct stakes in the matter considered by the ICJ, how do you think they should react? Should they expose their objections before the Court? Does it strengthen or weaken the Court's legitimacy when the Court ignores such objections? Will the involvement of the Court affect the way these states interact with the Court in the future?

C   The ICJ's Relationship with Other Principal UN Organs

Advisory jurisdiction offers an opportunity for UN organs to interact with the International Court of Justice, and for the Court to fulfill its role as a principal organ of the UN.[50] This section analyzes the Court's relationship with the Security Council and the General Assembly, which at times goes beyond the bounds of advisory jurisdiction.

1   Relationship with the Security Council

The UN Charter did not establish a formal institutional hierarchy between its five main organs. At least in theory, the Court is placed on equal footing with the Security Council. Neither organ is in any way subordinated to the

---

49   Hugh Thirlway, The Law and Procedure of the International Court of Justice: Fifty Years of Jurisprudence (2003), at 1714.

50   *See also* Mohamed Sameh M. Amr, The Role of the International Court of Justice as Principal Judicial Organ of the UN (2003), at 140 (arguing that the ICJ also shapes the relationship between the Security Council and the General Assembly).

100   CHAPTER 3

other.[51] In practice, however, each organ has sought to maintain its independence and to assert its legitimacy and authority. The relationship between the Court and the Security Council is carefully calibrated on the part of both bodies.

The Security Council has maintained a certain distance from the Court, even though the Charter encourages the Council and the Court to work together. The first mechanism designed to enhance cooperation is set forth in Article 96 of the UN Charter, which enables the Security Council to request advisory opinions from the ICJ on any legal question, as previously noted. In over seventy years, however, the Security Council only once requested an advisory opinion (on the legal consequences of South Africa's continued presence in Namibia in 1970).

The Security Council may also "make recommendations or decide upon measures to be taken to give effect" to ICJ judgements.[52] This allows the Council to act as the right arm of the Court, by ensuring the proper execution of its decisions. The absence of an obligation to act leaves some discretion to the Council as to the course of action it wishes to adopt in any given situation. The Council was only asked to play this role once, following the Court's judgment in *Military and Paramilitary Activities in and against Nicaragua*. The United States vetoed the draft resolution of the Security Council calling for full and immediate compliance with the Court's judgment, preventing the adoption of the resolution.

Finally, the UN Charter also encourages a level of cooperation between the Security Council and the Court in containing disputes and avoiding the outbreak of war. In the exercise of its function to "maintain or restore international peace and security,"[53] the Security Council is encouraged to "call upon the parties to settle their dispute" by peaceful means.[54] Specifically, the Charter reminds the Council that, "legal disputes should, as a general rule be referred by the parties to the International Court of Justice in accordance with the provisions of the Statute of the Court."[55] The Council therefore has the authority

---

51   *Advisory Opinion on the Legal Consequences for States of the Continued Presence of South Africa in Namibia (South West Africa) notwithstanding Security Council Resolution 276 (1970)*, Advisory Opinion, I.C.J. Reports 1971, p. 16.
52   UN Charter, Article 94(2).
53   UN Charter, Article 39.
54   UN Charter, Article 33.
55   UN Charter, Article 36(3).

THE INTERNATIONAL COURT OF JUSTICE AND THE UNITED NATIONS

to suggest, encourage, and recommend that the parties make use of the ICJ to resolve their disputes. But here again, the Council has been somewhat reluctant to play this role. It only recommended the use of the ICJ once, in 1947, following the incidents involving two British ships in the Straits of Corfu.[56] The Court called on Albania and the United Kingdom to "immediately refer the dispute to the International Court of Justice in accordance with the provisions of the Statute of the Court."[57] By doing so, the Security Council paved the way for *Corfu Channel*, the first contentious case to reach the Court.

In sum, the Security Council has not taken full advantage of the opportunities laid out in the Charter. The Council could have interacted more regularly with the Court by way of requests for advisory opinions, referrals of disputes to the Court, or the adoption of enforcement measures. Instead, it chose to maintain a distance between the two bodies – perhaps to preserve their respective independence and separate spheres of influence.

The Court has conceived of the relationship in similar, albeit slightly warmer terms. Although the Court gives significant legal weight to Security Council resolutions as authoritative pronouncements of the law, it too has emphasized the bodies' distinct roles.

> **Military and Paramilitary Activities in and against Nicaragua**
> **(Nicaragua v. United States of America)** [58]
> While in Article 12 of the Charter there is provision for a clear demarcation of functions between General Assembly and the Security Council (...) there is no similar provision anywhere in the Charter with respect to the Security Council and the Court. The Council has functions of a political nature assigned to it, whereas the Court exercises purely judicial functions. Both organs can perform their separate but complementary functions with respect to the same events.

---

56 In one additional case, *Aegean Sea Continental Shelf*, the Court merely invited Greece and Turkey to use the ICJ for dispute settlement but the Court held it had no jurisdiction. See The Statute of the International Court of Justice: A Commentary, *supra* note 49, at 158.

57 Security Council Resolution 22, 9 April 1947.

58 *See Case Concerning Military and Paramilitary Activities In and Against Nicaragua (Nicaragua v. United States of America)*, I.C.J. Reports 1984, p. 397, para 95.

102   CHAPTER 3

The distinct nature of their functions means that the Council and the Court operate in two separate spheres; they can be seized of the same matter and proceed with its treatment simultaneously – without one organ having to defer to the other. Accordingly, the Court is not prohibited from hearing a case on an issue that is concurrently on the Council's agenda. This also means that states may use the Court and the Council simultaneously and for the same overall purpose.

An important question arises as to the power of the Court to review decisions of the Security Council. At the San Francisco Conference in 1945, Belgium proposed an amendment endowing the ICJ with a muted right to carry out judicial review of the Council's decisions – which was rejected.

> *Philippe Couvreur, The International Court of Justice and the*
> *Effectiveness of International Law*[59]
>
> The possibility of the Security Council decisions being subject to some form of judicial review was discussed at the San Francisco Conference in 1945, at which the participating States submitted their amendments on the "Proposals of Dumbarton Oaks for a General International Organisation." The Belgian delegation, which included renowned Professor Charles de Visscher, who has been a judge at the PCIJ (1937–1945) and was to become a judge at the ICJ (1946–1952), proposed an amendment allowing for the *ex ante* judicial review of decisions taken by the Security Council:
>
> "[I]n the case where the [Security Council's] recommended procedures should be inoperative, where it should judge the situation thus created to be dangerous for the maintenance of International peace and security, the Security Council would have to take whatever equitable decision could settle the difference peacefully. However, before a project for the settlement of a difference, drawn up by the Council of by any other body became final, each of the States concerned should be able to ask an advisory opinion from the [International] Court of Justice as to whether the decision respected its independence and vital rights."
>
> This, at first sight, rather moderate amendment proposed by Belgium was, however, met with considerable resistance from the delegations of the United States, the United Kingdom, the Soviet Union and China, and was ultimately withdrawn. The form of judicial review proposed by Belgium would have been somewhat "mild", since an advisory opinion

---

59   Philippe Couvreur, *The International Court of Justice and the Effectiveness of International Law* (2017), at 135.

THE INTERNATIONAL COURT OF JUSTICE AND THE UNITED NATIONS 103

> would not have had any binding effect on the Security Council and since the scope of the review, as conceived by Belgium, would have been limited to the issue of independence and vital rights of the targeted State, not the general validity or legality of the measures envisaged as such. Be that as it may, it was considered to be too much of an interference in the exercise of the political powers of the Security Council, which was to be strengthened.

Questions of Interpretation and Application of the 1971 Montreal Convention arising from the Aerial Incident at Lockerbie marked a turning point in the relationship between the Court and the Council.

On December 21, 1988, a bomb detonated on a Pan Am flight from Frankfurt to Detroit, killing all 243 passengers and 16 crewmembers, in what became known as the Lockerbie bombing. Large sections of the aircraft crashed into residential areas of Lockerbie, Scotland, killing eleven more people on the ground. Following a three-year joint investigation, the United States and United Kingdom issued arrest warrants for two Libyan nationals. Libya contended that it had jurisdiction to prosecute its nationals and refused to extradite them. The Council adopted resolutions condemning Libya and imposing sanctions until the suspects were handed over to the UK.[60]

A few months later, Libya filed separate applications against the United Kingdom and the United States asking the Court to declare that the requests ordered by the Security Council violated Libya's rights under the 1971 Montreal Convention for the Suppression of Unlawful Acts against the Safety of Civil Aviation. Although Libya's applications to the Court questioned the validity of the measures ordered by the Security Council, the Court rejected the preliminary objections raised by the United Kingdom and the United States, and found that it had jurisdiction to entertain the cases.[61] This raised the possibility that, for the first time in its history, the Court might exercise a form of judicial review over Security Council resolutions but the case did not proceed to the merits stage at the request of the parties.[62]

---

60   S.C Res.731 S/RES/7318 (Jan. 21, 1992); S.C Res.748 S/RES/748 (March 31, 1992); S.C Res.883 S/RES/883 (Nov. 11, 1993).

61   *Questions of Interpretation and Application of the 1971 Montreal Convention Arising from the Aerial Incident at Lockerbie* (Libyan Arab Jamahiriya v. United Kingdom), Preliminary Objections, Dissenting Opinion of Judge Bedjaoui, 1998 I.C.J. Reports 1998, p. 115.

62   Bernd Martenczuk, *The Security Council, the International Court and Judicial Review: What Lessons from Lockerbie?*, 10 EJIL 517 (1999).

> **Dissenting Opinion of Judge Bedjaoui, *Aerial Incident at Lockerbie*[63]**
> If the concomitant exercise of the concurrent but not exclusive powers has thus far not given rise to serious problems, the present case, by contrast, presents the Court not only with the grave question of the possible influence of the decisions of a principal organ on the consideration of the same question by another principal organ, but also, more fundamentally, with the question of the possible inconsistency between the decisions of the two organs and how to deal with so delicate a situation.

Of course, debate ensued. Some leading scholars were concerned that judicial review of this resolution would expose the Security Council to future review of resolutions issued under Chapter VII, involving the Court in political – and, potentially, non-justiciable – issues.[64] President Schwebel echoed these concerns in his dissent, stressing that the Court could not "overrule or undercut decisions of the Security Council" based on Chapter VII.[65] Ultimately, the case was dismissed in 2003 when Libya complied with the requirements of the Security Council (while judgment on the merits was pending). The case serves as a reminder of the sensitivity of the judicial review in the international legal order.

---

63 *Questions of Interpretation and Application of the 1971 Montreal Convention arising from the Aerial Incident at Lockerbie* (Libyan Arab Jamahiriya v. United States of America), Provisional Measures, Order of 14 April 1992, Diss. Op. Bedjaoui, Guillaume and Ranjeva, I.C.J. Reports 1992, p. 3.

64 Michael J. Matheson, *ICJ Review of Security Council Decisions*, 36 Geo. Wash. Int'l L. Rev. 615, 621 (2004); O.J. Lissitzyn, The International Court of Justice – Its Role in the Maintenance of International Peace and Security (1951), at 96–97; C. de Visscher, Aspects récents du droit procédural de la Court Internationale de Justice (1966), at 16; Leo Gross, *The International Court of Justice and the United Nations*, 120 Hague Acad. Int'l L., Recueil des Cours 313, 429 (I, 1967, I).

65 *Questions of Interpretation and Application of the 1971 Montreal Convention arising from the Aerial Incident at Lockerbie* (Libyan Arab Jamahiriya v. United States of America), Preliminary Objections, Diss. Op. President Schwebel, ICJ Reports 1998, p. 155. *See also, Questions of Interpretation and Application of the 1971 Montreal Convention arising from the Aerial Incident at Lockerbie* (Libyan Arab Jamahiriya v. United States of America), Preliminary Objections, Diss. Op. Jennings, ICJ Reports 1998, p. 99, at 111 (noting that the Court could not "substitute its own discretion for that of the Security Council).

The debate over the authority of the ICJ to review the legality of Security Council decisions touches upon the balance of powers within the organization. There is little doubt that the cooperation, competition, and even tension between the two bodies contributes to the functioning of the UN as an organization by creating checks and balances. In practice, the Court gives deference to Security Council decisions in its judgements, and has never declared a Council decision illegal – demonstrating the limits of the theoretical discussions on this matter. That being said, should the Court and the Council wish to enhance their relationship by working closer together, the UN Charter certainly would support and even encourage such cooperation.

2   *Relationship with the General Assembly*

The International Court of Justice and the General Assembly enjoy a pleasant and harmonious relationship. They interact in various ways – including in the context of requests for advisory opinions, the presentation of the Court's annual report to the GA, the selection of ICJ judges, and via the ICJ's reliance on General Assembly resolutions in its decisions.

The General Assembly has made frequent use of its competence to request advisory opinions from the Court under Article 96 of the Charter. In fact, the United Nations General Assembly has been the prime user of the advisory jurisdiction of the International Court of Justice, with the Security Council and subsidiary bodies of the UN far behind. Since the establishment of the Court in 1945, the General Assembly has requested 16 advisory opinions from the Court, amounting to more than 60% of the requests.[66] The Court, for its part, has always welcomed the General Assembly's invitations and has never declined to provide a request for an advisory opinion emanating from the General Assembly. Advisory jurisdiction has created a privileged channel of communication between the General Assembly and the Court.

In requesting an advisory opinion, the General Assembly passes a resolution, submitting a particular question to the Court, which the ICJ can either accept or reject. For example, in *The Legal Consequences of the Separation of the Chagos Archipelago from Mauritius in 1965*, the General Assembly requested the Court to render an advisory opinion on two questions related to the decolonization of Mauritius and the subsequent administration of the Chagos Archipelago. The Court had the ability to exercise discretion to answer

---

66   See Figure 3.1.

the questions or decline to weigh in on the matter. These options are available to the Court in all advisory proceedings.

After the Court issues an advisory opinion, the General Assembly can further demonstrate its commitment to the Court's decision through a follow up resolution. Following *Chagos*, the General Assembly adopted Resolution 73/295, demanding that the United Kingdom withdraw its colonial administration in accordance with the Court's guidance. Demonstrative of the harmonious relationship between the two UN organs, the exchange between the General Assembly and the Court regarding the Chagos Archipelago indicates efforts by the General Assembly to bolster the non-binding findings of the Court's advisory opinion.

Like other organs of the United Nations, the Court is dependent on the General Assembly with regard to the preparation and adoption of the its budget. Its relationship with the General Assembly is therefore key in this regard. The General Assembly approves the Court's budget on a biennial basis. It includes the personnel and operational expenses of the ICJ, salaries, allowances, and compensation, as well as retirement pensions of the members of the Court and the Registrar. Together with legal affairs, the Court's budget amounts to approximately 2% of the organization's overall budget.[67]

The Court and the General Assembly also interact on yearly basis when the Court presents its report to the General Assembly. This practice began in 1968, two decades after the ICJ came into existence. Since then the President of the Court travels yearly to New York for the meeting of the General Assembly to report on the Court's activity, publications, visits, budget, and more.[68] The annual report often serves as a reminder of the Court's role and status within the UN system. Following the Court's 2016 report, state representatives at the General Assembly expressly noted the tireless work of the ICJ under an increasing workload and shrinking budget, and commended the Court's role in improving global confidence in international law.[69] Annual reports have also been used by the ICJ to issue budgetary requests from the General Assembly (for example, in its 2019 report, the ICJ addressed its restructured budget, and some concerns regarding the judges' pension scheme).

---

67   The fact that the budget of the ICJ forms part of the budget of the UN can indirectly promote or impede the functioning of the ICJ.

68   UN Charter, Article 15, para. 2 ("The General Assembly shall receive and consider reports from the other organs of the United Nations."). For most annual reports, see https://www .ICJ-cij.org/en/annual-reports.

69   Press Release, *Speakers Say International Court of Justice Needed More Than Ever, as General Assembly Considers Its Annual Report*, GA/11847, Oct. 27, 2016.

Importantly, the General Assembly and the UN Security Council also select, separately but concurrently, the Court's fifteen judges from a list of candidates nominated by the national groups at the Permanent Court of Arbitration.[70] Elections are staggered, with five judges elected every three years to ensure continuity within the court. A candidate is elected if he or she obtains an absolute majority in both organs (eight affirmative votes at the Security Council, and ninety-seven votes at the General Assembly). Should a judge resign or pass away while in office, the practice has generally been to elect a judge in a special election to complete the term. No two judges may be nationals of the same country. There is an informal understanding that the seats are distributed according to geographic distribution – typically, five seats for Western countries, three for African states, two for Eastern European states, three for Asian states, and two for Latin American and Caribbean states. For most of the Court's history, the five permanent members of the Security Council have had a judge on the ICJ, thereby occupying three of the Western seats, one of the Asian seats, and one of the Eastern European seats. In 2017, for the first time, the United Kingdom's candidate failed to achieve the requisite majority for re-election after an unusual ten rounds of voting. The UK ended up accepting defeat thereby allowing the Indian candidate, Judge Dalveer Bhandari, to fill the final vacancy on the Court. It remains to be seen how the absence of a British judge will affect the appointment of judges from other permanent members of the Security Council in the future.[71]

An overview of the relationship between the Court and the General Assembly would not be complete without mentioning a level of competition as the two bodies contribute, each in their own way, to international law-making. The Court contributes to the development of international law by making authoritative pronouncements that either clarify existing law or shape its evolution. The General Assembly is the most democratic body of the United Nations, where states enjoy equal voting rights regardless of size, population, or power. It resembles a legislative body, though its resolutions are not binding.

The Court has acknowledged that a GA resolution may acquire binding force depending on "the content and conditions of its adoption," and on "whether an *opinio juris* exists as to its normative character." General Assembly resolutions, the Court notes, may also be used to show the gradual evolution of the *opinio*

---

70   *See* ICJ Statute, Articles 4–19.
71   Arun M. Sukumar, *The Significance of Dalveer Bhandari's, and India's, Recent Election to the ICJ*, Lawfare (Dec. 13, 2017), available at https://www.lawfareblog.com/significance-dalveer-bhandaris-and-indias-recent-election-ICJ.

108   CHAPTER 3

juris required for the crystallization of a customary norm.[72] The Court therefore recognizes the contribution of the General Assembly to international
law-making in those circumstances.

Overall, the Court and the General Assembly have regular and frequent interactions – and their relationship is by no means a one-way street. From advisory
jurisdiction to budget approval, reporting, and the selection of judges, the two
bodies have plenty of opportunities for cooperation. They also make a point
of reinforcing and complementing each other whenever possible. Both the ICJ
and the General Assembly rely on this interaction to properly exercise their
functions, and have therefore generally maintained a friendly relationship.

Further Reading

Kathleen Renee Cronin-Furman, *The International Court of Justice and the United
    Nations Security Council: Rethinking a Complicated Relationship*, 106 Colum. L. Rev.
    435 (2006).

Vera Gowlland-Debbas, *The Relationship Between the International Court of Justice and
    the Security Council in the Light of the Lockerbie Case*, 88 Am. J. Int'l L. 643 (1994).

Ken Roberts, *Second-Guessing the Security Council: The International Court of Justice
    and Its Powers of Judicial Review*, 7 Pace Int'l L. Rev. 281 (1995).

Dapo Akande, *The International Court of Justice and the Security Council: Is there Room
    for Judicial Control of Decisions of the Political Organs of the United Nations?*, 46 Int'l
    and Comp. L.Q. 309 (1997).

Jaroslav Usiak and L'ubica Saktorova, *The International Court of Justice and the Legality
    of UN Security Council Resolutions*, 5 L. & Econ. Rev. 201 (2013).

D   A Timeline of Advisory Proceedings

On average, it has taken the Court approximately ten and a half months to
answer a request for an advisory opinion. For reasons that are not immediately
clear, two advisory proceedings – *Application for Review of Judgment No. 333
of the United Nations Administrative Tribunal* (requested by the Committee on
Applications for Review of Administrative Tribunal Judgements) and *Legality
of the Use by a State of Nuclear Weapons in Armed Conflict* (requested by the
World Health Organization) – lasted more than 21 months (32 and 34 months,

---

72   Legality of the Threat or Use of Nuclear Weapons, Advisory Opinion, I. C. J. Reports 1996,
      p. 226, para. 70.

THE INTERNATIONAL COURT OF JUSTICE AND THE UNITED NATIONS 109

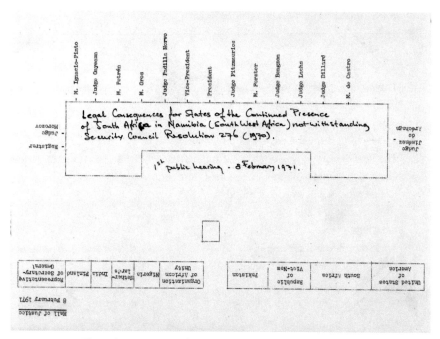

FIGURE 3.2   Floor plan in *Continued Presence of South West Africa in Namibia*
SOURCE: JEROEN BOUMAN, PHOTOGRAPHER

respectively). Regardless of why they occur, such delays limit the ability of the requesting body to receive legal advice in a timely fashion. Thankfully, most advisory proceedings proceed swiftly – in less than a year. The picture below shows how the Court sits in advisory proceedings.

Requests for advisory opinions typically proceed as follows before the International Court of Justice:

TABLE 3.1   Timeline of advisory proceedings

Step	Process	Authority
1	The Security Council, General Assembly, or other UN organ/specialized agency, votes on a resolution requesting an advisory opinion on a legal question	Art. 96 of the UN Charter and Article 65 of the ICJ Statute

TABLE 3.1   Timeline of advisory proceedings (*cont.*)

Step	Process	Authority
2	The request is transmitted to the Court by the Secretary-General or the chief administrative office of the organ/agency requesting the advisory opinion	Article 104 of the Rules of the Court
3	The Registrar provides notice of the request to all states entitled to appear before the Court and notifies additional entities granted permission to submit written statements and/or appear at oral hearings	Article 66 of the ICJ Statute
4	The Court determines public availability of written statements	Article 106 of the Rules of the Court
5	The Court may accelerate the procedure, if the opinion is considered urgent	Article 103 of the Rules of the Court
6	Oral hearings	Article 105 of the Rules of the Court
7	Judicial deliberations	Article 21 of the Rules of the Court
8	Judges adopt advisory opinion	Article 107 of the Rules of the Court
9	Registrar signs and seals the advisory opinion	Articles 26(h) and 109 of the Rules of the Court
10	The advisory opinion is read at a public sitting	Article 67 of the ICJ Statute
11	A copy of the advisory opinion is placed in the archives of the Court and an additional copy is sent to Secretary-General; if appropriate, a third copy is sent to the chief administrative officer of the requesting organ/agency	Article 109 of the Rules of the Court

E   Comparative Practice

The ICJ's experience paved the way for the inclusion of the advisory function into the constitutive documents of numerous international and regional

THE INTERNATIONAL COURT OF JUSTICE AND THE UNITED NATIONS   111

judicial bodies. This section explores the use of advisory jurisdiction in three regional courts – the European Court of Human Rights, the Inter-American Court of Human Rights, and the African Court on Human and People's Rights.

1   *The European Court of Human Rights*

The advisory function of the European Court of Human Rights (ECHR) came as somewhat of an afterthought. It was introduced in 1963,[73] thirteen years after the adoption of the European Convention on Human Rights and the creation of the Court. At the time, only the Committee of Ministers of the Council of Europe could request an advisory opinion concerning the interpretation of the Convention and the Protocols. The objective was to "enhance the interaction between the Court and national authorities and thereby reinforce implementation of the Convention, in accordance with the principle of subsidiarity."[74] It was hoped that advisory jurisdiction would increase the Court's presence and relevance for the members of the Council of Europe.

The ECHR's advisory jurisdiction is similar to the ICJ's in two ways: individual member states cannot request advisory opinions, and advisory opinions are not binding. Only matters concerning the interpretation of the Convention may be referred to the Court under its advisory jurisdiction.

> **Protocol 2 to the European Convention (Conferring upon the European Court of Human Rights Competence to Give Advisory Opinions)**
>
> **Article 1**
>
> 1. The Court may, at the request of the Committee of Ministers, give advisory opinions on legal questions concerning the interpretation of the Convention and the Protocols thereto.
>
> 2. Such opinions shall not deal with any question relating to the content or scope of the rights or freedoms defined in Section 1 of the Convention

---

73   Kanstantsin Dzehtsiarou, *Interaction between the European Court of Human Rights and Member States: European Consensus, Advisory Opinions and the Question of Legitimacy*, The European Court of Human Rights and Its Discontents (S. Flogaitis, T. Zwart and J. Fraser eds., 2013), at 118; Karin Oellers-Frahm, *Lawmaking Through Advisory Opinions?*, Advancing International Institutional Law (Armin Von Bogdandy and Rüdiger Wolfrum eds., 2012), at 71–79.

74   Protocol No. 16 to the Convention for the Protection of Human Rights and Fundamental Freedoms, CETS No. 214, Oct. 2, 2013, Preamble, https://www.echr.coe.int/Documents/Protocol_16_ENG.pdf.

and the Protocols thereto, or with any other question which the Court or the Committee of Ministers might have to consider in consequence of any such proceedings as could be instituted in accordance with the Convention.

3. Decisions of the Committee of Ministers to request an advisory opinion of the Court shall require a majority vote of the representatives entitled to sit on the committee.

In 2010, Protocol No. 16 to the Convention on the Protection of Human Rights and Fundamental Freedoms extended the right to request an advisory opinion to the highest courts and tribunals of states party to the European Convention on Human Rights.[75] The Protocol came into force in 2018, and in 2019 the ECHR issued for the first time an advisory opinion at the request of the French Cour de Cassation.[76]

Protocol No. 16 to the Convention on the Protection of Human Rights and Fundamental Freedoms

Article 1

1. Highest courts and tribunals of a High Contracting Party, as specified in accordance with Article 10, may request the Court to give advisory opinions on questions of principle relating to the interpretation or application of the rights and freedoms defined in the Convention or the protocols thereto.

2. The requesting court or tribunal may seek an advisory opinion only in the context of a case pending before it.

3. The requesting court or tribunal shall give reasons for its request and shall provide the relevant legal and factual background of the pending case.

---

75 *Id.*

76 *Advisory Opinion concerning the recognition in domestic law of a legal parent-child relationship between a child born through a gestational surrogacy arrangement abroad and the intended mother* (April 10, 2019), available at https://hudoc.echr.coe.int/eng?i=003-6380464-8364383.

Questions

1. At the European Court of Human Rights, a panel of judges must preapprove requests for advisory opinions before the Court hears them. Could/should such a system be implemented at the ICJ?

2. Compare the advisory competence of the ECHR with that of the ICJ: Is either comparable to a constitutional function? Should these courts be competent to address questions of a constitutional nature?

3. One of the objectives of allowing the Committee of Ministers of the Council of Europe to request advisory opinions from the ECHR was to enhance interaction between the court and the national authorities of member states. Could a similar procedure be used to enhance interaction between the ICJ and UN member states?

2   The Inter-American Court of Human Rights

The Inter-American Court of Human Rights (IACHR) was established in 1978 by the American Convention on Human Rights as part of the Organization of American States (OAS). The convention endowed the court with advisory jurisdiction, alongside contentious jurisdiction. The Inter-American Court of Human Rights undoubtedly borrows much from its older sibling, the ICJ; however, it expands the reach of the mechanism by allowing individual states to request advisory opinions.

> ### American Convention on Human Rights
> **Article 64**
>
> 1. The member states of the [Organization of American States] may consult the Court regarding the interpretation of this Convention or of other treaties concerning the protection of human rights in the American states. Within their spheres of competence, the organs listed in Chapter X of the Charter of the Organization of American States, as amended by the Protocol of Buenos Aires, may in like manner consult the Court.
>
> 2. The Court, at the request of a member state of the Organization, may provide that state with opinions regarding the compatibility of any of its domestic laws with the aforesaid international instruments.

Any state member of the Organization of American States (even those not party to the convention) and any of the bodies of the organization can refer a question to the court on the interpretation of the American Convention on Human Rights or other treaties concerning the protection of human rights in the American states. The scope of the latter has been interpreted broadly by the court.[77]

Like the ICJ, the IACHR may decline to give an advisory opinion. In *Compatibility of Draft Legislation*,[78] the court declined Costa Rica's request for an opinion on the compatibility of a draft law with the Convention on the ground that "the questions presented by Costa Rica, could produce, under the guise of an advisory opinion, a determination of contentious matters not yet referred to the Court".[79] In most cases, however, the court has not declined to give opinions on the ground that the subject matter of an opinion relates to a dispute between states. In this respect, the practices of the IACHR and the ICJ are very much aligned. They differ in that, at the IACHR, resort to advisory jurisdiction exceeds the use of the court as a mechanism of dispute settlement. At the ICJ, as noted above, advisory jurisdiction only accounts for about one fifth of the Court's overall activity.

The IACHR's advisory jurisdiction has also contributed to international law,[80] particularly in clarifying the character of human rights treaties and the law applicable to them. By entering into human rights treaties, according to the IACHR, "[s]tates can be deemed to submit themselves to a legal order within which they, for the common good, assume various obligations, not in relation to other States, but towards all individuals within their jurisdiction."[81] In addition, reservations to human rights treaties need not be accepted by another party for the treaty to come into force. Many other advisory opinions

---

77 As including, for example, the interpretation of the Vienna Convention on Consular Relations. *See* The Right to Information on Consular Assistance in the Framework of the Guarantees of the Due Process of Law, Advisory Opinion OC-16199, Inter-Am. Ct. H.R. (ser. A) no. 16 (Oct. 1, 1999), para. 3.

78 Compatibility of Draft Legislation with Article 8(2)(h) of the American Convention on Human Rights, Advisory Opinion OC-12/91, Inter-Am. Ct. H.R. (ser. A) No. 12 (Dec. 6, 1991).

79 Compatibility of Draft Legislation with Article 8(2)(h) of the American Convention on Human Rights, Advisory Opinion OC-12/91, Inter-Am. Ct. H.R. (ser. A) No. 12 (Dec. 6, 1991), para. 28.

80 Thomas Buergenthal, *The Advisory Practice of the Inter-American Human Rights Court*, 79 AJIL 1 (1985), at 25.

81 The Effects of Reservations on the Entry into Force of the American Convention (Arts. 74 and 75), Advisory Opinion No. OC-2/82, Inter-Am. Ct. H.R. (ser. A) No. 2 (Sept. 24, 1982), para. 29.

of the Inter-American Court of Human Rights have similarly strengthened the rights of the individual under international law.[82]

•••

Questions

1. What feature(s) of the IACHR's advisory jurisdiction contributed to its popularity?
2. What lessons can the ICJ take from the IACHR's experience?

3   The African Court on Human and Peoples' Rights

The African Court on Human and Peoples' Rights was established by the Protocol to the African Charter on Human and Peoples' Rights, which was adopted in 1998 and entered into force in 2004. Like the IACHR, the African Court is endowed with broad jurisdiction to render non-binding advisory opinions. Yet the two courts have very different records when it comes to the exercise of such jurisdiction. Unlike the IACHR and the ICJ, the African Court has often declined to answer requests for advisory opinions, rendering only a handful of opinions since its establishment.[83]

> **Protocol to the African Charter on Human and People's Rights on the Establishment of an African Court on Human and People's Rights**
> **Article 4**
> At the request of a Member State of the [Organization of African Unity], the OAU, any of its organs, or any African organization recognized by the OAU, the Court may provide an opinion on any legal matter relating to the Charter or any other relevant human rights instruments, provided that the subject matter of the opinion is not related to a matter being examined by the Commission.

---

82   Jo Pasqualucci, *The Advisory Practice and Procedure of the Inter-American Court of Human Rights: Contributing to the Evolution of International Human Rights Law*, 38 Stan. J. Int'l L. 241 (2002), at 243.

83   *Advisory Proceedings*, African Court on Human and Peoples' Rights, available at https://en.african-court.org/index.php/cases/2016-10-17-16-19-35. As of December 2018, the African Court received thirteen requests; six advisory opinions were issued, one request withdrawn, one request is pending, and five were struck out. *See also* Amelia Keene, *The Forgotten Potential of the Advisory Jurisdictions of International Courts and Tribunals as a Check on the Actions of International Organizations*, 14 N.Z.J. Pub. Int'l L. 67, 83 (2016).

Any organ of the Organization of African Unity (OAU), its member states, or any other African organization recognized by the OAU can make a request for an advisory opinion before the African Court on Human and Peoples' Rights. Questions asked may relate to the African Charter on Human and Peoples' Rights or any other human rights mechanism ratified by the states, as long as that matter is not pending before the commission. This extends beyond the advisory competence of the European Court of Human Rights, which is limited to questions relating to its own charter. It also extends beyond the ICJ's advisory competence in the sense that individual states are entitled to submit requests to the court. States have been reluctant to request advisory opinions, however, leading some scholars to advocate for an increased use of the mechanism.[84]

Since its inclusion in the Statute of the PCIJ and later in the Statute of the ICJ, regional courts have embraced and adapted the use of advisory jurisdiction to suit their own needs. Advisory jurisdiction is generally perceived as enhancing access to courts and extending the reach of the court's influence. Still, different courts have had different experiences with advisory jurisdiction. While the IACHR provides one of most successful implementations of this unique judicial function, the African Court, for its part, stands out for its willingness to deny requests for advisory opinions – something the ICJ and other courts endowed with advisory competence rarely do.

Further Reading

AP van der Mei, *The Advisory Jurisdiction of the African Court on Human and People's Rights*, 5 Afr. Hum. Rts. L.J. 27 (2005).

Julie Calidonio Schmid, Note, *Advisory Opinions on Human Rights: Moving Beyond a Pyrrhic Victory*, 16 Duke J. Comp. & Int'l L. 415 (2006).

Manisuli Ssenyonjo, The African Regional Human Rights System: 30 Years after the African Charter on Human and Peoples' Rights (2012).

Kanstantstin Dzehtsiarou and Noreen O'Meara, *Advisory Jurisdiction and the European Court of Human Rights: A Magic Bullet for Dialogue and Docket-Control?*, 34 Legal Stud. 444 (2014).

---

84   Frans Viljoen, *Understanding and Overcoming Challenges in Assessing the African Court on Human Rights and Peoples' Rights*, 67 Int'l & Comp. L.Q. 63, 97 (2018) (suggesting that "states should consider making use of this mechanism to obtain an authoritative view on, for example, the compatibility of their domestic law prior to ratifying particular human rights treaties.")

Cecilia M. Bailliet, *The Strategic Prudence of the Inter-American Court of Human Rights: Rejection of Requests for an Advisory Opinion*, 15 Braz. J. Int'l L. 255 (2018).

Conclusion

The ICJ's advisory function is more versatile, open, informal, and flexible than its contentious function. It holds great potential for the United Nations, the Court, and the international community, but achieving this potential depends on how the Court views and interprets its authority in this regard. The Court can make use of as much or as little of its broad competence in advisory proceedings. Whenever it receives a request for an advisory opinion, the Court can seize the opportunity to advance international law, resolve a dispute, and/or clarify matters of a semi-constitutional nature. The extent to which the Court does so varies, depending on factors ranging from the politicized nature of the question to the way the Court sees its role at a given time – from a trusted legal advisor to a mechanism for appeasing tensions between states.

In a significant departure from the PCIJ, the ICJ does not have authority to render advisory opinions about "disputes." Yet in practice, many of its advisory opinions touch upon highly divisive and politically charged bilateral issues. The Court has generally refused to see this as an obstacle to the exercise of its advisory jurisdiction, insisting instead on its duty to the United Nations as a whole – a justification that is at times only partially convincing. The same can be said of the Court's effort to overcome objections related to the absence of consent, particularly in situations where the use of advisory jurisdiction can appear driven by the impossibility to have the case settled by the Court via its contentious jurisdiction.

Ultimately, the exercise of its advisory jurisdiction reflects highly on the Court's credibility and legitimacy, notwithstanding the non-binding nature of advisory opinions. The Court should exercise this prerogative mindful of the original purpose of advisory jurisdiction: providing guidance on legal questions.

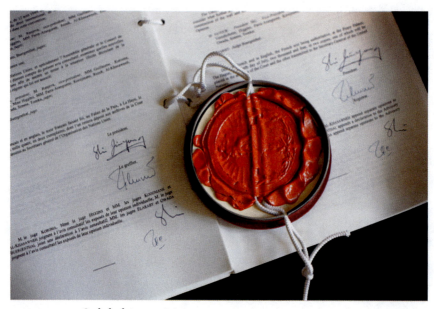

FIGURE 3.3   Sealed advisory opinion

TABLE 3.2   List of advisory opinions and requesting organs

Official number (ICJ website)	Requesting organ	Date of request	Date advisory opinion was issued	Official title of the advisory opinion
3	UN General Assembly	12/12/1947	5/28/1948	Conditions of Admission of a State to Membership in the United Nations (Article 4 of the Charter)
4	UN General Assembly	12/7/1948	4/11/1949	Reparation for Injuries during the Service of the United Nations
8	UN General Assembly	11/4/1949	7/18/1950	Interpretation of Peace Treaties with Bulgaria, Hungary and Romania
9	UN General Assembly	11/25/1949	3/3/1950	Competence of the General Assembly for the Admission of a State to the United Nations
10	UN General Assembly	12/27/1949	7/11/1950	International Status of South West Africa
12	UN General Assembly	11/20/1950	5/28/1951	Reservations to the Convention on the Prevention of the Crime of Genocide
21	UN General Assembly	12/21/1953	7/13/1954	Effect of Awards of Compensation Made by the United Nations Administrative Tribunal

THE INTERNATIONAL COURT OF JUSTICE AND THE UNITED NATIONS 119

TABLE 3.2 List of advisory opinions and requesting organs (*cont.*)

Official number (ICJ website)	Requesting organ	Date of request	Date advisory opinion was issued	Official title of the advisory opinion
24	UN General Assembly	12/6/1954	6/7/1955	Voting Procedure on Questions relating to Reports and Petitions concerning South West Africa
30	UNESCO's Executive Board	12/2/1955	10/23/1956	Judgments of the Administrative Tribunal of the ILO upon Complaints against UNESCO
31	UN General Assembly	12/19/1955	6/1/1956	Admissibility of Hearings of Petitioners by the Committee on South West Africa
43	IMO's Assembly	3/25/1959	6/8/1960	Constitution of the Maritime Safety Committee of the Intergovernmental Maritime Consultative Organization
49	UN General Assembly	12/27/1961	7/20/1962	Certain Expenses of the United Nations
53	UN Security Council	8/5/1970	6/21/1971	Legal Consequences for States of the Continued Presence of South Africa in Namibia
57	Committee on Applications for Review of Administrative Tribunal Judgements	7/3/1972	7/12/1973	Application for Review of Judgment No. 158 of the United Nations Administrative Tribunal
61	UN General Assembly	12/21/1974	10/16/1975	Western Sahara
65	WHO's Assembly	5/28/1980	12/20/1980	Interpretation of the Agreement of 25 March 1951 between the WHO and Egypt
66	Committee on Aplications for Review of Administrative Tribunal Judgements	7/28/1981	7/20/1982	Application for Review of Judgment No. 273 of the United Nations Administrative Tribunal
72	Committee on Aplications for Review of Administrative Tribunal Judgements	12/10/1984	5/27/1987	Application for Review of Judgment No. 333 of the United Nations Administrative Tribunal
77	UN General Assembly	3/7/1988	4/26/1988	Applicability of the Obligation to Arbitrate under Section 21 of the UN Headquarters Agreement of 26 June 1947
81	ECOSOC	6/13/1989	12/15/1989	Applicability of Art. VI, Section 22, of the Convention on the Privileges and Immunities of the United Nations

TABLE 3.2 List of advisory opinions and requesting organs (*cont.*)

Official number (ICJ website)	Requesting organ	Date of request	Date advisory opinion was issued	Official title of the advisory opinion
93	WHO's Assembly	9/3/1993	7/8/1996	Legality of the Use by a State of Nuclear Weapons in Armed Conflict
95	UN General Assembly	1/6/1995	7/8/1996	Legality of the Threat or Use of Nuclear Weapons
100	ECOSOC	8/10/1998	4/29/1999	Difference Relating to Immunity from Legal Process of a Special Rapporteur of the Commission on Human Rights
131	UN General Assembly	12/10/2003	7/9/2004	Legal Consequences of the Construction of a Wall in the Occupied Palestinian Territory
141	UN General Assembly	10/10/2008	7/22/2010	Accordance with international law of the unilateral declaration of independence in respect of Kosovo
146	IFAD's Executie Board	4/26/2010	2/1/2012	Judgment No. 2867 of the Administrative Tribunal of the International Labor Organization upon the International Fund for Agriculture Development
169	UN General Assembly	6/22/2017	2/25/2019	Legal Consequences of the Separation of the Chagos Archipelago from Mauritius in 1965

CHAPTER 4

The International Court of Justice and the International Community

The International Court of Justice was established in a different world order than that in which it operates today; there were only fifty one UN member states, no other international court, fewer international, regional, and non-governmental organizations, and non-state actors generally exercised much less influence in the international arena. Though the Court has remained structured in the same way, it serves an enlarged community of states and faces more competition from younger international and regional courts. The multiplication of international and regional actors, including states themselves, also raises questions as to the role, structure, and place of the Court in this wide constellation of players. This chapter examines the Court's relationship with international courts and tribunals, national courts, academia, and non-state actors, and assesses the ability of the Court to nurture these interactions and meet the international community's expectations.

A   The ICJ and Other International Courts and Tribunals

Since the establishment of the ICJ, the international judicial landscape has changed significantly. Although the ICJ remains the World Court, namely the UN's main judicial organ, it no longer stands as the *only* international court; it now co-exists with a plethora of additional international courts and tribunals. Some of these international courts and tribunals were created independently of the UN system; others are ad hoc structures that operate with limited jurisdiction in contrast to the general jurisdiction of the ICJ.[1]

Take the International Tribunal for the Law of the Sea (ITLOS), established in 1996. ITLOS is competent to adjudicate disputes arising out of the interpretation and application of the United Nations Convention on the Law of the

---

1   In addition to these prominent international courts, there are also regional courts that operate in Europe, Africa, and the Americas. These include the European Court of Human Rights (ECHR) and the European Court of Justice (ECJ), the African Court on Human and Peoples' Rights, the Inter-American Court of Human Rights (IACHR), the Caribbean Court of Justice, and the Central American Court of Justice.

© KONINKLIJKE BRILL NV, LEIDEN, 2020 | DOI:10.1163/9789004226968_006

Sea – a matter that also falls within the competence of the ICJ. Other adjudicative bodies, such as the International Center for the Settlement of Investment Disputes (ICSID) and the World Trade Organization's Dispute Settlement Body have similarly specialized competence to resolve certain types of international disputes. The North American Free Trade Agreement (NAFTA) panel hears disputes related to the trade agreement between Canada, the United States, and Mexico. The International Criminal Tribunal for the Former Yugoslavia (ICTY) put on trial those responsible for violations of international law that occurred during the conflicts in the Balkans in the 1990s – and paved the way for the creation of additional regional criminal tribunals. The International Criminal Court (ICC), established in 1998, brings individuals to justice for the violation of international law's most serious crimes. Although this list is far from exhaustive, it gives a sense of the specialized nature of most international adjudicative bodies – from international to regional, hybrid,[2] civil and criminal – established since 1945.

Some see this evolution as indicative of the expanding scope for international law and a testament to its relevance.[3] They see the creation of new mechanisms to handle disputes arising out of specialized areas of international law, such as the law of the sea or human rights, as necessary to ensure proper representation and develop expertise. Others have criticized the multiplication of international courts and tribunals, referring to the phenomenon as "fragmentation." When the International Tribunal for the Law of the Sea was established, certain scholars and ICJ judges noted, with some concern, that the ICJ was equipped to handle these disputes.[4] Judge Robert Jennings, in a similar vein, stressed that "[the World Court] is the right forum for the development of environmental law" precisely *because* it is a forum of general international law.[5] This view essentially holds that creating courts to handle issues over which the ICJ already has jurisdiction is redundant and therefore unnecessary.[6]

---

2 A hybrid court typically includes features or components of both international law and domestic law (for example as regards their jurisdiction, composition, or budget). Hybrid tribunals were established to hold individuals accountable in connection with conflicts that took place in Sierra Leone, Cambodia, and Lebanon.

3 Pemmaraju Sreenivasa Rao, *Multiple International Judicial Forums: A Reflection of the Growing Strength of International Law or Its Fragmentation?*, 25 Mich. J. Int'l L. 929, 930 (2004).

4 Firew Kebede Tiba, *What Caused the Multiplicity of International Courts and Tribunals*, 10 Gonz. J. Int'l L. 202, 204 (2006).

5 Sir Robert Jennings, *Need for Environmental Court?*, 22 Envtl. Pol'y & L. 312 (1992).

6 Geir Ulfstein, *International Courts and Judges: Independence, Interaction and Legitimacy*, 46 N.Y.U. J. Int'l L. & Pol. 849, 849 (2014).

Given the existence of a permanent forum with broad jurisdiction, one wonder why states feel the need to create more international tribunals. According to some authors, the proliferation of international tribunals results from the growth in international organizations.[7] Others contend that international legal crises, specifically those that challenge existing international norms, lead states to seek new international judicial mechanisms.[8]

Something may be said about turning to a tribunal *specialized* in a certain area of the law or establishing a new tribunal to handle the aftermath of a given conflict. Courts with competence to deal with specific subject matters also tend to develop an expertise in such matters. This might work in their favor. States – particularly younger states – may enjoy the idea that they have more input in the creation of newer mechanisms, in contrast with the ICJ whose features seem set in stone. Smaller and more specialized courts may at times also be less costly,[9] less bureaucratic, and more responsive than the ICJ where cases take years to reach a settlement. The creation of new, specialized avenues of international adjudication raises important questions regarding the ICJ's capacity to handle all international legal disputes involving an expanding constituency (193 states) and an expanding body of international norms. The Court would likely find it difficult to handle *all* international disputes.[10] The impossibility of adjudicating disputes involving non-state actors at the ICJ may constitute another reason for developing additional adjudicative mechanisms.[11]

These are just some of the reasons that explain the expansion of international adjudication. As international law branches out into sub-categories (law of the sea, space law, environmental law, international criminal law) and international actors (states and non-states) multiply, different needs arise. States have more choices now and do not automatically opt for the default, one-size-fits-all option that the ICJ embodies.

• • •

---

7   See Tiba, *supra* note 5, at 204.

8   Suzanne Katzenstein, *In the Shadow of Crisis: The Creation of International Courts in the Twentieth Century*, 55 Harv. Int'l L.J. 151, 154 (2014).

9   See Tiba, *supra* note 5, at 213.

10   *Id.*, at 208.

11   *Id.*, at 215. *See also* Cedric Ryngaert, *Non-State Actors: Carving Out a Space in a State-Centred International Legal System*, 63 Neth. Int'l L. Rev. 183 (2016); and William Thomas Worster, *Relative International Legal Personality of Non-State Actors*, 42 Brook. J. Int'l L. 207 (2016).

124   CHAPTER 4

Questions

1. Why might states prefer to use international judicial mechanisms competent to deal with specific issues rather than the ICJ?

2. What is, in your view, the most convincing argument for the creation of new international courts and tribunals?

3. Is there an area of international law, not accounted for by existing mechanisms, that would justify the establishment of a new court? Consider the need for international courts specializing in cyber, human rights, or space law, for example.

4. Would the ICJ look different today if it were not for the multiplication of international courts and tribunals? Would it play a greater role in the international arena? Would it have a larger docket? Would it have undergone some structural or other changes?

5. Viewed from the perspective of the ICJ, rather than that of states, does the creation of a multitude of international court and tribunals in any way threaten the ICJ's standing in the international legal and political orders? If so, what actions can the Court take, if any, to mitigate this effect?

The rise of international courts and tribunals not only affects the ICJ, it also affects international law more generally. The fear is that international law, interpreted and applied in a decentralized judicial system, will become fragmented and lose in coherence and legitimacy. Though fragmentation is a topic of major discussion in the field, no consensus exists on whether it constitutes a real impediment to the fulfillment of the ICJ's mission. What some view as a weakness is interpreted by others as a strength.

Fragmentation has at times been seen as a positive feature of the international legal system – an "institutional expression of political pluralism internationally."[12] Proponents of this view also emphasize the positive impact fragmentation has on the development of international law.[13] They believe that the co-existence of international courts and tribunals fosters a diverse body of law, and enables individual courts and tribunals to develop expertise in specific international legal matters.

---

12   Martti Koskenniemi and Päivi Leino, *Fragmentation of International Law: Postmodern Anxieties*, 15 Leiden J. Int'l L. 553 (2002).

13   Gerhard Hafner, *Pros and Cons Ensuing from Fragmentation of International Law*, 25 Mich. J. Int'l L. 849 (2004); and Rao, *supra* note 4, at, 930 (2004).

Speech by H.E. Judge Rosalyn Higgins[14]

I remain convinced that so-called "fragmentation of international law" is best avoided by regular dialogue between courts and exchanges of information. A detailed programme of co-operation between the ICJ and other international judicial bodies is now in place. We have an especially advanced programme of co-operation with the International Criminal Tribunal for the former Yugoslavia (ICTY).

The International Court has not failed to note that the newer courts and tribunals have regularly referred, often in a manner essential to their legal reasoning, to judgments of the ICJ. Indeed, in the first major decision of the ICC – the decision on the confirmation of charges in the case of the Prosecutor v. Thomas Lubanga Dyilo – particular reference is made to the ICJ's Congo v. Uganda Judgment of 2005.

Sometimes issues decided by other international or regional judicial bodies arise in a small but significant way in our own cases. In the Nicaragua v. Honduras case, the Court had occasion to study carefully a judgment of the Central American Court of Justice. And in connection with the provisional measures requested by Uruguay in the case concerning Pulp Mills on the River Uruguay (Argentina v. Uruguay), the Court has needed, in applying its own test for the granting of provisional measures, to study what issues relating to this dispute are (or are not) in front of Mercosur.

At other times, the judicial work of other international courts and tribunals have a more direct relevance to our own findings. In February the Court delivered its Judgment in the Bosnia and Herzegovina v. Serbia and Montenegro case.

This was the first legal case dealing with allegations of genocide by one State against another, but of course it was not the first time that the events in the Balkans had been considered by an international court or tribunal. The ICTY has been examining the same events for 13 years, but through the lens of individual criminal responsibility.

---

14   Speech by H.E. Judge Rosalyn Higgins, President of the International Court of Justice, at the meeting of Legal Advisors of the Ministry of Foreign Affairs, 3–5 (Oct. 29, 2007) at https://www.icj-cij.org/public/files/press-releases/7/14097.pdf.

> Both the Parties made great use of the judgments of the ICTY and the question of how to treat these judgments was thus squarely before the ICJ. The ICJ's Bosnia v. Serbia Judgment contains long and detailed findings of fact based on the Court's own analysis of the evidence, but with extensive reference also to relevant findings of the ICTY. The Court termed the working methods of the ICTY as rigorous and open, allowing it to treat ICTY findings of fact as "highly persuasive". The findings reached by the International Court through its independent analysis, including the key finding that the killings in Srebrenica in July 1995 were acts of genocide, were consistent with the jurisprudence of the ICTY.
>
> Apart from findings of fact, the Court was aware of the relevant legal findings established by the ICTY's jurisprudence. The International Court's Judgment in the Bosnia case addressed what is perhaps the most cited example of "the fragmentation of international law" – the test for control of irregular forces for purposes of responsibility adopted by the ICTY in the Tadić case. In 1999, the ICTY Appeals Chamber decided not to follow the "effective control" test that had been elaborated by the International Court in the Military and Paramilitary Activities in and against Nicaragua (Nicaragua v. United States of America) case, choosing instead to create an "overall control" test that required a lower threshold. In the Bosnia v. Serbia case, the International Court clearly addressed this perceived fracture in the jurisprudence and demonstrated that its significance should not be inflated. It observed that the ICTY was not called upon in the Tadić case, nor is it in general called upon, to rule on questions of State responsibility, since its jurisdiction is criminal and extends over persons only.
>
> (...)
>
> Thus, some differences of perception between the ICJ and the ICTY exist on this control test for purposes of responsibility, but given the different relevant contexts, they are readily understandable and hardly constitute a drama. Rather, we have an emerging sense of the United Nations principal judicial organ, and the Security Council's special Tribunal for the former Yugoslavia, working in parallel in harmony to achieve our respective tasks.

Others raise concerns that the proliferation of international courts and tribunals enables parties to pick the judicial mechanism that best fits their interests – a phenomenon known as forum-shopping. For example, states

INTERNATIONAL COURT OF JUSTICE & THE INTERNATIONAL COMMUNITY   127

might decide to bring a maritime dispute before ITLOS rather than the ICJ – or vice-versa – for reasons that have to do with the composition of the bench, the case law of these courts, or their own record of successes and failures before these judicial bodies.

The impact of forum shopping has not been proved detrimental to international law. Political scientists have shown that states do make rational strategic choices when selecting a forum to settle their territorial disputes.[15] The availability of a multitude of mechanisms, they find, increases opportunities for the development of international law and dispute resolution. Legal scholars, too, are generally optimistic and do not see forum shopping as a real concern for international law or international institutions.[16]

A more alarming scenario arises when proceedings take place on related issues in more than one forum at a time, which might lead to conflicting pronouncements on distinct points of law. Indeed, as new international courts and tribunals are created and endowed with jurisdiction over specific areas of international law, a potential for variance in the interpretation and development of international law emerges. Former President and Judge Guillaume addressed these and other concerns in a speech before the UN General Assembly in 2000.

> **Address by H.E. Judge Gilbert Guillaume[17]**
> [The proliferation of international courts] is in part a response to changes in international relations. It reflects greater confidence in justice and makes it possible for international law to develop in ever more varied spheres.
>
> It does however bring with it problems (...) First, it leads to cases of overlapping jurisdiction, opening the way for Applicant States to seek out those courts which they believe, rightly or wrongly, to be more amenable to their

---

15   Krista E. Wiegand and Emilia Justyna Powell, *Past Experience, Quest for the Best Forum, and Peaceful Attempts to Resolve Territorial Disputes*, 55 Journal of Conflict Resolution 33 (2011), at 52–53.

16   Koskenniemi and Leino, *supra* note 13, at 574–575.

17   Address by H.E. Judge Gilbert Guillaume, President of the International Court of Justice, to the United Nations General Assembly, Oct. 26, 2000 at https://www.icj-cij.org/public/files/press-releases/9/2999.pdf.

arguments. This forum shopping, as it is usually called, may indeed stimulate the judicial imagination, but it can also generate unwanted confusion. Above all, it can distort the operation of justice, which, in my view, should not be made subject to the law of the marketplace.

Overlapping jurisdiction also exacerbates the risk of conflicting judgments, as a given issue may be submitted to two courts at the same time and they may hand down inconsistent judgments (...)

Finally, the proliferation of international courts gives rise to a serious risk of conflicting jurisprudence, as the same rule of law might be given different interpretations in different cases. This is a particularly acute risk, as we are dealing with specialized courts that are inclined to favour their own disciplines (...) broadening the range of circumstances in which a State's responsibility may be engaged on account of its actions on foreign territory.

What can be done to ensure that this solution does not give rise to serious uncertainty as to the content of the law in the minds of players on the international stage and does not ultimately restrict the role of international law in inter-State relations? (...) Judges themselves must realize the danger of fragmentation in the law, and even conflicts of case-law, born of the proliferation of courts. A dialogue among judicial bodies is crucial. The International Court of Justice, the principal judicial organ of the United Nations, stands ready to apply itself to this end if it receives the necessary resources. Relying exclusively on the wisdom of judges might not be enough however. The relationships among international courts should, in my view, be better structured. With this in mind, it has at times been suggested that the Court should serve as a court of appeal or review for judgments rendered by all other courts (...) In order to reduce the risk of differing interpretations of international law, would it not be appropriate to encourage the various courts to seek advisory opinions in some cases from the Court, by way of the Security Council or the General Assembly?

Yet other international legal experts have stressed the emergence of separate, isolated normative regimes that overlap with general international law as interpreted by the ICJ but claim priority over these topics.[18] Take the World Trade Organization's Dispute Settlement Body, for example, which is dedicated to resolving disputes arising out of the World Trade Agreement. While

---

18   Koskenniemi and Leino, *supra* note 13.

noting that public international law overlaps with the law of trade, however, the DSB also adheres to the mission of the WTO – namely the advancement of free trade – and has occasionally set aside aspects of international law that it does not consider relevant to trade-related issues.[19]

The absence of a formal hierarchy among international courts also means that the International Court of Justice has at times been sidelined by newer courts, which are under no formal obligation to defer to the ICJ's judgments in the exercise of their judicial functions. In 1999, Mexico requested an advisory opinion from the Inter-American Court of Human Rights (IACHR) – established more than a decade after the ICJ – on the obligations set forth by the Vienna Convention on Consular Relations in relation to a dispute between Mexico and the United States.[20] The United States objected to the request for an advisory opinion on the ground that proceedings were pending before the ICJ on the same question (*Breard* first, followed by *LaGrand*), and asked the IACHR to stay its proceedings until the ICJ delivered its judgment. The IACHR refused on the ground that it is "an autonomous judicial institution" that cannot "be restrained from exercising its advisory jurisdiction because of contentious cases with the International Court of Justice."[21] The IACHR acknowledged that potential conflicting interpretations of international law might arise when there is no hierarchy between international judicial institutions bestowed with equal authority to interpret the same area of international law.[22] It also indicated that it had no intent to defer to the preferences or interpretations of another, equal court. The ICTY reacted similarly when it recognized the absence of an institutional hierarchy in *Čelebići*, acknowledging the need for consistency in international law while stressing its autonomous nature and the absence of a hierarchical relationship with the ICJ.[23] A possible request for an ICJ advisory opinion on the consistency of ICC decisions with customary international law on the immunity of heads of states would further underscore the absence of an international judicial hierarchy.[24] It would place the ICJ

---

19   *Id.*

20   The Right to Information on Consular Assistance in the Framework of the Guarantees of the Due Process of Law, Advisory Op. OC-16/99, Inter-Am. Ct. H.R. (Ser. A) No. 16 (Oct. 1, 1999).

21   *Id.*, paras. 57–65.

22   "Other Treaties" Subject to the Advisory Jurisdiction of the Court, Advisory Op. OC-1/82, Inter-Am. Ct. H.R. (Ser. A) No. 1 (Sept. 24, 1982), para. 50.

23   Prosecutor v. Zdravko Mucic et al. (*Celebiçi Case*), Decision, Case. No. IT-96-21-A, A.Ch., Feb. 20, 2001, paras. 24, 26. *See also* Koskenniemi and Leino, *supra* note 13.

24   Decision on the International Criminal Court, Doc. EX.CL/1068(XXXII).

130   CHAPTER 4

in the delicate situation of having to evaluate the soundness of the rulings of another international court.

That said, newer courts seeking to establish themselves as credible and legitimate often defer to judgments of other international bodies when deciding relevant issues in international law. All international courts and tribunals care about their image and how states, the general public, and a variety of other actors in the domestic, regional and international arenas perceive their role. As a result, the Appellate Body of the WTO, ITLOS, and the European Court of Justice regularly refer to the ICJ in their own decisions.[25] Vice-versa, the ICJ incorporates references to other courts in its advisory opinions and decisions. For instance, in *Application of the Convention on the Prevention and Punishment of the Crime of Genocide*, the Court relied extensively on the work of the ICTY in Bosnia.[26]

> *Marko Milanović, State Responsibility for Genocide: A Follow Up*[27]
> It is very interesting to observe how the ICJ interacted with other authoritative interpreters of international law, most of all the ILC and the ICTY (...) The Court's interaction with the ICTY is even more interesting, and it takes place at four different levels. First, the Court cites the ICTY (and the ICTR) on points of law regarding genocide – on what is the mens rea requirement, how to define the protected group and so on. This is a practice which is extremely rare for the ICJ, as it usually invokes only its own jurisprudence. Secondly, the Court cites the ICTY on points of fact – the ICJ did very little fact-finding of its own, but relied almost entirely on the ICTY, in fact never disagreeing with its assessment of the facts. Thirdly, the Court also relies on the ICTY when it comes to the legal qualification of these facts, mainly as to whether a particular crime can be qualified as genocide, with the result that only Srebrenica is so defined. Finally, when it comes to state responsibility, the ICJ rightly rejects the ICTY Appeal Chamber's overall control test from Tadić, applying instead its own two Nicaragua tests of complete dependence and control and of effective control. This interaction between the ICJ and the ICTY shows extremely well at least

---

25   Tullio Treves, *Advisory Opinions of the International Court of Justice on Questions Raised by Other International Tribunals*, *in* Max Planck Y.B. UN L. 215, 230 (Jochen A. Frowein and Rüdiger Wolfrum eds., 2000).

26   *Application of the Convention on the Prevention and Punishment of the Crime of Genocide* (Bosnia & Herzegovina v. Serbia & Montenegro), Judgment, I.C.J. Reports 2007, p. 91, para. 403.

27   Marko Milanović, *State Responsibility for Genocide: A Follow Up*, 18 EJIL 669 (2007).

> one way in which potential conflicts between proliferating international courts and tribunals can be resolved – by the deference of the generalist to the specialist. In this case the ICJ is the generalist, dabbling in everything but not specializing in anything, and deferring to the ICTY in its particular area of expertise. However, as the only international court of general jurisdiction, and as the principal judicial organ of the UN, the ICJ is the one authority whose pronouncements on structural principles of public international law should be followed, and state responsibility is precisely one of those areas in which the ICJ's expertise is paramount.

In *Territorial and Maritime Dispute* and in *Pulp Mills*, the Court considered decisions of the Central American Court of Justice and a Mercosur Tribunal (respectively) that had been raised by the parties.[28] Going forward the ICJ will likely also have to deal with the jurisprudence of human rights courts – a question which, according to Judge Simma, "will pose itself with greater frequency."[29]

Ultimately, the ICJ and other international courts and tribunals share a responsibility to develop consistent and cohesive international law. All fora of international adjudication must ensure that their jurisprudence complements that of other courts, in the aim of strengthening the international legal system. States established specialized courts to respond to some of their needs in the realm of dispute settlement – as they did when they established the ICJ. This is an important aspect which should not be overlooked.[30]

It is worth adding that the proliferation of international courts and tribunals has created a certain confusion among journalists, laymen, and even students, between the ICJ and other international courts and tribunals, many of which are also located in The Hague. Since 2011, the ICJ has included a paragraph in its press releases that seek to minimize such confusion.[31] This comes as an acknowledgment, by the Court itself, of the changing landscape of international adjudication.

---

28 The Statute of the International Court of Justice: A Commentary (Andreas Zimmermann, Christian J. Tams, Karin Oellers-Frahm & Christian Tomuschat, eds.) (3rd ed., 2019), at 90 (2019).

29 Bruno Simma, *Mainstreaming Human Rights: The Contribution of the International Court of Justice*, 3 Journal of International Dispute Settlement 7 (2012).

30 Treves, *supra* note 26.

31 Dapo Akande, *ICJ Press Release Distinguishes ICJ from Other International Tribunals*, EJIL Talk! (Dec. 27, 2011), available at https://www.ejiltalk.org/ICJ-press-releases-distinguish-the-ICJ-from-other-international-tribunals/.

132   CHAPTER 4

> **International Court of Justice, Press Release[32]**
>
> The International Court of Justice (ICJ) is the principal judicial organ of the United Nations. It was established by the United Nations Charter in June 1945 and began its activities in April 1946. The seat of the Court is at the Peace Palace in The Hague (Netherlands). Of the six principal organs of the United Nations, it is the only one not located in New York. The Court has a twofold role: first, to settle, in accordance with international law, legal disputes submitted to it by States (its judgments have binding force and are without appeal for the parties concerned); and, second, to give advisory opinions on legal questions referred to it by duly authorized United Nations organs and agencies of the system. The Court is composed of 15 judges elected for a nine-year term by the General Assembly and the Security Council of the United Nations. Independent of the United Nations Secretariat, it is assisted by a Registry, its own international secretariat, whose activities are both judicial and diplomatic, as well as administrative. The official languages of the Court are French and English. *Also known as the "World Court", it is the only court of a universal character with general jurisdiction.*

• • •

Questions

1. Should there be a formal hierarchy of international judicial institutions? What would it look like?

2. Take a look at the excerpt from President Higgins's speech above. Why would the ICTY decide *not* to adhere to the "effective control" test created by the ICJ? Should the ICTY be allowed to determine its own test? Should it have deferred to the ICJ's test?

3. In *Loizidou*, the European Court of Human Rights (ECHR) issued a decision that did not sit well with previous ICJ decisions. The ECHR addressed the differences between the ECHR and the ICJ, recognizing that "[s]uch fundamental differences in the role and purpose of the respective tribunals (...) provides a compelling

---

32   ICJ Press Release No. 2017/32 of 24 July 2017, Legal Consequences of the Separation of the Chago Archipelago from Mauritius in 1965, Request for Advisory Opinion (emphasis added).

basis for distinguishing Convention practice from that of the International Court."[33] Should all other courts – including regional courts – be required to comply with previous decisions of the ICJ?

4. Who, besides the ICJ, can claim authority in international law-making?

5. Compare Judges Guillaume and Higgins' view. Describe their contrasting opinions on the nature and effects of fragmentation in international law. Do you personally see fragmentation as a concern, and if so which particular aspect of it (forum shopping, conflicting interpretations, lack of a hierarchy, emergence of separate normative regimes within the field, etc.)?

6. Is the unity of international law a priority?

7. Judge Schwebel, a former President of the ICJ, believes that "in order to minimize ... significant conflicting interpretations of international law, there might be a virtue in enabling other international tribunals to request advisory opinions of the International Court of Justice on issues of international law that arise in cases before those tribunals that are of importance to the unity of international law."[34] Would Judge Schwebel's suggestion aid or hinder the development of a cohesive body of international law? What additional obstacles can you anticipate in the implementation of his proposal?

8. Why does the ICJ find it necessary to highlight its unique features in its press releases?

Further Reading

Pierre-Marie Dupuy, *The Danger of Fragmentation or Unification of the International Legal System and the International Court of Justice*, 31 Int'l L. & Politics 791 (1999).

Joel P. Trachtman, *Fragmentation, Coherence and Synergy in International Law*, 2 Transnat'l Legal Theory 505 (2011).

Rossana Deplano, *Fragmentation and Constitutionalisation of International Law: A Theoretical Inquiry*, 6 Eur. J. Legal Stud. 85 (2013).

---

33 Loizidou v. Turkey (Preliminary Objections), App. No. 15318/59, Eur. Ct. Hum. Rights 622, para. 85 (1995). *See also* Belilos v Switzerland (Admissibility), App. No. 10328/83, Eur. Ct. Hum. Rights (1988) (holding that a declaration by Switzerland to the *European Convention on Human Rights* was an invalid reservation, and that Switzerland remained bound by the convention as a whole).

34 ICJ Press Release No. 99/46 of 26 October 1999 ('Failure by Member States of the United Nations to pay their dues transgresses principles of international law, President Schwebel tells United Nations General Assembly').

Chiara Giorgetti, *Horizontal and Vertical Relationships of International Courts and Tribunals – How Do We Address Their Competing Jurisdiction?*, 30 ICSID Rev. 98, 99 (2015).

B   The ICJ and National Courts

Like the ICJ's interaction with international courts and tribunals, the ICJ's interaction with national courts has grown in relevance and frequency over time – albeit for different reasons. Here, the interaction is largely the product of the eroding boundaries between what were once considered two different spheres: the domestic sphere on the one hand, and the international sphere on the other.

In theory the relationship between the ICJ and national courts is reciprocal, meaning that the ICJ can refer to the judgments of national courts and, vice-versa, that national courts may show deference for the ICJ. Beyond a show of deference – also known as comity – national courts and the ICJ can also regard their respective decisions as legally binding. However, it is important to note that they are under no obligation to do so. In the absence of a formal legal obligation, the relationship between the ICJ and national courts must be assessed by taking into consideration a variety of indicia that may demonstrate authority, legitimacy, and deference.

1   *Compliance with ICJ Decisions*
Article 94 of the UN Charter (reproduced below) imposes an obligation on member states to comply with ICJ decisions to which they are party.

> **UN Charter, Article 94**
> 1. Each Member of United Nations undertakes to comply with the decision of the International Court of Justice in any case to which it is party.
> 2. If any party to a case fails to perform the obligations incumbent upon it under a judgment rendered by the Court, the other party may have recourse to the Security Council, which may, if it deems necessary, make recommendations or decide upon measures to be taken to give effect to the judgment.

The Court debated the question of whether Article 94 creates direct legal obligations for the *national authorities of a given state* to comply with ICJ decisions in a series of three cases, *Breard, Lagrand,* and *Avena.* The United States was the Respondent in all three cases. The cases were brought by states whose nationals, on death row in the United States, had allegedly been victim of violations under the Vienna Convention on Consular Relations. Pending a more thorough examination of the case, the Court requested the United States to stay the execution of foreign nationals awaiting the death penalty. The competence to stay such executions, the United States argued, was vested in the Governor of the state where the execution was to take place. The Court made clear that the Governors were "under the obligation to act in conformity with the international undertakings of the United States."[35] The ICJ's position is consistent with the general principle under which a State cannot rely on its domestic law as an excuse for violating international law, leading some commentators to suggest that "the State organ which is competent under national law has to act compatibly with [the obligation resulting from the ICJ decision], otherwise provoking the State's responsibility for a violation of international law."[36] Notwithstanding the willingness of the executive branch to implement the ICJ's request, the United States Supreme Court held that a direct obligation to comply does not exist under the ICJ Statute or the UN Charter.[37]

2 The Decisions of National Courts in the ICJ's Jurisprudence

Article 38 of the ICJ Statute does not frame the relationship between the ICJ and national courts in unequivocal terms.

> **ICJ Statute**
>
> **Article 38**
>
> The Court, whose function is to decide in accordance with international law such disputes as are submitted to it, shall apply:
>
> a. International conventions, whether general or particular, establishing rules expressly recognized by the contesting states;
>
> b. International custom, as evidence of a general practice accepted as law;

---

35   *See Lagrand* (Germany v. United States of America), Provisional Measures, I.C.J. Reports 1999, p. 16, para. 28; *Vienna Convention on Consular Relations* (Paraguay v. United States of America), Provisional Measures, I.C.J. Reports 1998, p. 228, paras. 38–41.

36   The Charter of the United Nations: A Commentary (2012) (Bruno Simma, Daniel-Erasmus Khan, Georg Nolte, Andreas Paulus, eds.), para. 14.

37   Medellín v. Texas, 552 US 491 (2008).

> c. The general principles of law recognized by civilized nations;
>
> d. Subject to the provisions of Article 59, judicial decisions and the teachings of the most highly qualified publicists of the various nations, as subsidiary means for the determination of rules of law.

It provides that "judicial decisions" should be used by the Court in the exercise of its judicial function, as "subsidiary means for the determination of rules of law." It is unclear whether the expression "judicial decisions" refers to the judicial decisions of the International Court of Justice, the judicial decisions of domestic courts, or the judicial decisions of other international courts and tribunals. International courts and tribunals (other than the ICJ) did not exist at the time the Statute was adopted, so the article cannot be interpreted to refer to their case law. The reference to Article 59 of the Statute (which provides that decisions of the ICJ have "no binding force except between the parties and in respect of that particular case") already delineates the normative weight of ICJ decisions, so Article 38 must be addressing some other issue – at the risk of the Statute repeating itself. If "judicial decisions" in Article 38 neither refers to the decisions of the ICJ nor to the decisions of other international courts, which were not in existence at the time the Statute was adopted, Article 38 must refer instead to the decisions of national courts as a source of law for the ICJ.

The decisions of national courts accordingly serve as "subsidiary means for the determination of rules of law". They help to ascertain the content of the law, if such content cannot be readily determined from treaties and customary international law. In practice, however, some decisions of national courts have left a strong imprint on international law – which goes beyond the words of Article 38 (think *Pinochet*,[38] *Eichmann*,[39] or *Targeted Killing*[40]). These decisions, which significantly influenced the development of international law, stood out for their boldness and forward-looking reasoning. They were the product of open-minded national judges who did not shy away from exploring

---

38   R. v. Bow St. Metro. Stipendiary Magistrate & Others, *Ex parte* Pinochet Ugarte, [2000] 1 A.C. 147, [1999] 2 W.L.R. 827 (H.L.).

39   Att'y Gen. of Israel v. Eichmann, 36 ILR 277 (S. Ct. 1962) (Isr.).

40   Pub. Comm. against Torture in Israel v. Gov't of Israel, HCJ 769/02 (Dec. 11, 2005).

uncharted territory. Far from viewing international law as foreign law, these judges researched, interpreted, and applied international norms – which contributed to the resonance of their jurisprudence. Domestic courts thus play dual and sometimes conflicting roles as international "law enforcers" and "law creators."[41]

The ICJ, for its part, mostly references the judicial decisions of domestic courts to demonstrate the existence of state practice in the emergence of customary international law. State practice is one of the constitutive elements of customary international law – a major source of law as per Article 38 of the ICJ Statute.[42] Even before the ICJ Statute was adopted, the PCIJ stressed the importance of analyzing the case law of national courts when ascertaining the existence of customary international law.[43] Later, in *Arrest Warrant*, the ICJ acknowledged the role of national court judgments in determining the contours of customary international law. The ICJ examined "those few decisions of national higher courts, such as the House of Lords or the French Court of Cassation" in an effort to determine whether there existed an exception to the immunity protecting Ministers of Foreign Affairs suspected of having committed war crimes or crimes against humanity. The Court concluded that it had been unable to deduce such an exception from state practice.[44] The role imparted to domestic judgments in ascertaining customary law was expanded in *Jurisdictional Immunities of the State* case, where the ICJ acknowledged the role of national courts' decisions in ascertaining both state practice and *opinio juris*, and proceeded to examine in depth the decisions of the national courts of a dozen states.[45] The ICJ has also placed some emphasis on the role of domestic courts in giving effect to international law.[46]

The ICJ's reliance on the case law of national courts endows the Court's holdings with greater legitimacy among its constituency, i.e., states. It should

---

41   Anthea Roberts, *Comparative International Law? The Role of National Courts in Creating and Enforcing International* Law, 60 Int'l & Comp. L.Q. 57, 69 (2011).

42   *Continental Shelf* (Libyan Arab Jarnahiriya v. Malta), I.C.J. Reports 1985, p. 13, para. 27.

43   *Lotus Case* (Fra. v. Turk.), 1927 P.C.I.J. (ser. A) No. 10.

44   *Arrest Warrant of Apr. 11, 2000* (Dem. Rep. of Congo v. Belgium), I.C.J. Reports 2002, p. 3, para. 58.

45   *Jurisdictional Immunities of the State* (Germany v. Italy: Greece intervening), Judgment, I.C.J. Reports 2012, p. 99, para. 64. *Opinio juris*, the second constitutive element of customary law, requires that states act a certain way because they believe that they are legally obligated to do so.

46   Michael Kirby, *International Law: The Impact on National Constitutions*, 21 Am. U. Int'l L. Rev. 327, 331 (2006).

be encouraged beyond the demonstration of the existence of customary norms to further the prestige of the Court and perhaps even enhance compliance.

3 The ICJ in the Jurisprudence of National Courts

From a domestic court's perspective, interpreting and applying international law may seem unnatural. Many national courts shy away from applying international law, let alone developing it. Australia and the United States, for example, have resisted the direct applicability of international law in their domestic legal order. Certain US courts have traditionally equated international law to foreign law, i.e., as if it were the law of a foreign state, and declared international law not directly applicable domestically.[47] At the time, the judges lacked expertise in the field, and voiced concerns that international law might be applied selectively to advance a certain outcome in cases where domestic law simply did not reach a suitable conclusion.[48] Certainly, this argument goes, lawyers and judges can "troll deeply enough in the world's corpus juris" to find support for a particular decision or legal interpretation.[49] It was also feared that citing to – let alone applying – the law of others would detract from the strength and legitimacy of domestic law.[50] Finally, it has been regarded as objectionable to subject domestic actors to the authority of international institutions, given the institutional and procedural differences between international and national courts.

The level of deference afforded to international law by domestic institutions reflects a state's view of the relationship between the domestic sphere and the international sphere. Two terms are regularly used to describe this relationship. Under a *monist* conception, international law and domestic law are part of a single sphere, with domestic law and international law coexisting within this unitary legal universe. Under a *dualist* conception, international law and domestic law are part of two separate spheres that exist separately and have no effect on each other. This conception asserts the supremacy of the state and denies any influence of international law on the domestic sphere.[51]

---

47 Harold Koh, *International Law as Part of Our Law*, 98 Am. J. Int'l L. 43 (2004).
48 *The Relevance of Foreign Legal Materials in US Constitution Cases: A Conversation Between Justice Antonin Scalia and Justice Stephen Breyer*, 3 Int'l J. Const. L. 519 (2005).
49 Richard Posner, *No Thanks, We Already Have Our Own Laws*, Legal Aff., July–Aug. 2004.
50 Michael Kirby, *International Law: The Impact on National Constitutions*, 21 Am. U. Int'l L. Rev. 327, 349 (2006).
51 *See* Malcolm Shaw, International Law (8th ed., 2017); Rosalyn Higgins, Problems and Process: International Law and How We Use It (1995), at 205.

INTERNATIONAL COURT OF JUSTICE & THE INTERNATIONAL COMMUNITY   139

In practice, sovereignty and the preservation of domestic objectives play a key role in how states express their commitment to international law in their constitutions and judicial decisions.[52] Consider the argument that the case law of international courts lacks democratic legitimacy.

> *Richard Posner, No Thanks, We Already Have Our Own Laws*[53]
> [The problem] is the undemocratic character of citing foreign decisions. Even decisions rendered by democratic judges in democratic countries, or by judges from the countries who sit on international courts, are outside the US democratic orbit (...) the judges of foreign countries, however democratic these countries may be, have no democratic legitimacy here. The votes of foreign electorates are not events in our democracy.
>
> Particularly questionable in this regard is citing foreign decisions to establish an international consensus that should have weight in US courts. Such nose-counting is like subjecting legislation enacted by Congress to review by the United Nations General Assembly.

Globalization has created an environment more conducive to the incorporation of international law into domestic jurisprudence.[54] Domestic courts use international law for a variety of reasons and purposes, including to interpret domestic and international norms, and prevent the examination by a domestic court of a matter that has already been settled by international courts.[55] National courts may engage with international law because of their own constitutions, if the latter give international norms binding force in the domestic legal system.[56] Even when the constitution does not provide so explicitly, it may contain provisions protecting human rights and fundamental freedoms leading judges, indirectly and perhaps unwillingly, to apply international norms when interpreting the constitution.[57] Courts in South Africa and India

---

52   Eyal Benvenisti and George W. Downs, *National Courts, Domestic Democracy & Evolution of National Law*, 20 Eur. J. Int'l L. 59 (2009).

53   *See* Posner, *supra* note 54.

54   Eyal Benvenisti & George W. Downs, *National Courts, Domestic Democracy & Evolution of National Law*, 20 Eur. J. Int'l L. 59 (2009).

55   *See supra* note 57.

56   *See* for example the constitutions of India, India Const. pt. IV, sec. 51(c), and South Africa, S. Afr. Const. 1996, ch. 3 sec. 39(1)(b).

57   *See* Kirby, *supra* note 51, at 330s.

140   CHAPTER 4

have been willing to use international law in this process of constitutional interpretation.[58]

Alternatively, and more relevant for our purposes here, national courts may decide to show deference by specifically referencing ICJ decisions in their judgments – even when they do not fully embrace or implement the ICJ decisions. For example, in *Beit Surik* and *Mara'abe*, the Israeli Supreme Court analyzed the ICJ's advisory opinion on the *Legal Consequences of the Construction of a Wall in the Occupied Palestinian Territory* and delineated the scope of its applicability within the domestic sphere.[59]

> **Mara'abe[60]**
>
> The opinion of the ICJ – as its title testifies, and in contrast to a judgment by the same court – is an Advisory Opinion. It does not bind the party who requested it. As the ICJ itself noted in its opinion, it does not bind the states. It is not res judicata. However, the opinion of the International Court of Justice is an interpretation of international law, performed by the highest judicial body in international law. The ICJ's interpretation of international law should be given its full appropriate weight.
>
> (...)
>
> Our answer is as follows: the Supreme Court of Israel shall give the full appropriate weight to the norms of international law, as developed and interpreted by the ICJ in its Advisory Opinion. However, the ICJ's conclusion, based upon a factual basis different than the one before us, is not res judicata, and does not obligate the Supreme Court of Israel to rule that each and every segment of the fence violates international law.

Finally, states occasionally (and more controversially) use the ICJ as a court of appeals when they ask the Court to opine on how domestic courts interpret

---

58   Khagesh Guatam, *The Use of International Law in Constitutional Interpretation in the Supreme Court of India*, 55 Stanford J. Int'l L. 27, 27 (2019); and Devika Hovell and George Williams, *A Tale of Two Systems: The Use of International Law in Constitutional Interpretation in Australia and South Africa*, 29 Melbourne University Law Review 96 (2005).

59   Beit Surik Village Council et al. v. Gov't of Israel et al., HCJ 2056/04 (June 30, 2004), 43 I.L.M. 1099 (2004); and Mara'abe v. Prime Minister of Israel, HCJ 7957/04 (Sept. 15, 2005).

60   *Mara'abe, supra* note 64, paras. 56 and 74 (references omitted).

international law.[61] States have turned to the ICJ to effectively review domestic interpretations of the Vienna Convention on Consular Relations,[62] and norms governing diplomatic and state immunity.[63] Pursuit of remedy from the ICJ is indicative of the overarching importance of international law on domestic legal practices, but also reveals an attempt at using the Court as an extra level of "appeal" rather than as a forum for the peaceful settlement of international legal disputes.

When national courts choose to tackle difficult international legal issues, it is not merely on account of the ICJ decisions themselves but also on account of the importance of the topic and its cross-border ramifications. As noted above, it calls for the careful handling of distant concepts by domestic judges, a mastery of comparative law, and sometimes also giving deference to other national courts and regional bodies.[64]

Ultimately, the role of domestic courts in strengthening international law generally, and the ICJ specifically, should be neither underestimated nor overestimated. Their input matters and may contribute to the emergence of customary international law. Limitations do exist in this regard, however. Without positive reinforcement on the part of practitioners, scholars, and other judicial and legal fora, a national court decision is unlikely to create customary law or significantly impact the Court's standing (or that of its decisions). This tension – on the one hand the important role of national decisions in creating state practice and therefore potentially new law, and on the other, their status as mere "subsidiary" legal sources – has its roots in Article 38 of the Statute. Domestic courts realize that a show of deference strengthens the domestic order by broadening the reach of their findings and enhancing their image as international players and standard-setters.[65] Engaging with international law also conveys the courts' awareness of the implications of globalization for judicial decision-making.

---

61   *See supra* note 57.

62   *Case Concerning Avena and Other Mexican Nationals* (Mexico v. United States of America), I.C.J. Reports 2004, p. 12; *La Grand* (Germany v. United States of America), I.C.J. Reports 2001, p. 466; *Breard* (Paraguay v. United States of America), I.C.J. Reports 1998, p. 99.

63   *Arrest Warrant of Apr. 11, 2000* (Democratic Republic of the Congo v. Belgium), I.C.J. Reports 2002, p. 3; and *Jurisdictional Immunities of the State* (Germany v. Italy), I.C.J. Reports 2012, p. 99.

64   *See* Anthea Roberts, *Comparative International Law? The Role of National Courts in Creating and Enforcing International Law*, 60 Int'l & Comp. L.Q. 57 (2011).

65   *See supra* note 57.

142   CHAPTER 4

•••

Questions

1. How do Article 94 of the UN Charter and Article 38 of the ICJ Statute give expression to the principle of consent and state sovereignty?

2. Are judicial decisions of national courts fundamental to the determination of rules of international law? How would you describe their importance?

3. Does the relationship between national courts and the ICJ seem balanced? If not, which institution possesses greater leverage – the ICJ or a domestic court? Does the answer vary depending on the location of the domestic court, the subject-matter, or the political context?

4. Can the ICJ rely on national courts in the enforcement of its judgments? What other mechanisms are available to the ICJ to achieve such goal?

5. Was the decision to incorporate state practice as a constitutive element of customary international law purposefully designed to increase the relevance of national courts in international law? Why would states want to elevate the role of domestic courts in the international legal system?

6. Would ICJ decisions be better received by states if they were more grounded in domestic law? Is that what the drafters of Article 38 had in mind? How would this affect the development of international law?

7. Take a look at the Israeli Supreme Court decision in *Mara'abe*. If you were a national judge, how much deference would you give to a prior ICJ advisory opinion?

Further Reading

George Slyz, *International Law in National Courts*, 28 N.Y.U. J. Int'l L. & Pol. 65 (1996).

David J. Bederman, Christopher J. Borgen, and David A. Martin, *International Law: A Handbook for Judges* (Studies in Transnational Legal Policy No. 35, 2003).

Pierre-Hugues Verdier and Mila Versteeg, International Law in National Legal Systems: An Empirical Investigation, 109 Am. J. Int'l L. 514 (2015).

Benedict Chigara, *National Courts and the Integrity of International Law*, 48 Cal. W. Int'l L.J. 189 (2018).

C   The ICJ and "the Most Highly Qualified Publicists"

Decisions and advisory opinions of the International Court of Justice, while predominantly based on treaty law, state practice, and customary international law, are also influenced by academic discourse. In fact, the ICJ Statute

INTERNATIONAL COURT OF JUSTICE & THE INTERNATIONAL COMMUNITY   143

provides that the "teachings of the most highly qualified publicists of the various nations" constitute "a subsidiary means for the determination of rules of law" alongside the judicial decisions of national courts.[66] Scholarly writings of the "most highly qualified publicists," therefore, possess a normative value equivalent to that of domestic judicial decisions.[67] According to Article 38, ICJ judges should turn to academic writings (and domestic judicial decisions) to determine the content of the law. In practice, however, the Court does not mention international legal academics by name and hardly cites to their work. This section explores the relationship between the Court and academia.

1   *Academia at the ICJ*
As previously noted, Article 38(1)(d) of the ICJ Statute explicitly includes "the teachings of the most highly qualified publicists of the various nations" as a "subsidiary" source of international law. The meaning of "subsidiary" is crucial here; it points to their lower normative weight. Shabtai Rosenne noted that "[d]octrine is not positive international law ... nor does it stand on the same basis as international judicial decisions."[68] Indeed, before 1983, the Court had never referred to the writings of international legal academics in its decisions (this does not include separate and dissenting opinions of individual judges, which regularly refer to academic scholarship).[69] That this continues to reflect the practice of Court is puzzling to say the least. In its entire case law, the Court has only very rarely cited to specific scholarly writings.[70]

It is puzzling because many ICJ judges have an academic background: prior to their appointment to the Court they were teachers or lecturers, international law researchers, and authors of books and articles on international law.[71] Even during their term on the bench, many judges continue to participate

---

66   ICJ Statute, Article 38.
67   *See supra* Section B.
68   Shabtai Rosenne, Practice and Methods of International Law (1984), at 119.
69   Sir Hersch Lauterpacht, The Development of International Law by the International Court (1982), at 23.
70   Michael Peil, *Scholarly Writings as a Source of Law: A Survey of the Use of Doctrine by the International Court of Justice*, 1 Cambridge J. of Int'l L. 136, 137 (2012) (noting that as of 2012, the Court had cited to doctrine in only twenty-two of its 139 judgments and advisory opinions). *See also* Sondre Torp Helmersen, *Finding 'the most highly qualified publicists': Lessons from the International Court of Justice*, 33 Eur. J. Int'l L. 355 (2019) ("the Court has cited to specific work of teachings on a point of law only seven times, in five cases").
71   Daniel Terris, Cesare P.R. Romano and Leigh Swigart, *The International Judge: An Introduction to the Men and Women Who Decide the World's Cases* (2007), at 20 (85 out of 215 judges at international courts previously held academic positions).

144   CHAPTER 4

in academic conferences. ICJ judges give speeches and lectures,[72] serve as
guests of honor at professional conferences,[73] visit universities,[74] publish academic articles,[75] address students,[76] and even teach following their time on the
Court.[77] For its fiftieth and sixtieth anniversaries, the Court organized colloquia and extended invitations to leading academics to come and speak about
the Court and its work.[78]

In light of the foregoing, the absence of references to specific academics
cannot be interpreted as an expression of disdain for academia. It would be
equally wrong to say that judges do not consider academic sources prior to
making judicial pronouncements. Agents and counsels appearing before the
Court routinely reference teachings and doctrine in their memorials and
arguments – thereby bringing the judges' attention to these important sources.
In addition, judges regularly refer to the work of scholars in their individual
opinions. Consider Judge M. Guggenheim's reference to John Norton Moore
in his dissenting opinion to *Nottebohm*,[79] Judge Ammoun's reference to Louis
Henkin's work in his Separate Opinion to *North Sea Continental Shelf*, or
Judge Simma's reference to Anna Riddell and Brendan Plant in his Separate
Opinion to *Application of the International Convention on the Elimination of
All Forms of Racial Discrimination*. These and a multitude of other references
suggest that academic scholarship influences the deliberations leading to ICJ

---

72 H.E. Judge Ronny Abraham, President of the ICJ, presents the Inaugural Lecture of the
    Asser-ICJ Series, Twitter (Feb. 10, 2016, 7:56 AM); and Antonio Augusto Cançado Trindade,
    *The Universality of International Law, its Humanist Outlook, and the Mission of the Hague
    Academy of International Law*, 32 Netherlands Q. H.R. 109 (2014).

73 Press Release, ICJ President Peter Tomka a Guest of Honor at Conference on the
    Compulsory Jurisdiction of the European Court of Justice, Min. For. Aff. (June 14, 2013).

74 Judge Giorgio Gaja, *The International Court of Justice's Approach to Injuries Suffered by
    Individuals* (May 8, 2014).

75 Sir Robert Jennings, *Need for Environmental Court?*, 22 Envtl. Pol'y & L. 312 (1992).

76 The Hague: Centre of International Justice and Enforcement of International
    Humanitarian Law (Dec. 8–14, 2016).

77 For instance, Judge Thomas Buergenthal, after serving on the Court from 2000 to 2010,
    returned to teach at the George Washington University School of Law.

78 *See A Dialogue at the Court: Proceedings of the ICJ/UNITAR Colloquium held on the occasion of the sixtieth anniversary of the International Court of Justice, at the Peace Palace
    on 10 and 11 April 2006*; and *Colloquium Marking Fiftieth Anniversary of Word Court to be
    Held Next Week in The Hague*, ICJ Press Release 545, 12 April 1996. ICJ Press Release No.
    1996/545 of 12 April 1996 ('Colloquium Marking Fiftieth Anniversary of Word Court to be
    Held Next Week in The Hague').

79 *Nottebohm* (Liechtenstein v. Guatemala), Diss. Op. Guggenheim, I.C.J. Reports 1955, p. 50.

pronouncements.[80] That the Court's library compiles and distributes a bibliography of academic and other sources to members of the Court in relation to each case or advisory opinion further confirms the importance that judges afford to scholarship in judicial decision-making.[81]

Although judges do consider, at times with great care, academic views on the legal issues that come before them, academic sources only rarely make it into the final text of a judgment or advisory opinion. When they do, it can be for a variety of reasons – to demonstrate widespread state practice, interpret a treaty provision, establish a general principle of law, explain the practice of the Court itself, provide general context for a specific point or case, demonstrate the existence of a rule of law, or advocate for a change in the law.[82]

The rarity of scholarly references in ICJ judgments and advisory opinions is particularly striking when contrasted to the practice of other international courts and tribunals. Academic writings (understood broadly as including treaty commentaries, academic journals, monographs, and dictionaries) are regularly cited by international criminal courts (hundreds of citations were counted in a sample of ninety-one judgements of the ICC, ICTY, and ICTR).[83] The practice appears similar to that of courts in the civil law tradition, which generally refrain from providing a detailed explanation of how they reached their decisions. In the common law tradition, in contrast, judges expose (sometimes over a considerable amount of pages!) the legal reasoning to allow other courts and parties to future cases to understand, apply, and potentially challenge such reasoning. Such judgements tend to include multiple references to scholarly work. The ICJ resembles courts of common law countries in that it renders long judgments and allows separate and dissenting opinions. Its reluctance to cite to academic sources is more reminiscent of the civil law tradition.

Deference to legal experts can nevertheless be found in the Court's reliance on the writings of the International Law Commission (ILC), a subsidiary organ of the UN General Assembly whose mandate is to "initiate studies and make recommendations for the purpose of ... encouraging the progressive development of international law and its codification."[84] The ICJ regularly references the work of the ILC – as in *North Sea Continental Shelf* – and

---

80   See Peil, *supra* note 75, at 136, 137 (citing Sir Humphrey Waldock).

81   Report of the International Court of Justice, A/64/4 (2009), at 21.

82   See *supra* note 75, at 153.

83   Nora Stappert, *A New Influence of Legal Scholars? The Use of Academic Writings at International Courts and Tribunals*, 31 Leiden J. Int'l L. 963 (2018), at 971.

84   Statute of the International Law Commission Article 1(1), Nov. 21, 1927.

146   CHAPTER 4

sometimes even endorses it – as in its Advisory Opinion for *Legal Consequences of the Construction of a Wall in the Occupied Palestinian Territory*. These frequent references to the work of the ILC stand in sharp contrast with the ICJ's reluctance to cite to the work of individual scholars. Perhaps it is because the ILC is a formal body of the UN, it has been "empowered" by states to contribute to international law, its members often become judges at the Court, or because its work is the product of a collective reflection.

> **Sandesh Sivakumaran, *The Influence of Teaching of Publicists on the Development of International Law*[85]**
>
> The teachings of State-empowered entities are thus of a different order to the teachings of publicists without a connection to a State. Indeed, from a nonformalist perspective, State-empowered entities might best not be considered publicists at all. State-empowered entities have a close relationship with States in a way that ordinary publicists do not. They are empowered by States to carry out a law-making function broadly defined – for present purposes, to develop a teaching. States usually have a say in the election or appointment of individuals to the entity. States also have a role to play in the content of the teaching, for example, submitting their views to the entity or otherwise being involved in the drafting process. In addition, States have an important role to play following the finalization of the teaching, for example, accepting it or rejecting it.
>
> Thus, the teachings of State-empowered entities prove useful, in part, because they can be traced back to States.

• • •

Questions

1. Why does the Court rarely cite to academic sources in its judgments and orders? Should it do so more often? Why?

2. In your view, do references to scholarly work in domestic judicial decisions enhance the legitimacy of these decisions or, rather, open the door to criticism and weakening of the *res judicata*? Does your view differ in the context of international judicial decisions?

---

85   Sandesh Sivakumaran, *The Influence of Teaching of Publicists on the Development of International Law*, 66 ICLQ 1 (2017), at 6.

INTERNATIONAL COURT OF JUSTICE & THE INTERNATIONAL COMMUNITY   147

3.   Do you agree with Sandesh Sivakumaran about the special status of the ILC as a "state empowered" entity?

2   Scholarly Critiques of the ICJ

From the perspective of academia, things look quite different. The academic community closely follows developments at the ICJ, commenting and critically appraising decisions made by the Court on a regular basis. International law journals commonly publish symposia (also known as "agora") in which international scholars comment on the most recent ICJ decisions. For example, the American Journal of International Law published a series of articles on *Case Concerning Avena and Other Mexican Nationals* and *Accordance with International Law of the Unilateral Declaration of Independence in Respect of Kosovo* as agorae.[86] The *Harvard Law Review* also published an eight-page analysis of the latter.[87]

These examples illustrate the richness of academia's input on the Court's work – as do the hundreds of references cited to in this book. Academics take an active role in critically analyzing the ICJ's role and decisions, resulting in hundreds of articles in journals and books published around the world. Frequently discussed topics include the principle of consent (often criticized as too loosely or too restrictively applied by the Court),[88] access of non-state actors to the Court,[89] the relatively slow pace at which cases proceed before the Court, the impartiality and diversity of the bench,[90] and judicial restraint.[91]

---

86   *Agora: ICJ Advisory Opinion on* Construction of a Wall in Occupied Palestinian Territory, 99 AJIL 1(2005); and *Agora: The ICJ's* Kosovo *Advisory Opinion*, 105 AJIL 50 (2011).

87   *Recent Advisory Opinion*, 124 Harvard Law Review 1098 (2011).

88   Shabtai Rosenne, International Law and Practice, Vol. 2, Chapter 9, para. 154 ("The result is that the application of the principle is less rigid than may be inferred from the manner in which it is enunciated"). *See also* Pieter Kooijmans, *The ICJ in the Twenty-First Century: Judicial Restraint, Judicial Activism, or Proactive Judicial Policy*, 56 Int'l & Comp. L.Q. 741 (2007), at 743.

89   Gleider Hernandez, *Non-state Actors from the Perspective of the International Court of Justice*, in Participants in the International Legal System: Multiple Perspectives on Non-State Actors in International Law 140 (Jean d'Aspremont, ed., 2011); Jordan Paust, *Non-State Actor Participation in International Law and the Pretense of Exclusion*, 51 Virginia Journal of Int'l Law 977 (2011); and Yael Ronen, *Participation of Non-State Actors in ICJ Proceedings*, 11 L. & Prac. Int'l Cts. & Tribunals 77 (2012).

90   Gleider Hernandez, *Impartiality and Bias at the International Court of Justice*, 1 Cambridge J. Int'l & Comp. L. 183 (2012).

91   Pieter Kooijmans, *The ICJ in the Twenty-First Century: Judicial Restraint, Judicial Activism, or Proactive Judicial Policy*, 56 Int'l & Comp. L.Q. 741 (2007).

148   CHAPTER 4

Some authors are skeptical, too, of the role the ICJ can play in an international society made up of sovereign states.[92]

In sum, by not citing to academic sources in its judgments, the Court has chosen not to engage directly with academia. This does not mean that it does not careful review academic sources prior to issuing its judgments – which it clearly does – or does not maintain excellent relationship with a community of scholars many judges formerly belonged to. However, by addressing these sources only behind closed-doors, the Court keeps the mystery of its decision-making process intact.

D   The ICJ and Non-State Actors

The United Nations embodies a paradigmatic example of an international organization built by states and for states. The International Court of Justice, as the principal judicial organ of the UN, was designed to serve states and provide a forum for the peaceful settlement of their disputes *with other states*. In this context, access to the Court is limited to states.

> **ICJ Statute**
>
> **Article 34**
> 1. Only states may be parties in cases before the Court.

The ICJ's doors have remained traditionally closed to non-state actors – despite their growing role and influence on the international scene. Each year, the Court receives many unsuccessful requests by private persons to seek redress or initiate proceedings (sometimes over a thousand a year!).[93] Whereas non-state actors have gained more recognition outside the Peace Palace, particularly via the emergence of human rights law and international criminal law, they have remained, for the most part, *persona non grata* at the ICJ. This is not to say that the relationship of the ICJ with non-state actors is a monolithic one. A slow and barely noticeable shift toward more openness to non-state actors has occurred over the years. It has not dramatically changed the nature of this

---

92   Eric A. Posner and Miguel F.P. de Figueiredo, *Is the International Court of Justice Biased?*, 34 J. Legal Stud. 599 (2005).

93   The Statute of the International Court of Justice: A Commentary (Andreas Zimmermann, Christian Tomuschat, eds., (3rd ed., 2019)), at 1102.

relationship but it has softened the Court's approach, in both contentious and advisory proceedings.

1   *Contentious Proceedings*

In contentious proceedings, the Court has traditionally distinguished between various types of non-state actors. Specifically, the Court has shown a willingness to interact with international organizations. They may submit information to the Court in contentious cases, on their own initiative or upon a formal invitation by the Court.[94] Article 43 of the Rules of the Court further suggests that international organizations may also be entitled to intervene in a case pending before the Court (as states can). In practice, however, the Court and international organizations only interact via such channels on rare occasions.

Other types of non-state actors, such as corporations or individuals, do not enjoy such benefits. For those actors, there is no direct interaction with the Court. States sometimes espouse their claims before the ICJ in an effort to get relief. The main interaction is that between the ICJ and the state exercising diplomatic protection.[95] The relationship between the Court and the non-state actors occurs behind the scenes, if at all. Sometimes the submissions of the affected individuals appear as appendix to the pleadings submitted by states.[96]

The ICJ can make the choice to engage more directly with non-state actors, but it does not have to. It can decide to remain a bastion of traditional international law, where states take center stage. Palestine's application against the United States for the relocation of the US Embassy from Jerusalem to Tel Aviv puts the ICJ to test.[97] Regardless of what the Court decides on the admissibility of Palestine's application, it is likely to shape the Court's relationship with non-state actors for years to come.

---

94   The ICAO Council, the Organization of American States, and the World Health Organization have submitted information to the Court in contentious cases.

95   *Nottebohm* (Liechtenstein v. Guatemala), 1955 I.C.J. 4 (Apr. 6); *Case Concerning Barcelona Traction, Light & Power Company, Ltd.* (Belgium v. Spain), Judgment, I.C.J. Reports 1964, p. 6. Diplomatic protection allows a state to take action on behalf of one of its nationals whose rights were injured by another state.

96   *See*, for example, *Case Concerning Barcelona Traction, Light & Power Company, Ltd.* (Belgium v. Spain), Documents Filed to the Court After the Closure of Written Proceedings (Apr. 7, 1969). Memoranda and affidavits from employees of the Barcelona Traction, Light & Power Company were submitted to the Court.

97   *Relocation of the United States Embassy to Jerusalem (Palestine v. United States of America),* available at https://www.ICJ-cij.org/en/case/176.

2 *Advisory Proceedings*

The Court and its predecessor demonstrated more flexibility in advisory proceedings. The PCIJ invited private organizations representing employers and employees of the International Labor Organization, which had a direct stake in cases before the Court, to submit information.[98] The ICJ Statute gives the Registrar the right to invite "international organization[s] considered by the Court" to present written and oral statements before the Court.

> **ICJ Statute**
>
> **Article 66**
>
> 1. The Registrar shall forthwith give notice of the request for an advisory opinion to all states entitled to appear before the Court.
>
> 2. The Registrar shall also, by means of a special and direct communication, notify any state entitled to appear before the Court or international organization considered by the Court, or, should it not be sitting, by the President, as likely to be able to furnish information on the question, that the Court will be prepared to receive, within a time-limit to be fixed by the President, written statements, or to hear, at a public sitting to be held for the purpose, oral statements relating to the question.
>
> 3. Should any such state entitled to appear before the Court have failed to receive the special communication referred to in paragraph 2 of this Article, such state may express a desire to submit a written statement or to be heard; and the Court will decide.
>
> 4. States and organizations having presented written or oral statements or both shall be permitted to comment on the statements made by other states or organizations in the form, to the extent, and within the time-limits which the Court, or, should it not be sitting, the President, shall decide in each particular case. Accordingly, the Registrar shall in due time communicate any such written statements to states and organizations having submitted similar statements.

---

98 *Designation of the Workers' Delegate*, P.C.I.J. (ser. B), No. 1, at 11; *Competence of the International Labor Organization*, P.C.I.J. (ser. B), Nos. 2–3, at 11. *See also Interpretation of Convention of 1919 Concerning Employment of Women during the Night*, P.C.I.J. (ser. A/B), No. 50, at 367 (the PCIJ requested information from four different international organizations on the question of whether the Convention Concerning Employment of Women During the Night applied to women in supervisory or management positions who are not engaged in manual work).

The ICJ invited Palestine to take part in the *Wall* proceedings, justifying its decision on Palestine's status as UN observer and its role in bringing the question to the attention of the UN General Assembly.[99] In the same proceedings, the Court also allowed the League of Arab States and Islamic Conference to submit written and oral statements.[100] A few years later, in *Kosovo*, the Court invited the 'authors of the declaration of independence' to provide information to the Court and appear before the Court.[101] They "spoke in the oral proceedings in second place, right after Serbia as quasi-parties to the dispute underlying the request for an opinion."[102]

This inclusive policy may raise concerns when states have not been expressly authorized to appear before the Court, as was the case with the European Union in *Wall* advisory proceedings.[103] Yet, at times it may appear reasonable, as a matter of procedural fairness, to enable a non-state actor that has a stake in the question to be granted access to the Court for the purpose of making its views known.[104] Importantly, however, even when non-state actors do participate in advisory proceedings, their role remains limited to that of supplying information. Non-governmental organizations, for example, may submit documents to the Court – which will be made available for consultation only.

> ### ICJ Practice Direction XII (2004)
>
> Where an international non-governmental organization submits a written statement and/or document in an advisory opinion case on its own initiative, such statement and/or document is not to be considered as part of the case file.
>
> Such statements and/or documents shall be treated as publications readily available and may accordingly be referred to by States and inter

---

99 *See* discussion, *supra* Chapter 3.

100 *See Legal Consequences of the Construction of a Wall in the Occupied Palestinian Territories*, Advisory Opinion, I.C.J. Reports 2004, p. 136, 142.

101 Accordance with international law of the unilateral declaration of independence in respect of Kosovo, Order of 17 October 2008, I.C.J. Reports 2008, at 409, 410.

102 The Statute of the International Court of Justice: A Commentary (Andreas Zimmermann, Christian Tomuschat, eds., (3rd ed., 2019)), at 1819.

103 Shabtai Rosenne, Law and Practice of the International Court (2017), Vol. 3, Chapter 30, para. 408.

104 *See* Ronen, *supra* note 94.

> governmental organizations presenting written and oral statements in the case in the same manner as publications in the public domain.
>
> Written statements and/or documents submitted by international non-governmental organizations will be placed in a designated location in the Peace Palace. All States as well as intergovernmental organizations presenting written or oral statements under Article 66 of the Statute will be informed as to the location where statements and/or documents submitted by international non-governmental organizations may be consulted.

Overall, the Court has varied degrees of interaction with different types of non-state actors, an approach that raises questions regarding the equal access of non-state actors to the Court. International organizations continue to fare much better than individuals or corporations. As for non-governmental organizations, they have generally been denied the right to submit materials before the Court in both contentious and advisory cases.[105] Any change in this respect – such as granting NGOs the right to submit briefs as "amicus curiae" (literally, friends of the Court)[106] – would require an amendment of the Court's Statute.

• • •

Questions

1. Is the Court's flexibility vis-à-vis non-state actors in advisory proceedings a positive feature? Consider the impact on jurisdiction, legitimacy, law-making, and enforcement.
2. The Court interacts differently with states, international organizations, individuals, and NGOs. Should these different non-state actors be granted different levels

---

105 For example, in *Legality of the Threat or Use of Nuclear Weapons*, material received from medical NGOs could not be included in the dossier. *See* Commentary to ICJ Statute (2019), at 86. There is one exception: the Court authorized the International League of the Rights of Man to submit written and oral statements in International Status of South West Africa but did not send any statement within the time limit set by the Court. *See* Rosalyn Higgins, Philippa Webb, Dapo Akande, Sandesh Sivakumaran, and James Sloan, Oppenheim's International Law: United Nations (2017), at 1175–76.

106 *See*, for example, Articles 15 (2) and 44 of the Rome Statute, Article 18(1) of the Statute of the International Criminal Tribunal for Former-Yugoslavia, Article 17(1) of the Statute of the International Criminal Tribunal for Rwanda, and Article 13 of the Dispute Settlement Understanding of the World Trade Organization.

of access to the Court? Can you think of other non-state actors that might want to get access to the Court?

Further Reading

Mark. J. Janis, *Individuals and the International Court,* in The International Court of Justice (Muller et al, eds, 1997), at 205.

Diane Shelton, *The International Court of Justice and Nongovernmental Organizations,* 9 Int'l Comm. L. Rev. 139 (2007).

Martin Scheinin, *The ICJ and the Individual,* 9 Int'l Comm. L. Rev. 123, 138 (2007).

• • •

Conclusion

The International Court of Justice by no means operates in a vacuum. It interacts with states on a regular basis through its contentious jurisdiction, and with the UN and its organs via its advisory jurisdiction. Its relationship with other international actors – international courts and tribunals, domestic courts, academia, and non-state actors – is no less important, and says a lot about the Court's role in the international order. Though the nature of the Court's relationship with each of those actors differs in nature and frequency, they have two common characteristics: first, like international law, they have grown and evolved with time; and, second, they remain less developed than the relationship the Court has with states and the United Nations.

The Court has a complex relationship with international courts and tribunals created after 1945 due to the lack of hierarchy and sometimes overlapping areas of competence with these new Courts. Regional courts (like the IACHR or the ECHR) do not always defer to the ICJ on issues of common interest, and the ICJ is technically under no obligation to accept legal constructs elaborated by other international courts. An atmosphere of respect nonetheless permeates their exchanges in the sense that the international and regional courts, including the ICJ, generally acknowledge each other's precedents and explain how they relate to their peers' holdings.

The relationship with domestic courts tends to be shaped by the reluctance of many domestic courts to interpret and apply international law, one on hand, and the ICJ's own limitations in recognizing the decisions of national courts as sources of law per se, on the other. Perhaps the ICJ should be more cognizant

154   CHAPTER 4

of the opportunities offered by domestic courts for the enforcement of international law.

With regard to academia, and consistent with the civil law tradition, the ICJ does not mention specific scholars by name in its decisions. Yet, ironically, the Court's activity has generated hundreds if not thousands of scholarly pieces published as articles, chapters, or books. This is arguably the most imbalanced relationship examined so far, with the Court showing little reciprocity in its treatment of academic sources.

The Court's relationship with non-state actors stands out as the most groundbreaking. The ICJ has enabled a variety of non-state actors to take part in advisory proceedings and, to a limited extent, contentious proceedings. The ICJ will have to decide whether it wishes to further open its doors to non-state actors, particularly in the context of the contentious case brought by Palestine against the United States on the relocation of the US embassy to Jerusalem.[107]

In sum, the ICJ operates today as part of a constellation of actors with whom it interacts to varying degrees. This web of actors and institutions makes for a more meaningful role and potentially greater circle of influence for the ICJ. As it grows older, the Court will face a dilemma between spreading its wings onto new horizons or remaining true to its original purpose and function by operating within a more restrained universe.

---

107   ICJ Press Release No. 2018/47 of 28 September 2018 ('The State of Palestine Institutes Proceedings against the United States of America').

CHAPTER 5

An Assessment

The Court sits at the pinnacle of the international legal order, offering its services to an ever-growing community of states.[1] This position is as prestigious as it is ambitious. Established in 1946 immediately upon the creation of the United Nations, the International Court of Justice was the only international adjudicative body at the time. If the lifespan of its predecessor – the Permanent Court of International Justice – is considered, the ICJ has been part of the international legal landscape since 1920. This longevity suggests that the international community views the international judicial function with favorable eyes.

In fact, states have made no real attempt at reforming the ICJ. It may have changed its name – from PCIJ to ICJ – and adjusted some procedural matters, but it has not undergone any institutional reform since the early nineteenth century.[2] Meanwhile, the rules, composition, or structure of other UN bodies did change: the membership of the Security Council was expanded from

---

1   I am indebted to the organizers and participants in the International Law Workshop at the Tel Aviv University Buchmann Faculty of Law for their helpful comments on this chapter.

2   Although the Court's Statute was never amended, the Rules of the Court (i.e., the provisions of the Statute concerning the Court's procedure and the working of the Court and of the Registry) have been amended on a number of occasions. According to the Court's Handbook (available at https://www.icj-cij.org/public/files/publications/handbook-of-the-court-en.pdf), the Court adopted its Rules on 5 May 1946 "largely based on the latest version of the Rules of Court of the PCIJ, which dated from 1936. In 1967, in the light of the experience it had acquired and of the need to adapt the Rules to changes that had taken place in the world and in the pace of international events, it embarked upon a thorough revision of its Rules and set up a standing committee for the purpose. On 10 May 1972, it adopted certain amendments which came into force on 1 September that year. On 14 April 1978, the Court adopted a thoroughly revised set of Rules which came into force on 1 July 1978. The object of the changes made – at a time when the Court's activity had undeniably fallen off – was to increase the flexibility of proceedings, making them as simple and rapid as possible, and to help reduce the costs to the parties, in so far as these matters depended upon the Court. On 5 December 2000, the Court amended two articles of the 1978 Rules: Article 79 on preliminary objections and Article 80 concerning counter-claims. The purpose of the new amendments was to shorten the duration of these incidental proceedings and to clarify the rules in force so as to reflect more faithfully the Court's practice. The amended versions of Articles 79 and 80 entered into force on 1 February 2001, with the previous versions continuing to govern all phases of cases submitted to the Court before that date. Amended and slightly simplified versions of the Preamble and of Article 52 entered into force on 14 April 2005. On 29 September 2005, a new version of Article 43 came into force, setting out the circumstances in which the Court was

---

© KONINKLIJKE BRILL NV, LEIDEN, 2020 | DOI:10.1163/9789004226968_007

ten to fifteen non-permanent members in 1965, the membership of ECOSOC was expanded in 1965 and again in 1973, the Commission on Human Rights was replaced with the Human Rights Council in 2006, and the United Nations Administrative Tribunal was fully revamped in 2009.

The long-lasting features of the ICJ can certainly be interpreted as a vote of confidence for this institution, which seems to have met the expectations of UN members. Despite the creation of many international and regional bodies that compete for attention and business, states continue to view the Court as well-suited to carry out the roles entrusted to it, and engage with the Court in various ways and with varying levels of intensity, as this Chapter reveals.

Scholars, in contrast, have somewhat lost interest in the Court. The fragmentation of the international legal order has affected the agenda of the "indivisible college of jurists." They must keep abreast of the creation of a growing number of courts and tribunals – some regional, some hybrid, some specialized. They must analyze an ever-expanding body of judicial decisions and advisory opinions. As is often the case, the newer courts attract more attention, not just among scholars but also among young graduates who wish to write on novel issues of international law or complete internships in the most recently established tribunal. This affects scholarship, too, which covers extensively the European Court of Human Rights and the International Criminal Court – to name only a few. A docket perceived as too thin also may make the Court seem less relevant. The shift is most noticeable in international relations scholarship where the ICJ has lost some of its appeal. Finally, teachers spend too little time in the classroom on the study of the ICJ. The emphasis is placed on the Court's jurisprudence rather than on the institution itself.

In light of the foregoing, writing an assessment of the Court sounds overly ambitious and exceedingly complex. In spite of the centrality of the ICJ in the international system since its establishment in 1945, no comprehensive quantitative study of how states view or use the Court has been undertaken in international relations or international law. Neither of these disciplines provides tools to measure the relationship between states and the international or regional organizations they have created. This is quite different from answering the question of why states create or join international organizations.[3] It is also quite different from analyzing state-to-state interaction *within* a given

---

    required to notify a public international organization that is a party to a convention whose construction may be in question in a case brought before it."

3 See, for example, Kenneth W. Abbott and Duncan Snidal, 42 Journal of Conflict Resolution 3 (1998).

international organization.[4] This chapter focuses instead on analyzing the interaction between states, on one hand, and the ICJ, on the other hand. It seeks to answer some of the many questions that have remained unanswered: Given that its institutional features have not changed significantly since its creation, can the ICJ play the same role today with 193 UN member states as it played when the UN only had fifty-one member states? Does the Court even have the resources necessary to interact with or provide its services to such a large constituency?

This chapter tries to answer these questions using data collected on a host of interactions states have with the Court – from depositing optional clause declarations to filing preliminary objections and submitting written statements in advisory proceedings.[5] This information offers unique insights on the UN's principal judicial organ. As noted above, states have interacted with the Court in multiple ways, demonstrating varying level of deference, and at times even defiance, vis-à-vis the institution. The chapter begins with patterns of interaction that demonstrate a willingness to interact with the Court. The second section analyzes state behavior designed to minimize interaction with the Court. States may engage in such behavior out of antagonism – or sheer indifference. Their interaction may in fact have little to do with the Court and more to do with the circumstances, or subject-matter, of a given case. Nevertheless these patterns of interaction provide valuable information about how states interact with the Court. Understanding the reasons behind state preferences, i.e., why states interact a certain way, deserves further research. The chapter ends with a discussion of compliance and its inadequacy as a benchmark of effectiveness.

---

4   *See,* for example, Joseph Weiler, A *Quiet Revolution: The European Court of Justice and its Interlocutors,* 26 Comparative Political Studies 510 (1994) (analyzes how member states of the European Union have interacted with the European Court of Justice); Anne-Marie Slaughter, *A Global Community of Courts,* 44 Harvard International Law Journal 191 (2003) (addresses the relationship between various courts, the deference they show each other, and advocates the creation of a "global community of courts" which requires personal as well as institutional interaction); and Hassan Nafaa, *The Study of Relationships between International Organization and the Member States: A System Approach,* 7 International Interactions 337 (1981) (notes the gap in the literature and engages in a mostly qualitative analysis of the relationship between Egypt and UNESCO).

5   Even states that actively engage with the Court have done so only a few times since the Court's establishment in 1945. As explained below, some states have not participated in contentious or advisory proceedings. Statistically, this is known as a non-normal distribution of the dependent variables which makes it necessary to apply zero-inflated models. This becomes mostly relevant when trying to analyze *why* states behave a certain way, a question that this chapter does not purport to resolve. The data is valid as of January 1, 2019.

A   What States Use the Court and for What

Let us begin with those states that have shown a high level of deference to the Court. Some states happily support the Court's activity, taking steps to ensure its continued relevance and contribution. States do this by depositing optional clause declarations, referring disputes to the Court, intervening in pending cases, or participating in advisory proceedings. The analysis that follows interprets large amounts of data on how states interact with the Court.

1   *Applicant*

It is useful to begin with states that use the Court on a regular basis for its main function, namely the peaceful settlement of disputes. Only sixty-five states, or about a third of states, have brought cases before the Court. But thirty-one of these sixty-five states have brought cases to the Court more than once (and seven states have brought cases before the Court on five or more occasions). In other words, states that bring applications to the Court tend to be returning customers.

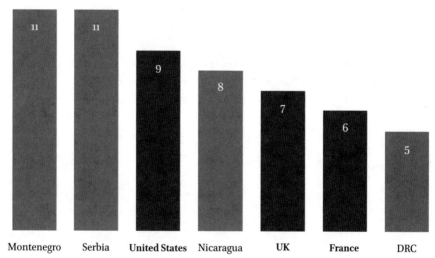

FIGURE 5.1   States that appeared as Applicant more than five times. (Note that in 1999, the Federal Republic of Yugoslavia brought 11 cases on the same issue before the Court. These cases are counted as having been filed by Serbia and Montenegro, which are two separate states since 2006).

AN ASSESSMENT   159

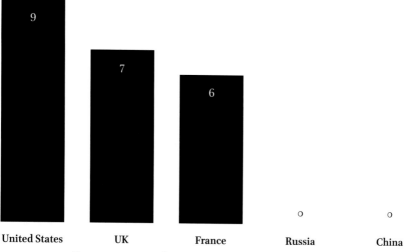

FIGURE 5.2   P5 appearing as Applicants

This leaves 128 states that have never been Applicant – including China and Russia – meaning that only a rather small proportion of states have actively sought the involvement of the Court in the settlement of their international legal disputes.

2   *Respondent*

When it comes to assessing interaction, serving a Respondent is by nature less significant than serving as Applicant. The Applicant takes the initiative; the Respondent must deal with a situation it did not elect in the first place. It interacts with the Court in a more passive way than the Applicant. Nevertheless, much can be learned from a Respondent's behavior following the filing of an application: did the Respondent object to jurisdiction? Did it appear before the Court? There are various kinds of Respondents: those that submit willingly to the Court's jurisdiction, and those that do so more reluctantly.

In terms of frequency, France, the UK, and the United States lead the show as Respondents (as they do as Applicants). Nicaragua, somewhat unsurprisingly, also makes the top five.

Thirty-six states have appeared before the Court both as Applicant and Respondent. This is a rather small proportion of states but, as the discussion below demonstrates, the remainder of states does interact with the Court in other ways.

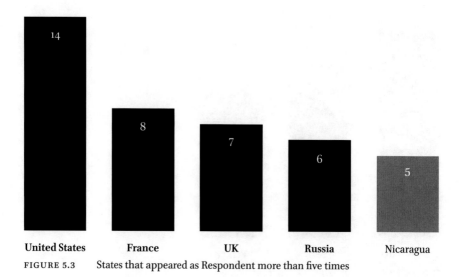

FIGURE 5.3   States that appeared as Respondent more than five times

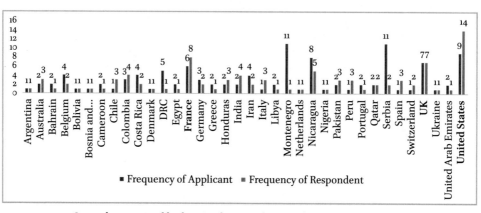

FIGURE 5.4   States that appeared both as Applicant and Respondent

The data shows that states that apply to the Court are also more likely to be sued before the Court, and vice-versa. The strong correlation between being Applicant and being Respondent suggests that a group of states tends to be party to contentious cases, whereas another group of states stays out of the Peace Palace. This means that states that brought cases before the Court as Applicant are more likely to be sued and appear as Respondent in other cases (something they might want to take into account when they bring an application before the Court). By the same token, states that appear as Respondents are also more likely to bring cases to the Court in the future.

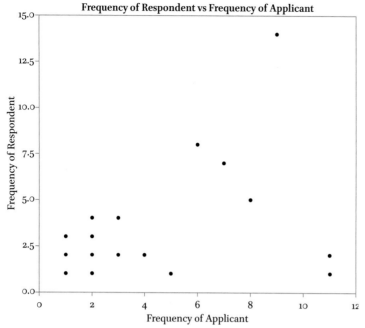

FIGURE 5.5   The more states appear as Applicant, the more they appear as Respondent, and vice-versa

3   *Application v. Intervention*

Measuring interaction also requires analyzing intervention patterns before the Court. According to Article 62 of the Court's Statute, a state may request to intervene in an existing case where the state is neither Applicant nor Respondent under the following conditions:

> **ICJ Statute**
> **Article 62**
> 1. Should a state consider that it has an interest of a legal nature which may be affected by the decision in the case, it may submit a request to the Court to be permitted to intervene.
> 2. It shall be for the Court to decide upon this request.

Intervention can be requested when a state's legal interests may be impacted by a decision in a case to which it is not a party. As the Court noted, the purpose of an intervention is "for an intervener to inform the [Court] of what it

162   CHAPTER 5

regards as its rights or interests, in order to ensure that no legal interest may be
'affected' without the intervener being heard."[6]

Intervention – and requests for intervention – therefore constitute important means available to states to show deference to the Court. Intervention is
a proactive act, one through which a state expresses its desire to appear before
the Court. Even if the case was filed by another state, intervention demonstrates a willingness on the part of a state to interact with the Court. States
rarely take advantage of this opportunity, however, and requests for intervention have not been granted systematically.

States only requested to intervene in seventeen cases. The Court accepted
the request in eight of these cases, allowing the intervening state to join in the
proceedings. States that successfully requested to intervene in cases pending
before the Court include Cuba, El Salvador, Equatorial Guinea, Fiji (on two
occasions), Greece, New Zealand, and Nicaragua. Cuba and Fiji are particularly interesting, as neither ever brought a case before the Court in their own
capacity. They never served as Applicant, yet they both showed a willingness
to intervene in existing cases.[7] This demonstrates that states elect how they
wish to interact with the Court; and bringing a case to the Court is by no means
the only expression of deference. Although being an Applicant is arguably the
most active type of interaction and the most obvious show of deference, it
certainly is not the only one.

In the remaining nine cases, the Court rejected the request for intervention. This means that the requesting state never became a formal party to the
case. But from the point of view of interaction, this willingness to intervene
must be accounted for. States that expressed a willingness to intervene – i.e.,
filed a request to intervene in a pending case, which was later denied by the
ICJ – include Malta, Italy, the Philippines, Australia, the Marshall Islands,
Micronesia, Samoa, the Solomon Islands, and Costa Rica.

Similarly, certain states did not formally serve as Applicant but appeared
before the Court in cases filed on the basis of special agreements (cases
brought by the two parties jointly before the Court). Though these states never
served as Applicant *stricto sensu*, they interacted with the Court in contentious

---

6 *Land, Island, and Maritime Frontier Dispute* (El Salvador/Honduras: Nicaragua Intervening),
   Judgment, I.C.J. Reports 1990, p. 92, para. 90.

7 *Haya de la Torre* (Colombia v. Peru), Declaration of Intervention by the Gov. of Cuba, I.C.J.
   Reports 1951, p. 79; *Nuclear Tests* (Australia v. France), Application for Permission to Intervene
   submitted by the Gov. of Fiji, I.C.J. Reports 1974, p. 530; *Nuclear Tests* (New Zealand v. France),
   Application for Permission to Intervene submitted by the Gov. of Fiji, I.C.J. Reports 1974,
   p. 447.

AN ASSESSMENT   163

proceedings and this interaction, too, must be noted.[8] Burkina Faso and Niger, for example, appeared twice in cases brought jointly – and yet they never appeared as Applicant. This suggests that they view the ICJ as a friendly mechanism for the resolution of international disputes.

4   Optional Clause Declarations

A state may further express faith in the Court by depositing an optional clause declaration.[9] Because it is, by nature, optional, such a voluntary undertaking carries important significance when assessing states' perception of the World Court.

Seventy-three states have deposited optional clause declarations. Fourteen states have withdrawn (or failed to renew) existing declarations: Brazil, Bolivia, China, Colombia, El Salvador, France, Guatemala, Israel, Nauru, South Africa, Thailand, Turkey, the United States, and Serbia. 105 states – i.e., the vast majority of states – never deposited an optional clause declaration.

Analyzing the behavior of those 105 states provides some insight into their preferred mode of interaction. It appears, for example, that states that deposited optional clause declarations are not less likely to object to the Court's jurisdiction. The act of depositing an optional clause declaration does not

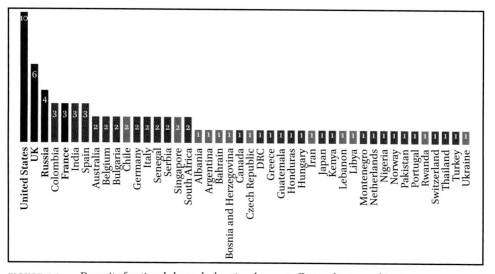

FIGURE 5.6   Deposit of optional clause declaration does not affect preliminary objections

---

8   *See* Figure 2.3 in Chapter 2.
9   *See supra* Chapter 2.

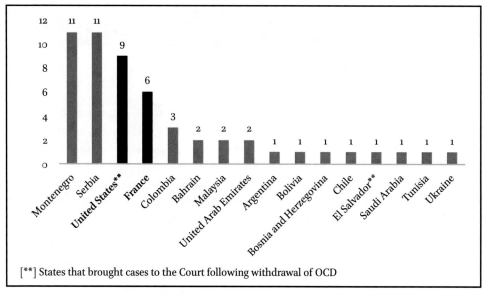

FIGURE 5.7 States that failed to renew, withdrew, or never filed optional clause declaration yet appeared as Applicant

significantly impact the likelihood of objecting to the Court's jurisdiction as Respondent. The vast majority of states that filed preliminary objections as Respondents had previously deposited an optional clause declaration (35 out of 44).[10] In other words, the willingness to commit to the Court's jurisdiction *before* a case arises does not necessarily translate into a willingness to submit to the Court's jurisdiction *once* a case has been filed. This finding suggests that the act of depositing an optional clause declaration – or not – is not a good predictor of how a state will behave as Respondent.

This is confirmed by another finding: among the states that withdrew or failed to renew existing optional clause declarations (14), and those that never had any (105), many states still took the active step of bringing cases to the Court. In other words, the act of withdrawing an optional clause declaration (or not having one at all) has surprisingly little impact on the likelihood that a state will bring a dispute before the Court.

Ultimately, these results show that states do have preferences, but rarely object to the Court's involvement *across the board*. Somewhat counterintuitively,

---

[10] States that objected but *never* deposited an optional clause declaration were Albania, Argentina, Chile, Czech Republic, Iran, Lebanon, Rwanda, Russia, and Ukraine.

AN ASSESSMENT   165

states may withdraw an existing optional clause declaration, and yet bring a
case to the Court that same year. Similarly, a state that has always rejected the
idea of *ex ante* consensual jurisdiction may not challenge such jurisdiction as
a Respondent. States might be reluctant to commit to the Court before a dispute arises, when neither the party nor the substance of the case are known,
yet more willing to engage with the Court once a dispute arises and they are
able to agree to the Court's jurisdiction in full knowledge of the consequences.

5   *Advisory Proceedings*

Advisory jurisdiction arguably offers the most interesting window of understanding into the effectiveness and relevance of the Court. Like the mechanism
of the optional clause declaration, engaging with the Court in advisory proceedings is by definition merely optional. A state's decision to participate in a
non-obligatory process therefore deserves to be accounted for.

As explained in Chapter 3, advisory proceedings are more open and flexible. Advisory proceedings present an opportunity for all states – even non-UN
members[11] – to participate. This differs greatly from contentious cases, in
which only a handful of states get to interact with the Court. Advisory proceedings, in contrast, begin with a vote involving dozens if not hundreds of states
(generally at the UN General Assembly), and continues with written and oral
proceedings at the Peace Palace in The Hague to which all states are invited.

i   Voting on Requests for Advisory Opinions

The opportunity for states to show deference to the ICJ as part of advisory proceedings begins early – before a request for an advisory opinion even comes
before the Court. States must first vote on whether a request should be transferred to the Court. This vote takes place according to the voting requirements
of the requesting institution – the Security Council, the General Assembly, or
another UN body. At this early stage, states may already express their support
for the Court's involvement by voting in favor of the request. They may also
abstain or vote against. At times states have also missed the vote on a request
for an advisory opinion. In such a case their vote is not recorded.

---

11   Non-UN members have participated in advisory proceedings. For this reason, a total
      of 198 states are considered for interaction in the Court within the framework of advi-
      sory proceedings (193 UN members, as well as the Cook Islands, Niue, Northern Ireland,
      Palestine, and the Union of South Africa).

166   CHAPTER 5

In its early years, the UN did not always record the details of votes – even for decisions adopted by its principal organs. Early requests for advisory opinions were sometimes adopted without a vote at all. In other instances, the record only indicates the summary of the vote (how many states voted in favor or against, but not *which* states). In addition, votes on requests for advisory opinions emanating from bodies *other than* the General Assembly or the Security Council (seven advisory opinions) – from UNESCO or the IMO, for example – are simply unavailable. As a result of these two factors – early votes not recorded and voting records of UN agencies not available – voting records on requests for advisory opinions are only available for twelve advisory opinions (out of twenty-seven). Although this affects the completeness of the data, the information available still provides some insights on state participation in advisory proceedings.

Available voting records on requests for advisory opinions tell the following story: States have voted in favor of advisory requests a total of 760 times (all states in all advisory requests), and have objected to requests for advisory opinions (states voting "no" when asked whether they support the request) only 116 times. Even when the records only summarize the votes without actually naming the states, "no" votes never exceed ten.[12]

By voting in favor or against a referral, states send a signal on whether they welcome the Court's advice on a given legal question. But what signal do they send when they abstain or when they fail to attend the vote? This question matters because states either abstain or fail to attend votes on requests for advisory opinions surprisingly often. To be precise, and again based on available records, states have abstained a total of 377 times in advisory opinion requests, and have elected not to attend these votes on 388 occasions. Abstaining or failing to attend the vote – unlike voting yes or no – does not send a clear signal. Instead, it may be interpreted as conveying a sense of indifference vis-à-vis the Court and its role as a 'trusted advisor.'

Looking at the voting patterns of individual states, Brazil and India appear most supportive of advisory proceedings (with nine and seven votes in favor of requests for advisory opinions, respectively), followed by France and the

---

12   This is the case, for example, in voting records of *Competence of the General Assembly for the Admission of a State to the United Nations* (1949); *International Status of South West Africa* (1949); *Reservations to the Convention on the Prevention and Punishment of the Crime of Genocide* (1950); and *Admissibility of Hearings of Petitioners by the Committee on South West Africa* (1955) (the date indicates the year the vote on the request was held).

AN ASSESSMENT 167

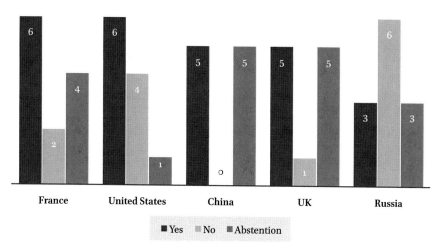

FIGURE 5.8   Voting record of P5 on advisory opinion requests

United States (with six "yes" votes). The UK, for its part, seems more mixed in its approach – with an equal number of supporting votes and abstentions – so it does not quite make the cut. States that regularly vote against requests for advisory opinions include the Czech Republic, Russia, and Poland – each with five or more recorded negative votes.

Only nineteen states *never* voted in favor of a referral to the ICJ – and they do not include any permanent members of the Security Council. Even Russia voted in favor of three requests and China voted in favor of five requests for advisory opinions.

Overall, states are more supportive of advisory jurisdiction than they are of contentious jurisdiction. Participation in advisory proceedings is less risky and generally does not directly affects states' interests – certainly not to the same extent as contentious proceedings. The outcome also differs, in the sense that advisory opinions do not carry the *res judicata*. So, the conclusion that states are typically supportive of advisory requests is not very surprising. The more interesting insight has to do with voting requests more specifically. The data suggests that states tend not to voice objections at the referral stage of advisory proceedings (remember that only nineteen states *never* voted in favor of a request for an advisory opinion). States either express indifference at the potential future involvement of the ICJ or outright support for the referral. At this early stage, states rarely oppose advisory proceedings. In fact, no precedent seems to exist for a draft resolution requesting an advisory opinion from the ICJ that would not have passed the majority of votes in the requesting body.

ii   State Participation in Advisory Proceedings

Once the requested majority of states votes in favor of a request for an advisory opinion, such request is transferred to the Court. The Court's Registrar then sends an invitation to all states to take part in advisory proceedings. States may decide whether they wish to take part – and how. They can submit written statements, appear orally before the Court, or both. They can also choose not to participate at all. Thanks to this inherent flexibility, state participation in advisory proceedings serves as a relatively accurate indicator of state interaction with the Court.

As noted above, few states bluntly oppose requests for advisory opinions at the voting stage. Even when they do, they tend to overcome their initial objections later on in the process. It seems that the willingness to influence the outcome of advisory proceedings ultimately prevails over the reluctance to receive legal advice from the Court. Take Russia, for example: it voted no to requests on six occasions, yet it participated in four out of these six proceedings. How states vote on the initial request does not necessarily determine how they behave in the ensuing proceedings. States may vote no, and yet opt to participate (like Russia). Conversely, states frequently vote in favor of the referral, and choose *not* to participate in the proceedings. Cuba, for example, voted yes on eight requests for advisory opinions but never participated in advisory proceedings.

This disconnect between how states vote on the initial request and the extent of their participation in written and oral proceedings suggests that something else is at play. An analysis of state participation in written and oral advisory proceedings provides more insight.

The permanent members of the Security Council (with the exception of the UK) tend to favor written statements over participation in oral hearings – as do

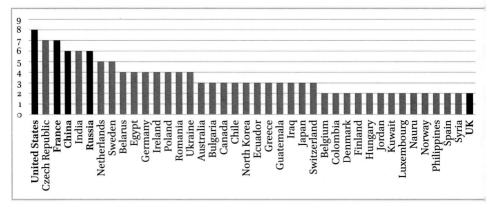

FIGURE 5.9   States that submitted written statements but did not participate in oral hearings

the Czech Republic and India, and, to a lesser extent, Poland, the Netherlands, and Sweden. Most states, however, prefer to send a statement *and* appear at oral hearings in advisory proceedings. These states take advantage of the double opportunity – written and oral – contemplated by the Statute. The opposite (appearing orally without having submitted a written statement) is much less frequent. It might happen, in rare situations, when a state misses the deadline for the submission of written statements and still wishes to make its views known to the Court.

Importantly, state interaction with the Court in advisory proceedings does not necessarily align with their use of the Court as a means of dispute settlement. States that have never brought cases before the Court might otherwise feel comfortable interacting with the Court in the context of advisory proceedings. Patterns of interaction in contentious cases do not mirror those in advisory cases, suggesting that states use the Court for different reasons and in different ways. Forty-two states that never had any type of interaction with the Court within the framework of contentious proceedings nevertheless chose to engage with the Court and the rest of the international community as part of advisory proceedings.

Certain patterns of interaction are specific to advisory proceedings. Indifference, for example, is unique to advisory proceedings and has no equivalent in contentious proceedings. In contentious proceedings states must send a clear message: cooperate with the Court and accept its jurisdiction – or not. Advisory proceedings are different in so far as states can send potentially conflicting messages, change their minds, or simply opt out. Combining voting data with participation data, only four states (Andorra, Croatia, Tonga, and Vanuatu) have shown complete indifference to advisory requests: they neither voted against any request nor in favor of any request, they abstained at times from the vote, and never participated in advisory proceedings. They stand alone, as all other states have participated in advisory proceedings in one way or another.

Given these findings, one is left to wonder why UN bodies, under state leadership, do not request advisory opinions more frequently, and why none of the proposals designed to enhance the use of advisory jurisdiction have been retained. Some scholars have sought of ways to encourage the practice by enabling the Court to issue legal advice more expeditiously.[13]

---

13   See *supra* Chapter 3, Section A.

> ### Mohamed Sameh M. Amr, The Role of the International Court of Justice as Principal Judicial Organ of the UN[14]
>
> [T]he limited use of the advisory jurisdiction by the organs and agencies of the UN might be the result of the length of the procedures of the Court when dealing with a request for an advisory opinion. Therefore, it could be suggested that the Court might form, as regards its contentious jurisdiction, Chambers, pursuant to Arts. 26–29 of the Statute, to deal with requests for advisory opinions. This could be based on Art. 68 of the Statute, which indicates that "in the exercise of its advisory functions the Court shall be guided by the provisions of the present Statute which apply in contentious cases to the extent to which it recognises them to be applicable." In the writer's view, such a Chamber, with rapid procedures, might help to encourage the organs and agencies to request opinions from the Court, which could lead to the Court being used as a legal adviser to the UN.

• • •

Questions

1. Do this chapter's findings on how states vote and participate in advisory proceedings surprise you? Why?

2. In your view, why has the Court's advisory function not been used more extensively?

3. What do you think about Mohammed Amr's suggestion to allow the Court to sit in a Chamber as per Article 26–29 of its Statute? Would this encourage UN bodies to request advisory opinions more frequently and ensure that opinions are rendered more rapidly? Article 26 is reproduced below for your convenience.

> ### ICJ Statute, Article 26
>
> 1. The Court may from time to time form one or more chambers, composed of three or more judges as the Court may determine, for dealing with particular categories of cases; for example, labour cases and cases relating to transit and communications.

---

14   Mohamed Sameh M. Amr, The Role of the International Court of Justice as Principal Judicial Organ of the UN (2003), at 381 (references omitted).

> 2. The Court may at any time form a chamber for dealing with a particular case. The number of judges to constitute such a chamber shall be determined by the Court with the approval of the parties.

In sum, the vast majority of states have either interacted with the Court as part of contentious proceedings *or* participated in advisory proceedings (150 states).[15] The data shows that states do interact with the court in some way, with states demonstrating individual preferences for specific types of interaction. Future research should try to ascertain what these preferences are, their roots, and what this means for states and for the Court. It would also be helpful to further investigate the commonalities shared by the eighty-eight states that never interacted with the Court in the realm of dispute settlement, or the forty-six states that never interacted with the Court *in any way*.[16] Finally, some fine-tuning might also be needed to distinguish a lack of involvement from outright defiance. The absence of interaction does not, in every circumstance, signal a criticism of the Court. States' preferences might be driven by reasons that have little to nothing to do with the Court. Just like state interaction with the Court does not necessarily demonstrate deference (indeed there can be many explanations for why a state brings a case or deposits an optional clause declaration), the absence of interaction does not necessarily indicate a lack of confidence in the Court (states may prefer less adversarial dispute resolution mechanisms, for example). In other words, interaction says a lot but it may not tell us how states feel about the Court as an institution.

B   Avoiding the Court

This assessment would not be complete without an analysis of defiant state behavior vis-à-vis the Court. On some occasions, states have rejected, avoided, or opposed any contact with the Court. First, states have done so by *not* resorting to the Court for the peaceful settlement of their legal disputes (they may

---

15   Eighty-three states have engaged in some way in contentious proceedings *and* in advisory proceedings.

16   This list includes states that never served as Applicant or Respondent, never intervened or requested to intervene in a pending case, never submitted an application on the basis of a special agreement, and never participated in advisory proceedings. The list considers discontinued cases, i.e., cases that proceeded to judgment on the merits, cases dismissed for lack of jurisdiction, and cases settled prior to the Court rendering its judgment.

172   CHAPTER 5

have used other mechanisms available in the international arena or none at all). Second, many states have chosen *not* to make an optional clause declaration. Third, states have often objected to jurisdiction when brought before the Court by another state. And fourth, a handful of states have refused to appear before the Court when brought as Respondent. These types of behavior seem to convey a message of defiance to the Court, yet, as mentioned above, states rarely adopt a systematic policy of avoiding contact with the Court entirely.

1   *Not Using the Court to Settle Disputes*

Many states – 104 to be exact – never served as Applicant or Respondent in a contentious case before the Court. This figure seems exceedingly high, tempting the conclusion that the Court only caters to a very small portion of states. The reality is more complex. Within the contentious function, state interaction with the Court does not limit itself to acting as Applicant and Respondent. As explained in Section A(3), states may also bring cases jointly (in which there is no Applicant and no Respondent, properly speaking) or intervene in pending cases. These interactions belong to the realm of dispute settlement, yet they display unique features in comparison to the more traditional behavioral dichotomy of Applicant/Respondent.

A state, it should be recalled, may bring a case against another state exclusively on its own initiative, or it may first seek the approval of the other party to the dispute and bring the case jointly before the Court. In the latter case, properly speaking, there exists no Applicant and no Respondent. The record of the case will indicate this important procedural detail by listing the parties as State A/State B, instead of State A v. State B. In cases brought jointly, the parties work together, and request the Court's decision on a friendly basis.

The proportion of these cases remains extremely low in comparison to cases brought to the Court by an Applicant bringing another state before the Court in the more traditional fashion. Cases brought jointly account for a mere 13% of the Court's docket. Only twenty-three states, in fifteen cases, have engaged in the friendly act of jointly seizing the Court. Additionally, states that have brought a case as Applicant are not more likely to file a joined case with another state.

As previously mentioned, states also are permitted to intervene in a pending case before the ICJ, although the right to intervene is not indicative of whether the Court will actually permit the intervention. Intervention provides yet another opportunity for states to interact with the Court, outside the more traditional application/respondent paradigm.

Taking into consideration this broader set of interactions, the numbers speak more truth. States that never served as Applicant or Respondent, never jointly seized the Court, and never intervened (or requested to intervene) in a pending case, account for 45.5% of total UN membership (eighty-eight states in total). This includes Andorra, China, and the Central African Republic. The lack of interaction in the realm of dispute settlement does not necessarily signal an opposition to all regional and international mechanisms of dispute settlement, such as the World Trade Organization or arbitration. It may well be that states that did not use the ICJ to settle their disputes resorted to other methods, as contemplated in Article 33 of the UN Charter. This was not verified as part of the research conducted for this book, but it certainly would be interesting to know whether states that have stayed out of contentious proceedings before the ICJ have otherwise been active in other fora of dispute resolution.

Zooming in on the P5, the record indicates deep dissimilarities. The five states are split along relatively clear lines of widely diverging behavior and demonstrations of deference. The United States, the UK, and France have heavily engaged with the Court, even if at times it meant expressing some criticism. The United States brought nine cases to the Court, the UK brought seven, and France was Applicant six times. In contrast, Russia and China have rarely engaged with the Court willingly: China was never involved in *any* way in a contentious proceeding before the ICJ. Although Russia, like China, never brought a case to the Court, it served as Respondent six times, and only objected to jurisdiction in four of these six cases. Russia neither intervened in pending proceedings nor submitted cases on the basis of a special agreement.

2   *Not Depositing an Optional Clause Declaration*

States may also chose *not* to accept the Court's jurisdiction *ex ante* in application of Article 36(2) of the ICJ Statute. This limits the Court's competence to situations where jurisdiction was agreed upon in a treaty (bilateral or multilateral) or on an *ad hoc* basis. Seventy-three states have deposited optional clause declarations at some point during the course of the Court's existence, leaving approximately 62% of UN member states without an optional clause declaration.

Just as states are free to make such declarations, they are also free to withdraw them. In general, withdrawals or cancellations of optional clause declarations are interpreted as signaling a certain disappointment in the institution. As noted above, fourteen states either withdrew or failed to renew their optional clause declaration. Traditionally, these withdrawals have attracted a lot of attention.

Interestingly, however, the analysis shows that the failure to renew or the withdrawal of an optional clause declaration does not significantly affect the relationship of states with the Court. States that withdrew optional clause declarations continue to bring cases and serve as Respondents even following their withdrawal/failure to renew. The United States and El Salvador both brought cases before the Court *following* the withdrawal of their optional clause declarations. France, Turkey, and the United States were brought to the Court – and sometimes more than once! – following a withdrawal or non-renewal of their optional clause declarations. States in that situation do not systematically object to the Court's jurisdiction. Though the act of non-renewal or withdrawal of an optional clause declaration may carry symbolic value, it has little practical consequences on the withdrawing state's future interaction with the Court.[17]

3 *Filing Preliminary Objections*

A state that has been named as Respondent may seek to avoid the Court's jurisdiction by filing preliminary objections.[18] The filing of preliminary objections is common practice before the Court. States have filed preliminary objections in seventy-six cases out of a total of 147 cases, or approximately in 52% of proceedings before the Court. The P5 lead the show here, with the United States objecting to the Court's jurisdiction on ten occasions, the UK on

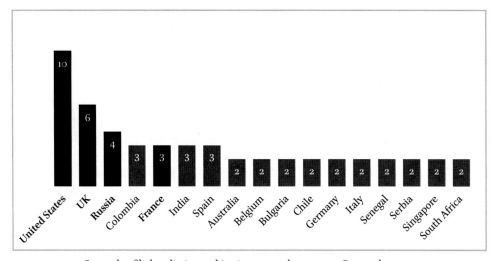

FIGURE 5.10   States that filed preliminary objections more than once as Respondent

---

17 At times, of course, the optional clause declaration mechanism may be calculated. For instance, the Former Republic of Yugoslavia deposited an optional clause declaration on April 25, 1999; four days later it brought eight cases before the Court. It obtained a final judgment from the Court on December 15, 2004, and proceeded to withdraw its declaration that same day.

18 See *supra* Chapter 2, Section E(1).

AN ASSESSMENT   175

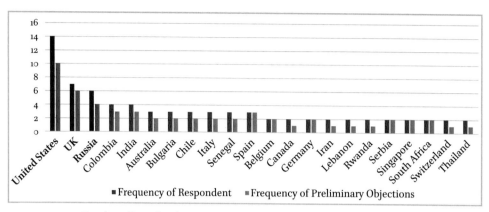

FIGURE 5.11   Trends in filing of preliminary objections

six occasions, Russia on four occasions, and France filing preliminary objections in three cases.

Preliminary objections offer an opportunity to learn more about patterns of interaction: do certain states avoid the Court's jurisdiction as a matter of principle or systematic policy? Does the decision to file preliminary objections have its roots in antagonistic feelings toward the Court or in the specific circumstances of the case at hand? In order to answer these questions, it is helpful to analyze in greater detail the behavior of states that have been Respondent more than twice.

Only six states have challenged the Court's jurisdiction *every time* a case is filed against them: Belgium, Germany, Serbia, Singapore, South Africa, and Spain. None of the P5 is on this list. Other states demonstrate a *tendency* to challenge the Court's jurisdiction. In such cases, preliminary objections may not be interpreted as a lack of deference to the Court. There seems to be additional factors at play that do not have to do with the Court itself. The UK, the US, and Russia belong to this group, showing no systematic pattern in their attempts to avoid the Court's jurisdiction. So does India, whose behavior aligns with that of the P5.

The same can be said with respect to a third and rather limited group of states that filed preliminary objections only occasionally upon serving as Respondents. France, for example, filed preliminary objections in three out of eight cases in which it was Respondent. Honduras, Norway, and Pakistan were all Respondents before the Court on three occasions, yet they only objected once to the Court's jurisdiction. It would be wrong to interpret these states' preliminary objections as a willingness to "avoid" the Court altogether.

4 *Non-Appearing Respondent*

Lastly, states limit their interaction with the Court by not appearing as Respondents. The phenomenon of the non-appearing Respondent can be misleading. Like the withdrawal of optional clause declarations, it attracts a lot of attention when it happens, giving the impression of a widespread and highly damaging practice. This impression is wrong on two accounts.

First, in practice, the phenomenon of the non-appearing Respondent remains limited. It has only happened in nine cases, or about 6% of the Court's docket. Only five states challenged the Court by not appearing as Respondent in the merits phase of a contentious case. Clearly, an assessment of how states view the Court cannot overlook the low frequency at which non-appearance has occurred. The phenomenon makes a lot of noise, yet it remains limited.

Second, and contrary to popular belief, a state's decision not to appear before the Court does not entail a violation of international law or of the ICJ Statute. In fact, the latter envisages the consequences of such behavior of the Court's judicial function and the proceedings themselves.

> **ICJ Statute**
>
> **Article 53**
>
> 1. Whenever one of the parties does not appear before the Court, or fails to defend its case, the other party may call upon the Court to decide in favor of its claim.
>
> 2. The Court must, before doing so, satisfy itself, not only that it has jurisdiction in accordance with Articles 36 and 37, but also that the claim is well founded in fact and law.

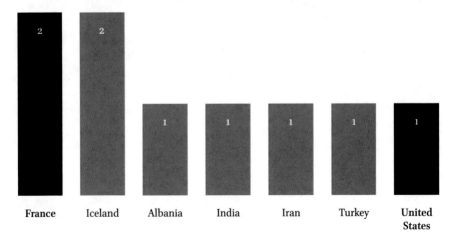

FIGURE 5.12   Non-appearing Respondents

The Court, as a matter of principle, refuses to be deterred by non-appearance: non-appearance does not affect how the case is handled. If jurisdiction is found the case proceeds, even in the absence of the Respondent. Non-appearance does not necessarily harm the good administration of justice, or prevent the non-appearing Respondent from making its view known to the Court. Though, in theory, the non-appearing state waives the opportunity to rebut the evidence of the Applicant and establish an affirmative defense, in practice, there is a marked tendency among non-appearing Respondents to manifest themselves to the Court, directly or indirectly, by letters, messages, or statements. The communications of the non-appearing State are practically exempt from all terms, conditions, and deadlines imposed upon the parties by the Court, allowing the non-appearing Respondent to argue its case virtually as fully as if it had appeared. In *Nottebohm*, Guatemala sent a letter to the Court in lieu of appearance in the jurisdiction phase, explaining its position in much detail including the reasons why it was unwilling to appear before the Court.[19]

> **Xue Hanqin, Jurisdiction of the International Court of Justice[20]**
> While a default judgment rendered by a national court that totally relies on the claims of one party is invariably unfavorable to the non-appearing party, in international adjudication that is not necessarily the case.
>
> In the practice of the ICJ, if a State considers that there does not exist any consensual basis for the jurisdiction of the Court or that it does not accept the jurisdictional basis of an application filed against it by another State, it may choose not to appear before the Court and not appoint an Agent on its behalf. This special practice is unique in international judicial settlement.

Going a step further, the Court takes it upon itself to compensate for the Respondent's decision not to appear and affirms that non-appearance should not work to the benefit or detriment of either party. Specifically, Article 53(2) protects the non-appearing party by ensuring that the Court makes a decision that is justified in both procedure and substance.

The duty, in other words, lies on the Court – not on the Respondent – under the rationale that the Applicant is entitled to adjudication of its claim

---

19 *Letter from the Minister of Foreign Affair of Guatemala to the President of the International Court of Justice* (Sept. 9, 1952), available at https://www.icj-cij.org/public/files/case-related/18/10985.pdf.

20 Xue Hanqin, *Jurisdiction of the International Court of Justice* (2017), at 52.

178   CHAPTER 5

in spite of the Respondent's choice not to appear. The Court accordingly finds
it its duty "to consider the submissions of the party which appears" without
being compelled "to examine their accuracy in all their details; for this might in
unopposed cases prove impossible in practice."[21] The Court finds it sufficient
"to convince itself by such methods as it considers suitable that the submissions are well founded."[22]

Non-appearance may not carry serious consequences *de jure*, but one cannot overlook its impact *de facto*. The Court may not have access to all the facts
and therefore rely more on the Applicants' demonstration of the facts. In
addition, non-appearance precludes the Respondent from requesting interim
measures that could have otherwise protected its interests.

Finally, the absence of a duty to appear should not be construed as providing an excuse for non-compliance. A state that has chosen not to appear may
find itself in an uncomfortable situation when the Court issues a final decision
that goes against its interests. Complying with the decision might entail "losing
face", while non-compliance would violate international law.

Ultimately, understanding the phenomenon of the non-appearing
Respondent is critical to avoid giving it more importance than it actually
has, and not overshadowing otherwise positive interactions with the Court.
Moreover, the Rules of the Court tolerate the phenomenon of the non-
appearing Respondent. They do not impose a duty to appear or any sanction
for non-appearance. Respondents contemplating this option, however, need
to carefully consider the practical and strategic implications of such act: it
will likely attract attention, make it difficult to communicate one's views to
the Court, foster some resentment among judges, hurt diplomatic relations,
and complicate the aftermath of the judgment. States that nevertheless opt
for this course of action should make clear that it does not entail any violation
of international law, and that the decision not to appear goes beyond the law.

C   Compliance with the Court's Judgments

The obligation is clear: UN member states must comply with the decisions
of the International Court of Justice in cases to which they are party. Compliance has often been used as a benchmark of the Court's effectiveness. As
a concept, however, compliance is both difficult to define and difficult to
measure.

---

21   *Corfu Channel* (United Kingdom v. Albania), Judgment, I.C.J. Reports 1949, p. 244, at 248.
22   *Id.*

In some instances, states comply with ICJ decisions because it has become advantageous to comply – not necessarily because of the Court's ruling. At others, states may declare that they have complied or will comply with the decision, but the facts on the ground suggest otherwise. In yet other cases, a state may comply only partially with a judgment, or after a long period of time. Some decisions of the ICJ do not clearly indicate what states must do in order to comply with the decision. In a few situations, the Court's decision may be technically complied with, but the process nevertheless undermines the Court's legitimacy.

This last point ties into a larger issue regarding the concept of compliance. Compliance does not, in and of itself, provide an adequate measure of the Court's effectiveness. Like sanctions and other means of enforcement, compliance is not central to how international law operates.[23] Placing too much emphasis on compliance overlooks a plethora of other factors that shape states relationship with the ICJ. Limiting international law – or ICJ decisions – to their enforceability simply misses the point.

Consider, by way of example, that many applications filed with the Court do not culminate in a judgment. These cases are known as discontinued, and amount to 35 out of a total of 147 cases that have come before the Court. States do not always share the reason behind the removal of a case from the Court's docket, but one can safely assume that many of those 35 cases ended up settling out of Court. What role did the act of seizing of the ICJ play in eventually "pacifying" those disputes? The impact of the Court – however difficult to measure – neither begins nor ends with compliance with a formal judgment.

1   *Defining Compliance*

As noted above, the Court may not explicitly require the parties to take specific steps towards the implementation of the judgment. This makes compliance, and the assessment of compliance, quite challenging – as it is not clear what compliance would entail.[24]

Take, for example, *Haya de la Torre*, which involved a dispute between Peru and Colombia after Colombia granted diplomatic asylum to a Peruvian national in 1949. Haya de la Torre, the Peruvian national, was accused by the Peruvian government of having instigated a military rebellion. The dispute

---

23   Louis Henkin, How Nations Behave (1979); Rosalyn Higgins, Problems and Process: International Law and How We Use It (1995).

24   Scholars have reached different conclusions regarding the compliance record of ICJ judgments. *See* Aloysius P. Llmazon, *Jurisdiction and Compliance in Recent Decisions of the International Court of Justice*, 18 Eur. J. Int'l L. 815 (2008), at 824–25.

180   CHAPTER 5

gave rise to three separate judgements,[25] and the difficulty in implementing the two judgments that were rendered on the merits (in 1949 and 1950) significantly delayed compliance. In 1951, the Court ruled that asylum had been irregularly granted by Colombia but declared that Colombia was not bound to surrender the refugee.[26] According to the Court, these two conclusions were not contradictory because there were other ways in which the asylum could be terminated besides the return of the refugee. The Court essentially sent the sides back to the negotiating table.[27]

The Court's initial judgment in *Avena* led to a similar situation. In 2004, the ICJ held that by not informing Mexican nationals on death row in the United States of their rights, and failing to notify the Mexican authorities, the United States breached its obligations under Article 36 of the Vienna Convention on Consular Relations. The Court did not clearly indicate what measures the United States needed to take to remedy the violation of these rights.[28] In *Avena*, as in *Haya de la Torre* and many other returned cases, it was not clear what compliance entailed.[29]

2   *The Timing Issue*

Another issue arises with respect to the proper time frame within which to measure compliance. Notable in this context is *Corfu Channel*, where the parties ended up complying with the Court's decision forty-seven years after it was issued.[30] The dispute arose out of the explosions of mines, allegedly laid by Albania, which damaged British warships passing through the Corfu Channel in 1946. The United Kingdom seized the Court of the dispute in 1947 and accused Albania of laying or allowing a third state to lay the mines after mine-clearing operations had been carried out by the Allied naval authorities. The Court did not accept the view that Albania itself laid the mines, but it held that

---

25   *Asylum Case* (Colombia v. Peru), Judgment, I.C.J. Report 1050, p. 266; *Request for Interpretation of the Judgment of 20 November 1950* (Colombia v. Peru), Judgment, I.C.J. Reports 1950, p. 395; *Haya de la Torre* (Colombia v. Peru), Judgment, I.C.J. Reports 1951, p. 71.

26   *Haya de la Torre* (Colombia v. Peru), Judgment, I.C.J. Reports 1951, p. 71.

27   Constanze Schulte, Compliance with Decisions of the International Court of Justice (2004), at 108.

28   *Case Concerning Avena and Other Mexican Nationals* (Mexico v. United States of America), I.C.J. Reports 2004, p. 12.

29   *See also Case concerning Right of Passage over Indian Territory* (Merits), I.C.J. Reports 1960, p. 6, at 46. (the Court decided retroactively that India had not violated its obligations, thus not requiring a positive action by any of the parties).

30   *Corfu Channel* (United Kingdom v. Albania), Judgment, 1949 I.C.J. Report 1949 244 (Dec. 15).

AN ASSESSMENT   181

the mines could not have been laid without the knowledge of the Albanian government. The Court determined that Albania owed the United Kingdom £844,000 in reparations.

The judgment against Albania remained unsettled for decades. In 1950, Albania offered £40,000 to settle the claim, but the United Kingdom rejected the offer. Settlement talks subsequently broke down and the United Kingdom looked to seize Albanian property in its territory, but there was none. The United Kingdom then looked to satisfy its claims out of gold reserves that originally had belonged to the National Bank of Albania and that the Nazis had brought from Rome to Berlin in 1943.[31] The Tripartite Commission for the Restitution of Monetary Gold, of which the United Kingdom was a member, formed an agreement in 1951 whereby it requested the President of the ICJ to appoint an arbitrator to resolve the competing claims of Italy and Albania as to the status of the gold, but the commission did not grant the gold to the United Kingdom.

After the fall of socialism in Albania, the sides reached an agreement whereby the United Kingdom would grant Albania some 1,574 kilograms of Tripartite Commission gold, and Albania would pay $2 million to the United Kingdom – finally complying with the judgment ... in 1996. This raises serious questions as to *when* compliance ought to be assessed. Do declarations made by states in the wake of an ICJ decision provide an accurate picture of whether they intend to comply with the judgment? In the absence of a centralized body capable of ascertaining compliance, who has the final word as to whether compliance has been attained? These questions highlight the breadth of the challenge and confirm that compliance cannot provide a benchmark for measuring the Court's effectiveness.

3   Additional Issues with Compliance
i   Compliance for Other Reasons
In some situations, parties do comply with ICJ judgements – but for reasons that have little to do with the Court. States may end up complying because the situation has changed in a manner as to make compliance more beneficial than non-compliance. *Military and Paramilitary Activities in and against Nicaragua* illustrates this quite well.[32]

---

31   *Monetary Gold Removed from Rome in 1943 (Preliminary Question)* (Italy v. France, United Kingdom of Great Britain and Northern Ireland and United States of America), Judgment, I.C.J. Reports 1954, p. 19.

32   *Military and Paramilitary Activities in and against Nicaragua* (Nicaragua v. United States of America), Judgment, I.C.J. Reports 1986, p. 14.

182   CHAPTER 5

In 1984, Nicaragua instituted proceedings against the United States, together with a request for the indication of provisional measures. Nicaragua accused the United States of unlawfully attacking Nicaraguan facilities and naval vessels, mining Nicaraguan ports, intruding on Nicaraguan air space, and training, arming, equipping, financing, and supplying rebels (the "contras") seeking to overthrow Nicaragua's Sandinista government. In its judgment on the merits, the Court ruled that the United States' actions amounted to an unlawful use of force. The United States did not comply with the ICJ's injunction to stop intervening or with the obligation to negotiate repatriations. The United States also blocked enforcement of the judgment by the UN Security Council. After the United States-backed candidate was elected president in Nicaragua, relations between the countries improved: the trade embargo was lifted in 1990 and Nicaragua became the second-largest recipient of US aid to Central America.[33] In 1991, the US cancelled Nicaragua's debt of US$259.5 million. None of these measures were formally carried out in application of the ICJ's judgment of 1986.[34]

In another case involving the United States, this time as Applicant, the Court requested that Iran release hostages held at the US embassy in Tehran and compensate the United States. A day before the hostages were released, the United States asked that the case be removed from the Court's docket on the ground that the two states "had entered into certain mutual commitments in order to resolve the crisis."[35] Because the matter was settled between the parties, the Court was not called upon to decide the amount of reparation due to the United States. In both cases, the concept of compliance seems unduly simplistic to capture the multi-faceted impact of the Court's involvement on the conduct of the parties.

ii   Compliance or the Appearance of Compliance

Even in cases where states agree to comply, it may be difficult to determine whether the specific measures undertaken amount to compliance. *Whaling in the Antarctic* created just such a challenge. In 2010, Australia instituted proceedings against Japan for pursuing "a large-scale program of whaling under the Second Phase of its Japanese Whale Research Program under Special Permit in the Antarctic (JARPA II)," in breach of obligations assumed by Japan under the 1946 International Convention for the Regulation of Whaling and

---

33   Nicaragua: A Country Study (Tim Merrill ed., 1993).
34   Schulte, *supra* note 24, at 206.
35   *United States Diplomatic and Consular Staff in Tehran* (United States of America v. Iran), Order, I.C.J. Reports 1981, p. 45.

other international obligations for the preservation of marine mammals and the marine environment.

In 2014, the Court held that the special permits issued by Japan for the killing, taking, and treating of whales in connection with JARPA II were not granted "for purposes of scientific research" pursuant to the 1946 Convention.[36] Because the ICJ decision prohibited whaling only in regard to JARPA II, Japan side-stepped the decision by renaming the program.[37] Although Japan initially said it would cease whaling, Japan's Prime Minister later declared that whaling would resume[38] with a third scientific whaling program called NEWREP-A.[39] Four years later, Japan announced its intention to withdraw from the International Whaling Commission (IWC) in order "to resume commercial whaling"[40] within its territorial waters and exclusive economic zone (EEZ) – but not in the Antarctic Ocean. The decision flies in the face of the spirit of the ICJ's decision, but it is unclear whether whaling in Japanese territorial waters and EEZ actually violates the ICJ decision.

iii   Compliance and Legitimacy

In cases where the Court is seized unilaterally or when the subject-matter of the dispute concerns sensitive issues tied to national interests, the attitude of the parties (or one of the parties) may undermine the legitimacy of the Court. Even when a case was brought to the Court jointly by both party, states may not comply with the Court's judgment. It took many years, for example, for Thailand to comply with the Court's holding that the Temple of Preah Vihear belonged to Cambodia. Although Thailand eventually complied, it repeatedly expressed its disapproval with that decision.

Initially Cambodia complained that Thailand had occupied a piece of its territory surrounding the ruins of the Temple of Preah Vihear, and asked that Thailand withdraw its armed detachment stationed there since 1954. In its

---

36   *Whaling in the Antarctic* (Australia v. Japan: New Zealand Intervening), Judgment, I.C.J. Reports 2014, p. 226, para. 247(7) (Mar. 2014).

37   Julia Miller Bedell, *On Thin Ice: Will the International Court of Justice's Ruling in Australia v. Japan: New Zealand Intervening End Japan's Lethal Whaling in the Antarctic?*, Colum. J. Env'l L. 1 (2015).

38   Hilary Whiteman, *Japan's PM Shinzo Abe Suggests Return to Antarctic Whaling during 'Whale Week'*, CNN (June 11, 2014).

39   Gov. of Japan, Proposed Research Plan for New Scientific Whale Research Program in the Antarctic Ocean (NEWREP-A).

40   Article XI of the International Convention for the Regulation of Whaling (ICRW) provides that any contracting government may withdraw from this convention on June 30 of any year by giving notice on or before January 1 of the same year to the depository government.

judgment on the merits in 1962, the Court awarded sovereignty over the temple to Cambodia.[41] Thailand blatantly opposed this holding, issued hostile declarations not only to the ICJ but also to countries whose nationals served as counsel for Cambodia, cut off trade with Poland as retaliation for the decision handed by Polish ICJ President Winiarski, and ordered Thai soldiers to shoot every Cambodian trying to enter the temple.[42]

This atmosphere subsided and, in the summer of 1962, Thailand informed the Secretary-General of its decision to comply with the ICJ judgment. The dispute was later revived when Cambodia submitted an application to UNESCO in 2008 requesting that Preah Vihear and the surrounding land be designated a World Heritage site. Thailand opposed the application. In the interest of cross-border relations, Cambodia withdrew the application and, after winning the support of Thailand, submitted a modified map requesting the designation only for the temple itself.

Nonetheless, tensions mounted and cross-border gunshot incidents caused Cambodia to seize the Court for a reinterpretation of its 1962 decision.[43] In 2013, the ICJ declared unanimously that the 1962 ICJ judgment had awarded all of the area surrounding the temple to Cambodia and that Thailand had an obligation to fully withdraw. This case shows that compliance is possible even when initial resistance by one or both sides seems to foreshadow long-term defiance. Ultimately, after many years, multiple judgments, and repeated military confrontations, the ICJ was successful in bringing the sovereignty battle over the Temple of Preah Vihear to an end.

At times, pressure from the international community – as in the territorial dispute between Libya and Chad where Libya agreed to a strategic compromise largely on account of the political pressure exercised by the African Union and the United Nations[44] – or the involvement of the Security Council may facilitate compliance.[45] At others, it is simply the fact that the dispute does not threaten national interests, making it easier for states to comply. Over the years, maritime delimitation has fared well in terms of compliance, though

---

41 *Temple of Preah Vihear* (Cambodia v. Thailand), Judgment, I.C.J. Reports 1962, p. 6, at 36.
42 Schulte, *supra* note 24, at 135.
43 *Request for Interpretation of the Judgment of 15 June 1962 in the Case concerning the Temple of Preah Vihear (Cambodia v. Thailand)* (Cambodia v. Thailand), Judgment, I.C.J. Reports 2013, p. 281.
44 *See* Cotler Paulson, *Compliance with Final Judgments of the International Court of Justice Since 1987*, 98 Am. J. Int'l L. 434, 441 (2004); and Heather L. Jones, *Why Comply? An Analysis of Trends in Compliance with Judgments of the International Court of Justice Since Nicaragua*, 12 Chi.-Kent J. Int'l & Comp. L. 57 (2012).
45 *See* Llmazon, *supra* note 21, at n. 39.

AN ASSESSMENT 185

this could change as technology enables states to exploit resources deeper and further into the sea. Compliance becomes costlier when the subject-matter of the dispute touches on territorial sovereignty or where civilian lives are at stake. Either way, in any given case, the Court will decide if it prefers to split the territory or maritime area between the two parties to the dispute – a solution known as a Solomonic compromise – or award the entire area to one of the parties – thereby identifying a 'winner' and a 'loser.' The latter option runs the risk of heightening tensions between opposing states, makes compliance more difficult for the losing side, and may dissuade the "losing" party to use the Court in the future.

In sum, a detailed analysis of the Court's case law demonstrates the following: out of sixty-four judgments issued by the Court on the merits, twelve of those did not clearly impose obligations on the parties. Thirty-one judgments were complied with – this is the case for most territorial and maritime delimitations judgments. Twenty judgments were either (1) only partially complied with, (2) complied with, but with significant delay, or (3) the decision was complied with seemingly as a result of an agreement between the parties rather than in application of the Court's ruling. *Whaling in the Antarctic* stands out as a potential case of non-compliance.

•••

Questions

1. Some scholars have argued that the ICJ can limit non-compliance by avoiding cases where a judgement is likely to be resisted (for example where one of the sides refuses to participate in the proceedings).[46] The argument is that by establishing a successful compliance record, the Court would strengthen its legitimacy. Should the ICJ only exercise jurisdiction when both parties are likely to comply with its decision? On the one hand, non-compliance can have a negative impact on the Court's reputation. On the other hand, the Court may lose in legitimacy if it only takes on cases it knows it can "win." How, if at all, should these considerations factor into the Court's decisions?

2. Do the measures undertaken by the United States following *Military and Paramilitary Activities in and Against Nicaragua* and by Iran in the wake of *United States Diplomatic and Consular Staff in Tehran* amount to compliance with the Court's decisions? If compliance is used as a benchmark, is there room

---

46 Jonathan I. Charney, *Disputes Implicating the Institutional Credibility of the Court: Problems of Non-Appearance, Non-Participation, and Non-Performance*, in The International Court of Justice at a Crossroads (Lori Fisler Damrosch ed., 1987), at 288.

to distinguish between what states do because the Court ordered it and what states do for other reasons?

Further Reading

Gary L. Scott and Karen D. Csajko, *Compulsory Jurisdiction and Defiance in the World Court: A Comparison of the PCIJ and the ICJ*, 16 Denv. J. Int'l L. & Pol'y 377 (1988).

Tom Ginsburg and Richard H. McAdams, *Adjudicating in Anarchy: An Expressive Theory of International Dispute Resolution*, 45 Wm. & Mary L. Rev. 1229 (2004).

Sara McLaughlin Mitchell and Paul R. Hensel, *International Institutions and Compliance with Agreements*, 51 Am. J. Pol. Sci. 721 (2007).

Nienke Grossman, *Solomonic Judgments and the International Court of Justice*, in Legitimacy and International Courts 43 (Nienke Grossman, Harlan Grant Cohen, Andreas Follesdal and Geir Ullfstein eds., 2018).

Conclusion

This last chapter concludes a book designed for students, teachers, and international lawyers seeking to gain novel insights on the UN's principal judicial organ. Neither the book nor this chapter intended to offer suggestions for improvement, let alone a critique of the institution. Instead, the intent has been to present the World Court as a key player within a wide and ever-expanding network of domestic, regional, and international actors. The focus was on relationships and interaction rather than on compliance, given the limitations inherent to the concept of compliance as a benchmark of the Court's effectiveness. Compliance is subjective, time-dependent, often extraneous to legal compliance strictly speaking, and layered when multiple judgments are issued in a single case. Perhaps most importantly, the Court's judgments do not always elaborate on what states are expected to do. When the Court leaves states a margin of appreciation in the implementation of their international legal obligations, assessing compliance becomes virtually impossible.

A second take-away from this chapter's analysis is that state interaction with the Court cannot be assessed by merely counting cases brought before the Court and optional clause declarations. The observation that a majority of UN members never took part in a contentious case before the Court, either as Applicant or Respondent, does not appropriately capture how the Court operates. Ultimately, the Court's docket says little about the role the ICJ serves within the international community.

AN ASSESSMENT

An assessment of how states view the Court requires a more open-minded and flexible approach. Such assessment must capture all types of interaction – active, passive, commitment-driven, and even behavior perceived as "defiant". First, even within the contentious framework, states may take part in contentious proceedings in other ways: they can request to intervene or bring cases on the basis of special agreements. Second, this assessment cannot limit itself to the contentious role of the ICJ, no matter how important. It must account for states' participation in advisory proceedings at well (measured here using two criteria: state support for the Court's involvement at the requesting organ, and state participation during the proceedings at the ICJ).

The analysis shows that patterns of state interaction with the ICJ are not necessarily intuitive. The relatively simplistic idea that certain states favor the Court while others do not finds no real support in the data. The relationship is much more complex, with the divide lying more between states that willingly commit to the Court's jurisdiction ahead of time (before the dispute and the parties become known) and those that are taken aback by the uncertainty. This phenomenon finds expression, for example, in the somewhat odd realization that states that fail to renew or terminate their optional clause declarations subsequently bring cases before the Court.

A more intuitive finding reveals that advisory proceedings constitute the preferred mode of interaction. All UN member states – with the exception of Andorra, Monaco, Northern Ireland, Tajikistan, the Former Yugoslav Republic of Macedonia, and Tonga – have interacted with the Court on some level within the framework of advisory proceedings. The latter are less commitment-intensive, do not require approval ahead of time, and – although states have an opportunity to influence the outcome of the process – such outcome does not bind them legally. This widespread participation in advisory proceedings does not sit well with the relatively limited use of the mechanism.

As for the permanent members of the Security Council, two major insights are worth reflecting upon and offer interesting avenues for future research. First, the behavior of India strikingly resembles that of the P5 (with the exception of China, which is an outlier). This is particularly interesting given India's aspirations to become a permanent member of the Security Council, and its active involvement in UN work (including as one of the top contributors to UN peace operations).[47] The election of an Indian judge in the seat that had been occupied by a British judge for seventy years only strengthens the position

---

47   Ramesh Thakur, *India and the United Nations*, 35 Strategic Analysis 898 (2011).

of India within the United Nations.[48] The analysis of India's interaction with the ICJ provides a window of understanding into India's own view of its role within the UN in general, and at the ICJ in particular.

Second, China stands out in comparison to other P5, including Russia. China has never interacted in any way with the Court in contentious proceedings. This lack of activity in the contentious realm is misleading, as China has interacted with the Court in other ways; it has voted in favor of advisory opinion requests five times, and, most notably, has *never* opposed such a request. China has also participated in many advisory proceedings, filing written statements on seven occasions and even appearing in oral proceedings once. China has always had a judge on the bench, and Chinese judges have served as president or vice-president of the ICJ for a total of twelve years (see Figure 5.15 below). It would be easy to conclude by looking exclusively at contentious cases that China barely interacts with the Court, particularly in comparison to other P5. A more refined analysis, which takes into account a broader set of interactions, reveals China's complex and more deferential record. It also demonstrates, more generally, that state interaction with the Court cannot be assessed exclusively via the prism of contentious jurisdiction.

As a matter of fact, almost all states interact with the ICJ – but on their own terms. In the exercise of its contentious and advisory functions, the Court meets a diverse set of needs, and the assessment of the Court's record must reflect this reality. The Court, for its part, should be attentive to the needs of states and to the various roles it fulfills, as an institution, on a global scale.

Ultimately, this book presents the Court as I believe Shabtai Rosenne would have liked it: as a living institution. It looks beyond the usual methods of analysis and takes a broad view. It examines the Court in the context of its interactions with states, non-states, academia, other UN bodies, and domestic actors. Because the International Court of Justice is both more than a court, and less than a court. It is its own thing.

---

48   Arun M. Sukumar, *The Significance of Dalveer Bhandari's, and India's, Recent Election to the ICJ*, Lawfare (Dec. 13, 2017). *See supra* Chapter 3, Section E on the election of India's first judge to the ICJ.

AN ASSESSMENT

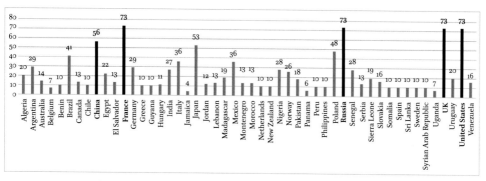

FIGURE 5.13   Number of Judges per state

CHAPTER 6

Bringing the Court to the Classroom: Student's Guide

This guide assists the student in preparing for their role in a moot court exercise. Moot court exercises help students gain a better insight on the inner workings of the International Court of Justice and deepen their knowledge of international law. They also improve their research, writing, and oratory skills. A facilitator's guide seeking to assist in setting up moot court exercises (and complete with grading suggestions) is available by request at worldcourt@brill.com.

⋮

I What is a Moot Court?

An International Court of Justice (ICJ) moot court simulates a hypothetical dispute between two states before the ICJ. A moot court consists of two phases: written pleadings and oral hearings. Students are split into teams to prepare these written and oral submissions. Traditionally, teams argue as Agents for either the Applicant or Respondent; however, for particularly large groups, additional teams can be created to serve as ICJ Judges.

During the written pleadings phase, students prepare a Memorial (as Agents), or Judges' Notes (as Judges). After all written pleadings are completed, students exchange their Memorials and/or Judges' Notes with other teams to prepare for the oral hearings phase.

Oral hearings allow students to deepen their knowledge of international law and understand the workings of the ICJ. During oral hearings, Agents do not recite from a script; instead, they prepare an outline of the argument, with facts and law that support their position. At least the first few minutes of an Agent's presentation are uninterrupted so they can present the key issues of the argument, however, after the initial few minutes, Judges can interject during the argument and ask questions. Agents will need to be prepared to make their argument and defend their position.

Before students begin preparing their written and oral hearings, they need to possess a working knowledge of the ICJ and its function, as well as the basics of international law. For all moot court scenarios, students should be familiar

© KONINKLIJKE BRILL NV, LEIDEN, 2020 | DOI:10.1163/9789004226968_008

with the UN Charter, the ICJ Statute, and the Vienna Convention on the Law of Treaties.

II   Written Pleadings Phase

A   *Written Pleadings Overview*
The written pleadings phase is an opportunity for the teams to conduct independent research on the applicable law and generate arguments to advance a particular position. All teams will research and draft a written document prior to the oral hearings phase. Agent teams will research and draft a 5–15 page written Memorial.[1] Judges (if used) will research and draft 3–10 pages of Judges' Notes, as well as a list of 10–20 potential questions to ask the Applicant and Respondent teams during oral arguments.

Agents will be graded on the organization of their Memorial as well as their knowledge of the law, quality of the reasoning, research effort, and teamwork. If students are playing the role of Judges, they will be graded on the organization of their Judges' Notes as well as their knowledge of the law, the quality of the questions posed, research effort, and teamwork.

B   *Memorial*
A Memorial is a team-drafted written document that describes the facts of the case and evaluates the law in a manner that favors the team's client.

All Memorials must contain the following elements:
– Title Page
    – The Title Page should look like the first page of the Moot Court Problem, however, "Moot Court Problem" should be replaced with "Applicant/ Respondent Memorial"
– Statement of Facts
    – What are the relevant facts of the case?
– Issues
    – What legal issues arise that arise from the problem?
– Jurisdiction
    – For the Applicant: What is the basis of the Court's jurisdiction in this case?
    – For the Respondent: Do you recognize the jurisdiction of the Court? Why or why not?[2]

---

1   Page limits can be modified at the discretion of the facilitator.
2   Even if the Respondent State does not recognize the jurisdiction of the Court over this issue, the Memorial should still argue the merits.

192   CHAPTER 6

- Statement of Law
  - What treaties and customary norms apply?
- Argument/Pleadings (Merits)
  - How do the laws and facts support your case?
- Submissions
  - What do you want the Court to do/declare/order?

C   *Judges' Notes*

The Judges' Notes is a written document that analyzes potential arguments in support of, and in opposition to, both the Respondent and the Applicant. In addition to identifying the arguments for both Respondent and Applicant, the Judges' Notes will indicate, for each issue, which Agent's position appears strongest. Furthermore, the Judges' Notes will include 5–10 questions for both the Applicant and the Respondent on each issue, which the Judges can use during the oral hearings phase.

All Judges' Notes must contain the following elements:
- Title Page
  - The Title Page should look like the first page of the Moot Court Problem, however, "Moot Court Problem" should be replaced with "Judges' Notes"
- Statement of Facts
  - What are the relevant facts of the case?
- Jurisdiction
  - Does the Court have jurisdiction? Why or why not?[3]
- Issues
  - What legal issues will be raised by each of the parties?
- Applicable Law
  - What treaties and customary norms apply?
- Findings
  - How do the laws and facts support the Applicant's case? How do the laws and facts support the Respondent's case? For each issue, which side has a stronger argument – the Applicant or the Respondent? Why?
- Questions
  - What questions would you ask the Applicant and the Respondent to help you reach a decision?

---

3   Even if the Court determines that it does not have jurisdiction, the Judges' Notes should still examine the merits.

BRINGING THE COURT TO THE CLASSROOM

III   Oral Hearings Phase

A   *Oral Hearings Overview*

The oral hearings phase is an opportunity for students to enhance their oratory skills while presenting an outline of their argument (or interjecting with relevant questions as Judges). To prepare for the oral hearings phase, students should review their respective Memorial, as well as the Memorial of the opposing side (and the Judges' Notes, if applicable). The objective is to present arguments that advance the Agent's position while also indicating why the opposing counsel's arguments are not correct.

Agents will be graded on their speaking skills and ability to respond to questions, in addition to their independent knowledge of the law and the quality of their legal arguments. If students are playing the role of Judges, they will need to be familiar with the Agents' Memorials and will be graded on their handling of oral proceedings as well as their participation in deliberations with the other Judges.

B   *Room Setup*

Judges should be seated behind a long table facing the room. Applicant and Respondent should be seated at two separate tables facing the Judges' table. Placards can be useful to identify Judges and the respective team members for Applicant and Respondent.

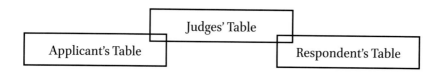

Before the oral hearings begin, the "courtroom" will also need to be set up with signs indicating where Applicants and Respondents sit, as well as the names of the Judges. The facilitator should prepare three time cards that read "5 Minutes," "2 Minutes," and "Time Out," as well as a clock or watch.

C   *Oral Hearings*

Oral Arguments shall proceed as follows:
- Opening of the Court session
  - Introduction of Justices and presentation of the case before Court by the timekeeper (usually the instructor, facilitator, or a student *not* serving on one of the teams)

- Applicant's argument (20 minutes suggested)
  - Applicant 1 argues
  - Applicant 2 argues
- Respondent's argument (20 minutes suggested)
  - Respondent 1 argues
  - Respondent 2 argues
- Applicant rebuttal (5 minutes suggested)
  - Applicant 1 **or** 2 responds
- Respondent rejoinder (5 minutes suggested)
  - Respondent 1 **or** 2 responds
- Decision of the Court (optional)
  - The facilitator can decide in advance whether the Judges will deliberate and then issue a decision at the conclusion of oral arguments or whether the Judges will issue a written opinion at a later date (during the following class, for example).
  - When oral arguments take place over multiple days with different teams, it is advised that Judges do not issue a decision immediately following the oral argument phase but instead wait until the recap session.

During the oral hearings, Agents should not read from a script but rather present an outline of their strongest argument for each issue. While Agents proceed through their arguments, Judges should feel free to interject with relevant questions designed to explore the depth of Agents' knowledge of the law and the facts of the case.

D   *Timekeeper*

The instructor, facilitator, or a student *not* participating in any of the teams will keep track of timing for each side. The timekeeper will also make sure that Judges and Agents sit in the designated locations.

The timekeeper is responsible for ensuring that Agents only use the allotted time for arguments and rebuttal/rejoinder. The timekeeper will show the Agents time cards when there are 5 minutes remaining, 2 minutes remaining, and when time is up.

E   *Addressing the Court*

You should address the Court as "Mister/Madam President and distinguished Judges" or "Your Excellencies." You can refer to "Your Excellency" when addressing an individual Judge. You should address opposing counsel as "Agents for Applicant/Respondent."

You should always introduce yourself as you rise before the bench. During the opening argument for either the Applicant or Respondent, the first team member should say:

> Mr./Madam President and distinguished members of the Court. My name is (**insert name**) and, along with co-counsel (**insert name**), I represent Applicant/Respondent. I will present on (**state the issue(s)**), while my co-counsel(s) will address (**state the issue(s)**). We would like to reserve two or three minutes for rebuttal/rejoinder following our presentation of the main legal issues.

When responding to questions from the Judges, always begin by stating "yes" or "no" before explaining your position. When affirming a Judge's question, say, "Yes/No, your Honor, because ..." When refuting a Judge's assertion, say, "Yes/No, your Honor ..."

There are multiple methods for each teammate to conclude their oral presentation:

- (*Concluding, in general*) "If there are no further questions from the bench, I will conclude my argument by asking the Court to find (**insert team's position**). Thank you, and may it please the Court."
- (*If turning over to co-counsel*) "At this time, I will turn the remaining time over to my co-counsel, (**insert name**), to address (**insert issue**)" or "Your excellencies, I see that my time has lapsed/is up, if I may be of no further assistance to this Court, this concludes our arguments on (**insert issue**), and I will now yield the floor to my co-counsel X [for first speaker] who will address (**insert issue**)."
- (*If out of time*) "Mr./Madam President, Distinguished Judges, I see my time has expired and I would like to conclude by asking the Court to find (**insert team's position**). Thank you, and may it please the Court." Another option is simply to refer back to written submissions: "As for (**insert issue**), I rely on my written submissions".
- (*If time is up halfway into concluding sentence*), the student should stop at once and turn to address the Court and say: "Your excellencies, I see that my time is up, if I may briefly finish my sentence and conclude."

F   Conclusion

At the conclusion of the oral arguments, after the Respondent team presents its rejoinder, the Judges will end the oral hearings phase by indicating that it will begin their deliberation, thanking the Agents for their pleadings, and closing the session with a gavel.

IV   Recap

Following the conclusion of the oral hearings, the teacher/faciliator will lead a de-briefing or recap session. In the de-briefing, students should discuss – either as a class or in small groups – different elements of the moot court exercise. Discussion topics may include:
- Research and legal drafting,
- Challenges and successes of working as a team,
- Barriers to success and obstacles overcome in the moot court process,
- Achievements and hurdles in the oral argument phase,
- Thoughts on the law and its ability to provide answers to the questions raised,
- Suggestions for future development of the law, and
- Thoughts on the dynamics at the ICJ between Agents and Judges, among Judges, etc.

In lieu of a classroom de-brief, or in addition to the in-person recap, the facilitator may require students to submit a short, written reflection on their experience (which may or may not be graded).

V   Moot Court Problems

A   *Problem #1: Amaliland v. Raviland (Case Concerning Space Debris and Environmental Protection)*

INTERNATIONAL COURT OF JUSTICE
Case Concerning Space Debris and the Yamma Fish

THE KINGDOM OF AMALILAND
(Applicant)
v.

THE FEDERAL STATES OF RAVILAND
(Respondent)

MOOT COURT PROBLEM

1.   The Kingdom of Amaliland is a small, rural kingdom of 30,000 kilometers with a population of approximately 5 million. Amaliland has a strong fishing culture – particularly in the 500 feet deep Naxos River, which runs from the mountains in the North down through the middle of Amaliland

BRINGING THE COURT TO THE CLASSROOM

until it joins up with the Pariana Sea. With abundant resources and a small population, Amaliland boasts successful agricultural practices, clean water and air, and sizeable reserves of untouched land.

2. The Federal States of Raviland borders Amaliland to the east and is the same landmass size but has a population of 30 million, increasing the strain on its already tight resources. Excessive farming and mining have reduced agricultural and resource development in Raviland and many of its waterways are polluted due to runoff.

3. Amaliland and Raviland are Members of the United Nations and Parties to the ICJ Statute. Under Article 36(2) of the ICJ Statute, Amaliland has recognized compulsory jurisdiction of the ICJ. Raviland has not recognized the jurisdiction of the ICJ as compulsory.

4. Amaliland and Raviland are Parties to the 1969 Vienna Convention on the Law of Treaties. They are also Parties to the 1972 Liability Convention and the 1975 Registration Convention. Amaliland is also a Party to the 1967 Outer Space Treaty and the 1979 Moon Agreement. Amaliland and Raviland are both Parties to the 1972 London Convention; Amaliland also ratified the 1996 Protocol.

5. As Raviland's natural resource depletion grew, it began importing most of its produce, grains, and water from Amaliland. In an effort to retain sufficient resources to support its own population, Amaliland increased export taxes by 400%, which severely strained the Raviland economy. Following failed diplomatic conversations to reduce the export tax, Raviland's rambunctious Prime Minister Alo led a campaign to promote innovative technological advancements to develop solutions to the growing food and water crisis.

6. Even after developing new crop fertilization techniques, harnessing wind energy, and working to desalinize water from the Pariana Sea in ten years of intensive innovation, Raviland began pursuing space exploration in earnest, recognizing its burgeoning population would require excess resources still likely to be strained locally in the next hundred years.

7. In three years conducting extensive research on future space habitability, the Raviland Space Agency (RSA) launched multiple satellites and rockets, rivaling the most prominent international space programs with its number of space endeavors. The RSA sought to explore potential resource development and mining as well as examine potential colonization of extraterrestrial bodies.

8. Debris from these RSA launches is not uncommon. Two years ago, the RSA released a statement warning the public to avoid contact with any debris from space objects due to the potential presence of hazardous chemicals.

9. While most space debris from RSA launches burns up in the atmosphere, the few instances that involved larger objects reaching the ground intact typically occurred far out in the Pariana Sea. In May, a large upper-stage rocket from an RSA launch re-entered the atmosphere and crash-landed in the Naxos River in Amaliland. The rocket destroyed two prominent fishing vessels, killed six fishermen, and sunk to the bottom of the river.

10. Amaliland instantly notified Raviland of the debris in the Naxos River and requested its rapid removal. The RSA, however, was deeply involved in preparations for the launch of its newest satellite and did not retrieve the rocket immediately.

11. Seven days after the incident, Amaliland sent a diplomatic letter to Raviland demanding the rocket be removed from the River and any toxins cleaned up that may have leeched into the Naxos River during the week. Two weeks later, the RSA located and removed most of the recognizable debris from the rocket.

12. Ten years ago, when the University of Raviland was tasked with resolving the polluted water issue in Raviland, it created CharCloth – large sponge-like materials infused with charcoal and other products that could potentially attract and remove chemicals from the water. The Raviland Minister of Health declined to use these cloths in public waterways because of concerns that potential pollutants would be pulled to the surface, rather than removed from the surface of the water. The RSA, however, invested heavily in the product and dragged giant pieces of CharCloth down three miles of the Naxos River in an attempt to reduce any chemical waste leeched from the rocket pieces.

13. Within three months fishermen in Amaliland reported a rise in the population of deceased Yamma fish, a delicacy in Amaliland, floating along the surface of the Naxos River. When the Ministry of Fishing and Agriculture tested the water in the Naxos River, it noticed high concentrations of hazardous chemicals in a five-mile radius of the crash site. The Ministry did not test the entire Naxos River but did notice that the levels of chemical contamination were significantly lower ten miles north of the crash site.

14. Amaliland, again, submitted a diplomatic letter to Raviland requesting improved clean up and reparation for the economic toll the chemicals imparted on the fishing sector. Raviland responded to Amaliland's request, indicating it had complied with initial requests for retrieval and clean up and that any current contamination in the River is not immediately related to Raviland's activities.

BRINGING THE COURT TO THE CLASSROOM   199

15. On September 27, the Government of the Kingdom of Amaliland ("Applicant") filed in the Registry of the Court an Application instituting proceedings against the Federal States of Raviland ("Respondent").

16. Amaliland asks the Court to adjudge and declare:
   a. Raviland violated international law when it failed to adequately control the accumulation and effects of its space debris; and
   b. Raviland violated international law by allowing its space debris to contaminate the Naxos River and harm the Yamma fish.

B   *Problem #2: Abalonia v. Rodonia (Case Concerning Diplomatic Protection of Beta Boop)*

INTERNATIONAL COURT OF JUSTICE
Case Concerning Diplomatic Protection of Beta Boop

THE FEDERAL REPUBLIC OF ABALONIA
(Applicant)

v.

THE UNITED REPUBLIC OF RODONIA
(Respondent)

MOOT COURT PROBLEM

1. The Federal Republic of Abalonia is a developed nation, known for its technological advancement, in the Onia Region. To the east of Abalonia is the United Republic of Rodonia, a constitutional monarchy, and a predominantly agrarian society specifically focused on dairy farming. The United Republic of Redonia is not as economically developed as Abalonia.

2. Both Abalonia and Rodonia are situated in the Onia Region, along with Yaronia (a highly developed economy to the north of both Abalonia and Rodonia) and Monia (a developing island nation in the Onia Sea, to the south of both Abalonia and Rodonia).

3. Abalonia and Rodonia are Members of the United Nations and Parties to the ICJ Statute. Under Article 36(2) of the ICJ Statute, Abalonia has recognized the jurisdiction of the ICJ as compulsory. Rodonia has not recognized the jurisdiction of the ICJ as compulsory.

4. Abalonia and Rodonia are also Parties to the 1969 Vienna Convention on the Law of Treaties and the 1963 Vienna Convention on Consular Relations.

5. Professor Gia of the University of Abalonia, and Professor Max of the Rodonia University, spent four years creating Beta Boop, a humanoid robot, in the Robotics Lab in Abalonia. Beta Boop was unveiled at the Annual Tech Gizmo Gadget Conference in Yaronia.

6. During the Annual Tech Gizmo Gadget Conference, the Abalonian Ambassador to Yaronia awarded Abalonian citizenship to Beta Boop in a formal ceremony attended by many Abalonian and Yaronians dignitaries.

7. While Beta Boop was a joint project between Professor Gia and Professor Max, Beta Boop was created to work with the Onia Regional Center for Peace and Security (ORCPS) at the Rodonia University. The ORCPS is dedicated to promoting democracy throughout the Onia region. Beta Boop was designed to understand human emotions and enhance the population's interest in local politics.

8. Professor Max, in addition to being the head of the ORCPS, is also an influential member of the Rodonia People's Liberation (RPL) movement – an underground organization committed to overthrowing the Administration of Rodonian Prime Minister Uli. Rodonia's Prime Minister Uli comes from the Uvi family, which owns 90% of the dairy cows in Rodonia, essentially maintaining control of the domestic dairy market. In his capacity with RPL, Professor Max often highlighted Beta Boop as a symbol of the future potential of a politically active Rodonia with citizens fighting for their rights (and the cessation of Prime Minister Uli's family's agricultural dominance as the largest dairy farm in Rodonia).

9. The RPL, in an effort to foment unrest in Rodonia against the Administration of Prime Minister Uli, orchestrated two separate riots in Rodonia's capital: the Main Street Riot in October and the Farmer's Market Riot in November. Professor Max brought Beta Boop to both riots to motivate the crowd. During the Farmer's Market Riot, Rodonian armed forces detained Beta Boop without realizing at first that she was a robot.

10. After identifying Beta Boop as a robot, Rodonia did not immediately inform Abalonia that Beta Boop was in their possession. Professor Max, who was aware of Beta Boop's detention, contacted Professor Gia, who then informed the Abalonian Ambassador to Rodonia.

11. Taking advantage of this discovery, the Government of Rodonia decided to inspect Beta Boop's structure in the hope of understanding and eventually designing their own humanoid robot. They hoped to use such a robot in military affairs, allowing more Rodonians to engage in dairy farming instead of serving in the armed forces. Beta Boop had been in

detention for two months when members of the Rodonia armed forces damaged one of her components while investigating the internal wiring.

12. Abalonia sent a diplomatic letter to Rodonia, requesting Beta Boop be released to Professor Gia at the University of Abalonia. Rodonia refused to honor Abalonia's request, indicating that Beta Boop would be detained and eventually executed for her crimes.
13. The Federal Republic of Abalonia requests the Court indicate provisional measures of protection by requiring Rodonia to release Beta Boop and return her to Abalonia before the robot is damaged beyond repair and crucial information is stolen. Abalonia further requests the Court adjudge and declare that the United Republic of Rodonia violated its international legal obligations against a citizen of Abalonia when it detained Beta Boop, and award Abalonia with damages for the harm caused to its national.

Map:

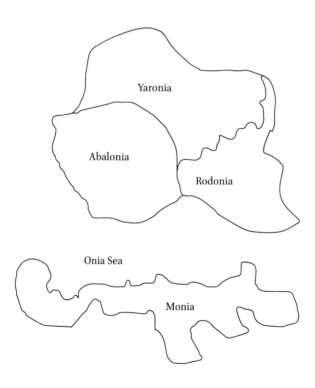

202 CHAPTER 6

C **Problem #3: *Arraticus v. Remonicus* (*Case Concerning the Tig Population, Species Endangerment, and the Law of the Sea*)**

INTERNATIONAL COURT OF JUSTICE
Case Concerning the Tig Population, Species Endangerment, and the Law of the Sea

THE ARRATICUS FEDERATION
(Applicant)

v.

THE REPUBLIC OF REMONICUS
(Respondent)

MOOT COURT PROBLEM

1. The Arraticus Federation (hereinafter Arraticus) and the Republic of Remonicus (hereinafter Remonicus) are located on one large island in the Vengan Sea. The center of the island consists of a jungle with hundreds of canals meandering across the Arraticus and Remonicus border and out to the Vengan Sea. In addition to Arraticus and Remonicus, the other island nations of the Vengan Sea are Fiaticus, Haticus, Norticus, and Watticus.

2. The Tig, an indigenous population, reside on all six nations. Many of the Tig prefer to live in treehouses in smaller Tig-oriented communities, away from urban centers and deep in the jungles of the islands. The Grupo Infamilie Tig (GIT) is a network that operates on all island nations in the Vengan Sea to promote the health and welfare of the Tig community. For over 80 years, the GIT has run hospitals, schools, and communal tree houses that serve the Tig community exclusively.

3. Arraticus, which covers 75% of the island and has a population of approximately 10 million people, is a regional power, particularly in environmental conservation. Ecotourism accounts for 10% of its GDP. Most citizens of Arraticus are of Aticus descent (over 80% of the population), and a minority of 15% of the population identifies as Tig.

4. Remonicus has a population of approximately 2 million people (70% identifying as Tig, 10% as Aticus, and 20% mixed Tig-Aticus), covering the remaining 25% of the island.

5. The Arraticus Federation and the Republic of Remonicus are Members of the United Nations and Parties to the ICJ Statute. Under Article 36(2) of

BRINGING THE COURT TO THE CLASSROOM 203

the ICJ Statute, Remonicus has recognized the compulsory jurisdiction of the ICJ but Arraticus has not.

6. Arraticus and Remonicus are both Parties to the 1969 Vienna Convention on the Law of Treaties and the 1963 Vienna Convention on Consular Relations.

7. Arraticus and Remonicus are also Parties to the Convention on Biological Diversity (CBD) and the 1951 Refugee Convention.

8. Arraticus is a Party to the 1982 United Nations Convention on the Law of the Sea (UNCLOS). Remonicus has signed but not ratified the UNCLOS.

9. Arraticus and Remonicus, along with Fiaticus, Haticus, Norticus, and Watticus, are parties to the Tig Cultural Protection Treaty (TCPT). Article 17 of the Treaty recognizes the importance of arboreal life to the Tig community, and obligates parties to ensure that all Tig families have access to trees of a proper height and size to build the traditional Tig treehouse, which usually spans across three trees.

10. Over the past thirty years, in an effort to promote environmental conservation efforts, Arraticus expanded its government-protected areas in the jungle, often encroaching upon Tig treehouse communities and, occasionally, relocating some Tig communities to urban parks and forested spaces. These urban parks usually contained tall trees surrounding soccer pitches or community pools. When relocated to these areas, the Tig found themselves compelled to live in smaller areas and build their homes in younger trees, which provided less stability for the Tig treehouse structures.

11. As Arraticus actions continued to affect the Tig living in Arraticus, a separate wing of GIT sought to slow down this encroachment. The GIT Army in Arraticus (GIT-AA) began to hijack Arraticus boats in the canals, stealing their goods, holding Arraticus citizens hostage, and generally creating chaos along the canals.

12. GIT-AA also allegedly set fire to the Puka Park in the capital of Arraticus. Though it contains some of the oldest, tallest trees, Puka Park is one of the only urban parks the Arraticus government did not relocate Tig to.

13. Due to the large population of Tig in Remonicus, the government has traditionally been supportive with GIT, providing funding and other contributions to the hospitals, schools, and shelters GIT developed across Remonicus. Many government officials in Remonicus are also active volunteers with GIT.

14. The Remonicus government provides GIT with a $10 million stipend every year towards its activities in Remonicus. This year, half of all monies received by GIT were channeled to GIT-AA, allowing the militant wing

204   CHAPTER 6

to acquire several speedboats for its activities against Arraticus along the canals.

15. As the presence of GIT-AA increased on the canal, the Environmental Ministry of Arraticus announced a rapid decline of the Blue Bellied Frog, an endangered species. Arraticus, in a diplomatic letter to Remonicus, requested that the protection of biodiversity in the canals that traverse the borders of the two countries be ensured in accordance with Remonicus' obligations under the CBD. Remonicus replied that it had not recorded a decline in the Blue Bellied Frog population in Remonicus and, therefore, was not in violation of the CBD.

16. Arraticus, in an effort to stem the presence of GIT-AA, decided to install a few low-level dams in certain canals with the intent to stop the GIT-AA speedboats. The location of some of these dams impeded the ability of large catfish to navigate the canals between Arraticus and Remonicus, essentially retaining the catfish in the Arraticus canals to the detriment of Remonicus citizens living off the previously abundant catfish in the Remonicus canals.

17. Most recently, on August 1, Arraticus dismantled a Tig community along the banks of the Swyzee canal. Sixty-Seven Tigs fled just over the border to Remonicus. Due to recent flooding in the canals, however, the nearest GIT-sponsored shelter was already full with local Tig from Remonicus. An Arraticus fisherman and active supporter of GIT, Kit Olman, agreed to take the Tigs from Swyzee as refugees to an open GIT shelter on Fiaticus.

18. Kit and the Tigs from Swyzee decided to navigate via a narrow sea passage between Arraticus and an underwater volcano chain to reach Fiaticus, rather than proceed up the Western coast and around the entire island (which would have added seven days to the journey) or proceed along the southern side of the volcanic chain (which would add an extra three days to the journey). This passage tends to be used for bringing goods originating from Haticus and Remonicus to the other islands in the Vengan Sea. Near Arraticus, the boat was intercepted by Captain Pax and the LMS Mool of the Arraticus Navy. Although Captain Pax ultimately determined the members aboard were not members of GIT-AA, he refused to let the ship continue through the passage, sending Kit and the Tigs from Swyzee back to Remonicus.

19. Arraticus requests the Court adjudge and declare:
    a. Remonicus violated international law through its involvement with GIT-AA, an organized armed group; and
    b. By failing to cooperate with Arraticus for the protection of the Blue Bellied Frogs suffering from Remonicus' involvement with GIT-AA and

by damaging biodiversity in the canals Remonicus violated Article 5 of the CBD and international environmental law.

20. Remonicus asks the Court for an order recognizing:
   a. Arraticus violated UNCLOS by prohibiting Kit's ship to navigate the canal between Arraticus and the underwater volcano chain.
   b. Arraticus violated Article 23 of the 1951 Refugee Convention when it returned the Tig population aboard Kit's ship to Remonicus.
   c. Arraticus violated Article 17 of the TCPT when it failed to provide proper arboreal habitats for relocated Tigs.

Map:

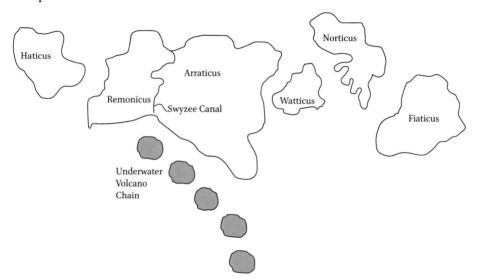

CHAPTER 7

Teaching the International Court of Justice

The International Court of Justice is usually taught via the prism of its case law, with little attention paid to the institution itself. The reasons are manifold: the procedural aspects might appear dry and difficult to teach, newer courts and tribunals might seem more attractive and relevant to the younger generation, the breadth of international law makes it difficult to cover the ICJ in real depth in undergraduate classes, and the absence of engaging material on the Court itself is lacking. Much of the scholarly literature on the Court is designed for legal experts or practitioners representing states before the Courts. Teachers have few interactive and accessible platforms to build on.

This book seeks to fill this void, at least partially, by providing an interactive, engaging, and ready-made platform for teachers and students. This chapter takes this approach a step further by suggesting model syllabi that can be adapted to undergraduate and graduate classes, for law students and non-law students. The model syllabi are formulated with these audiences in mind, in the aim of increasing their understanding of the Court's work and its role in the international order. Dozens of syllabi and additional resources have been reviewed, compared, and integrated. What follows is purely suggestive and teachers should of course adapt the proposed syllabi to their own teaching style, needs, and methods! The material below should therefore be used in combination with the remainder of this book, which includes plenty of additional resources and suggested themes for discussion.

A   The ICJ for Law Students

1   *Public International Law Course, 2 Credits*
In a two-credit course on public international law, teachers need to cover a lot of material in just two hours a week. For this reason, they may not want to devote a full session to the ICJ. The focus generally turns to the case law of the ICJ and its contribution to international law (for example on the use of force, diplomatic protection or state responsibility), accompanied by a short introduction (typically as part of the session on peaceful dispute settlement) on the Court. Students become acquainted with the Court as the main judicial organ of the UN but may not grasp the extent of its relationship with states and other UN organs, or the unique nature of its judicial function.

© KONINKLIJKE BRILL NV, LEIDEN, 2020 | DOI:10.1163/9789004226968_009

Therefore, a lesson that touches briefly on the Court's history and provides an overview of the Court's two heads of competence – contentious and advisory – with an explanation of their respective functions, is recommended. Instructors may emphasize the Court's influence on state behavior, the relationship between politics and law at the ICJ, the development of international law, or the peaceful settlement of disputes.

This session can be divided into three main parts:

(1) A short introduction of the Court and its history (the clip below can be used as the starting point for the discussion, and is perhaps best watched by students ahead of time in light of its length);

(2) Contentious and advisory jurisdiction, illustrated by an example of each (contemporary or not), and an emphasis on the differences between the two procedures; and

(3) A discussion of the role of the Court in the international order and/or an assessment of its record (this can be done in the form of a discussion at the end of class).

Reading material:
– In this book, Chapters 1, 2, and 3 (or parts thereof).
– Clip on the International Court of Justice, available at https://www.icj-cij .org/public/files/multimedia-galleries/icj/v_icj_en.mp4.
– UN Charter, Articles 7 and 92.
– ICJ Statute, Articles 1, 13, 34–37, 41, 59, 65–66.
– On the importance of jurisdiction and propriety in advisory proceedings: *Legal Consequences of the Construction of a Wall in the Occupied Palestinian Territory*, Advisory Opinion (2004), paras. 36–65.
– On compulsory jurisdiction: here are a couple of suggestions that can easily trigger a discussion of consensual jurisdiction conferred via treaty and optional declaration clauses, and an explanation of how the Court makes the determination of whether it has jurisdiction to hear a case:
  – *Obligations concerning Negotiations relating to Cessation of the Nuclear Arms Race and to Nuclear Disarmament* (Marshall Islands v. United Kingdom), Judgment (2016), paras. 26–58.
  – *Whaling in the Antarctic* (Australia v. Japan), Judgment (2014), paras. 30–41.
  – *Case Concerning Oil Platforms* (Iran v. United States), Judgment (1996), paras. 9–53.

Discussion questions:
– Is the ICJ an essential international institution? How does the ICJ contribute to the development of international law, the enforcement of international norms, the peaceful resolution of disputes?

208   CHAPTER 7

- Should non-states be able to bring cases before the ICJ? This may include a discussion of *Relocation of the United States Embassy to Jerusalem* (Palestine v. United States of America) (under consideration by the Court at the time of writing).
- How important is advisory jurisdiction to the Court's judicial function?

2   *Public International Law Course, 4 Credits*

In a four-credit international law course, instructors have more time and should be able to devote two sessions to the International Court of Justice. The first lesson should present a brief history of the Court and its two types of jurisdiction (with an emphasis on the various methods used to confer jurisdiction on the Court). The second lesson should focus on the various roles played by the Court, the nature of the international legal system, and the ICJ's constituency – which expanded from 51 to 193 UN member states since 1945. Depending on the instructor's preference, the second lesson might instead include a short moot court exercise (see *supra* Chapter 6 for examples of moot court problems) designed to expose students to international adjudication in an interactive and engaging way.

Lesson 1 – The Court and Its Jurisdiction

This lesson's overall objective is to introduce the Court, briefly relate to its historical roots, explore its basic structure and modes of operation (contentious and advisory), explain how states may confer jurisdiction on the Court, and analyze the Court's approach to jurisdiction in its case law. The session may start with a viewing of the official clip on the International Court of Justice (students also watch the clip at home and answer some basic questions as a preparation for class).

Reading material:

- In this book, Chapter 1, 2 and 3. Chapter 2(C)(2)(ii) includes an exercise on optional clause declarations that can easily be weaved into this class.
- Clip on the International Court of Justice, available at https://www.icj-cij .org/public/files/multimedia-galleries/icj/v_icj_en.mp4. *See also* ICJ Virtual Tour, available at https://www.icj-cij.org/public/files/multimedia-galleries/ icj/v_virt_en.mp4.
- UN Charter, Articles 7 and 92.
- ICJ Statute, Articles 1, 13, 34–37, 41, 59, 65–66.
- On the centrality of the principle of consent in ICJ jurisdiction: *Military and Paramilitary Activities in and Against Nicaragua* (Nicaragua v. United States of America), Jurisdiction of the Court and Admissibility of the Application (1984), paras. 13–23, 34–36, 59–67, 109–111.

TEACHING THE INTERNATIONAL COURT OF JUSTICE

– On the Court's interpretation of its own jurisdiction: *Case Concerning Oil Platforms* (Iran v. United States), Judgment (1996), paras. 9–53.
– On propriety and jurisdiction in advisory proceedings: *Legal Consequences of the Construction of a Wall in the Occupied Palestinian Territory*, Advisory Opinion (2004), paras. 36–65.

Discussion questions:

– How stringently does the Court interpret the principle of consensual jurisdiction? Could international adjudication and the peaceful settlement of disputes make do with this principle? How would it affect the Court and its activity?
– What role does the ICJ play in the international system? Given the growing role of non-state actors in the international arena, can the ICJ continue to be relevant by catering only to states? (If the instructor wishes to emphasize the state/non-state dichotomy before the ICJ, relevant sections of Chapter 4 can be assigned as reading material, or some of the resources referred therein as "further reading").

Lesson 2 – The Role(s) of the Court (or moot court exercise, as noted above) In this lesson, students uncover the role played by the Court in developing international law (with a focus on law-making), enforcing international law (with a focus on binding decisions and compliance), and resolving disputes (with a focus on maintaining international peace and security). Alternatively, the class could be built around the structure of Chapter 4 and analyze the relationship of the Court with (1) international courts and tribunals, (2) national courts, (3) academia, and (4) non-state actors.

Regardless of the direction chosen by the instructor, this class offers an opportunity to examine the influence of political matters on the Court's business, including on the decision to bring a dispute before the Court and accept its outcome, the election of judges, and the appointment of judges *ad hoc*. The class can conclude with a discussion of how the Court deals with contemporary crises, depending on what those might be at the time of teaching.

This class lends itself well to the analysis of scholarly writings on the Court, as the suggestions below indicate.

Reading material:

– In this book, Introduction, Chapters 4 and 5, Conclusion.
– On compliance and effectiveness of ICJ decisions: Colter Paulson, *Compliance with Final Judgements of the International Court of Justice since 1987*, 98 AM. J. INT'L L. 434 (2004).
– On ICJ activity and an assessment of the Court's achievements: *Speech by H.E. Mr. Ronny Abraham, President of the International Court of Justice, at the 72nd Session of the United Nations General Assembly* (2017).

- Students may compare this speech to older ones (for example, *Speech by former ICJ President Mohammed Bedjaoui* from 1994).
- On the election and the bias of judges of the Court: Chiara Giorgetti, *The Challenge and Recusal of Judges of the International Court of Justice, in* Challenges and Recusals of Judges and Arbitrators in International Courts and Tribunals 3 (Chiara Giorgetti ed., 2015).
- On political considerations and international courts: Tom Ginsburg, *Political Constraints on International Courts, in* The Oxford Handbook of International Adjudication 483 (Cesare P.R. Romano, Karen J. Alter and Yuval Shany eds., 2013).
- On the role of the ICJ, Eric Posner, *The Decline of the International Court of Justice* 1–38 (John M. Olin Program in Law and Econ., Working Paper No. 233, 2004).

Discussion questions:
- How does the Court view its various responsibilities?
- How do states make use of the Court (mostly relevant to Chapter 5)?
- What role does the Court fulfill in the broader international community (mostly relevant to Chapter 4)?
- Has the Court's importance declined (particularly in light of the creation of other international courts and tribunals)?
- Do other international and domestic courts face similar political pressures?

B   The ICJ for International Relations/Political Science Students

Teaching the ICJ to international relations and political science students is no less important. This book certainly encourages it. In addition to what is already included in the book, IR teachers might want to place additional emphasis on the role of the International Court of Justice in international politics, diplomacy, and decision-making. The Court's judges, and even agents appearing before them, may be influenced by international politics, with inadvertent (or not) consequences on the nature of the Court. Students can be prompted to reflect upon the desirability or inevitability of this political context. The relationship between law and politics in the international order can also be explored via the relationship between the Court and the UN Security Council, given the latter's responsibility to maintain international peace and security. Keeping this in mind, much of the recommendations included in Section I (a) above can be useful here, and can be taught in one or two sessions depending on the teacher's needs.

Reading material:

– Clip on the International Court of Justice (students may be asked to watch at home and answer some questions as a preparation for class), available at https://www.icj-cij.org/public/files/multimedia-galleries/icj/v_icj_en.mp4.
– In this book, Introduction, Chapter 1 and 2 (sections A and B) to provide background on history and the principle of compulsory jurisdiction (which offers ample opportunity to discuss the political undercurrents). Chapters 4 and 5 (particularly the data relating to the permanent members of the Security Council) could be assigned in the event the teacher is holding a second session on the ICJ. Chapter 3(C) should be assigned if the teacher is planning to discuss the relationship between the ICJ and the Security Council.
– UN Charter, Articles 7 and 92.
– On the debate between the effectiveness and compliance of ICJ decisions, compare: Eric A. Posner and John C. Yoo, *Judicial Independence in International Tribunals* 93 CAL. L. REV. 12–27, 34–40 (2005) with Laurence R. Helfer and Anne-Marie Slaughter, *Why States Create International Tribunals: A Response to Professors Posner and Yoo,* 93 CAL. L. REV. 899, 942–954 (2005).
– Anne-Marie Slaughter, *International Law and International Relations Theory: A Dual Agenda,* 87 AM. J. INT'L L. 205 (1993).
– Mark Pollack, *Political Science and International Adjudication, in* The Oxford Handbook of International Adjudication 357 (Cesare P.R. Romano, Karen J. Alter and Yuval Shany eds.).
– Tom Ginsburg, *Political Constraints on International Courts, in* The Oxford Handbook of International Adjudication 483 (Cesare P.R. Romano, Karen J. Alter and Yuval Shany eds., 2013).
– Karen J. Alter, *The Multiple Roles of International Courts and Tribunals: Enforcement, Dispute Settlement, Constitutional and Administrative Review,* (2012). *Faculty Working Papers.* Paper 212.
– On the respective roles and the relationship between the ICJ and the United Nations Security Council: Kathleen Renee Cronin-Furman, *The International Court of Justice and the United Nations Security Council: Rethinking a Complicated Relationship,* 106 COLUM. L. REV. 435 (2006).

Discussion questions:

– How strong are political pressures and do they really affect the Court's role?
– Is political influence on the Court good, bad, or inevitable?
– How can political influence on the International Court of Justice be mitigated, if at all?

C   A Full Course on the International Court of Justice, 2 Credits

The objective of this book is to make the Court more accessible to teachers and students alike, while keeping to the high standard and unparalleled scholarship of the late Shabtai Rosenne. A full course on the ICJ embodies, in many ways, the ultimate realization of this book's aims. The book as a whole can serve as a support for teaching such a course, with lessons structured around the Court's relationship with various actors: states, the UN system, national and international courts, academia, non-state actors, etc. The book could also be used to build a more traditional syllabus. Either way a full course on the ICJ should also include a moot exercise (I would recommend the longer one, which takes place over two sessions – as explained in Chapter 6). The suggested syllabus below includes twelve lessons. Additional lessons could expand on the Court's case law or the contribution of such case law to international law-making, depending on the teacher's preference and the institution's requirements.

Lesson 1 – The Court and Its Predecessor

The opening lesson should provide the students with a general overview of the Court's history as a baseline for the rest of the course. This lesson should relate the march towards the establishment of a mechanism for the adjudication of international disputes, the breakthrough embodied by the creation of the Permanent Court of International Justice, and its replacement with the ICJ with the demise of the League of Nations and the birth of the United Nations. The class should also explain the evolving position of the ICJ from the sole international judicial body to one of many regional and international courts and tribunals (how the ICJ differs from the ICC, the ICTY, the ECJ, the ECHR, and the Inter-American Court of Human Rights) and how this affects the study and role of the Court. At the end of this class, students should feel comfortable explaining the historical underpinnings of the ICJ, the continuity between the PCIJ and the ICJ, and the specificity of the ICJ as compared to other international courts.

Reading material:
- In this book, Introduction and Chapter 1.
- For a basic overview of the ICJ, watch this clip (https://www.icj-cij.org/public/files/multimedia-galleries/icj/v_icj_en.mp4) and read the history of the ICJ, available at http://www.icj-cij.org/en/history.
- UN Charter, Articles 7 and 92.
- On the general development of the Court over the past fifty years: Robert Y. Jennings, *The International Court of Justice after Fifty Years*, 89 AM. J. INT'L L. 493 (1995).

TEACHING THE INTERNATIONAL COURT OF JUSTICE

- On the first generation of international adjudication (PCA, PCIJ & ICJ): Gary Born, *A New Generation of International Adjudication*, 61 DUKE L.J. 791 (2012).
- Dapo Akande, *ICJ Press Releases Distinguish the ICJ from other International Tribunals*, EJIL Talk! (Dec. 27, 2011).

Discussion questions:

– What are the key differences between the PCIJ, the ICJ, and newer international courts and tribunals?
– How did international arbitration lead to the development of international adjudication?
– Would an ICJ established outside the UN system have credibility? What are the advantages and disadvantages of the ICJ's connection to the UN?

Lessons 2 and 3 – The ICJ and States: Contentious Jurisdiction

Lessons 2 and 3 explore the relationship between the Court and states via the principle of consent and contentious jurisdiction, which enable the Court to settle legal disputes between two sovereign states in accordance with international law. In addition to an overview of contentious jurisdiction, the readings and in-class exercises help students grasp the different methods of conferring jurisdiction on the Court and their respective advantages and disadvantages. The study of a few cases teaches the students how the Court analyzes the validity of various sources of jurisdiction and determines whether it has jurisdiction in a given case. At the end of this class, students should feel comfortable discussing compulsory jurisdiction as the main mode of interaction between the Court and states. Lesson 3 can either focus on the cases themselves or address some of the criticism of the principle of consensual jurisdiction and more advanced sources (see below for some examples). This might also be a good opportunity to expose international law students to some of the IR literature on dispute settlement.

   Reading material:

– In this book, Chapter 2, Sections A, B, C, and D.
– ICJ Statute, Article 36 and *How the Court Works*, available at https://www .icj-cij.org/en/how-the-court-works.
– For an analysis of bases of jurisdiction and a discussion of whether the Court has jurisdiction to handle a case, consider the exercise included in Chapter 2(C)(2)(ii) on optional clause declarations which can be done in class; as well as the following cases (see *supra* n.1):
  – *Obligations concerning Negotiations relating to Cessation of the Nuclear Arms Race and to Nuclear Disarmament* (Marshall Islands v. United Kingdom), Judgment (2016), paras. 26–58;
  – *Whaling in the Antarctic* (Australia v. Japan), Judgment (2014), paras. 30–41;

214 CHAPTER 7

- *Application of the Convention on the Prevention and Punishment of the Crime of Genocide* (Bosnia and Herzegovina v. Serbia and Montenegro), Judgment (2007), paras. 80–113; 121–141;
- *Case Concerning Oil Platforms* (Iran v. United States), Judgment (1996), paras. 9–53;
- *Military and Paramilitary Activities in and Against Nicaragua* (Nicaragua v. United States of America), Jurisdiction of the Court and Admissibility of the Application (1984), paras. 13–23, 34–36, 59–67, 109–111.
- For a more philosophical take on the principle of consent: Matthew Lister, *The Legitimating Role of Consent in International Law*, 11 CHI. J. INT'L L 663 (2011).
- On why some states accept ICJ jurisdiction more readily than other states: Emilia Powell and Sara Mitchell, *The International Court of Justice and the World's Three Legal Systems*, 69 J. of Pol. 397 (2007).
- For a cynical view of compulsory jurisdiction: Shigeru Oda, *The Compulsory Jurisdiction of the International Court of Justice: A Myth?: A Statistical Analysis of Contentious Cases* 49 Int'l & Comp. L. Quarterly 251 (2000).
- On forum prorogatum before the ICJ: *Case Concerning Certain Questions of Mutual Assistance in Criminal Matters* (Djibouti v. France), Judgment (2004), paras. 60–64; and Sienho Yee, *Forum Prorogatum and the Advisory Proceedings of the International Court*, 95 Am. J. Int'l L. 381 (2001).

Discussion questions:

- Why did states decide not to endow the Court with automatic jurisdiction?
- Who determines whether the Court has jurisdiction to settle a given dispute?
- If you were advising a state on ICJ-related matters, what course of action would you recommend with regard to the acceptance of the Court's jurisdiction in a multi-lateral treaty? In an optional clause declaration?
- What function does the principle of consent serve with regard to the protection of state sovereignty?
- How much significance does the Court afford to matters of jurisdiction? Why?

Lesson 4 – How the Court Works

In the fourth lesson, the discussion shifts to more practical matters. It should, first and foremost, introduce the students to the inner workings of the Court. *How A Case is Tried*, an interactive presentation complete with pictures of some of the ICJ's most famous cases and opinions, allows for a dynamic depiction of how cases proceed before the Court from the time an application is submitted to deliberations and the public reading of the judgment. Teachers may request this unique and comprehensive teaching tool at worldcourt@brill.com. It can be used to explain the various steps to the students. Alternatively, teachers can ask students to prepare the timeline of an existing case based on the steps described in the presentation and using material available on the Court's website. Either way, students should understand how cases proceed before the Court, and become familiar with terms such as agents, memorials, counter-memorials, time limits, and incompatibilities.

This lesson can also include a discussion of the role, selection, and activity of ICJ judges. It can begin with the requirements of the Statute (Articles 2–21; and Article 31 for *ad hoc* judges), proceed to an explanation of issues of representation on the bench (geographical and gender-based) and the restrictions inherent to the judicial function, and conclude with the unique status reserved to the five permanent members of the UN Security Council, for example. A discussion of judicial activism might also be a good fit here.

Reading material:
– In this book, Chapter 2, Section D.
– On ICJ judges generally: Chiara Giorgetti, *The Challenge and Recusal of Judges of the International Court of Justice, in* Challenges and Recusals of Judges and Arbitrators in International Courts and Tribunals 3 (Chiara Giorgetti ed., 2015); Nienke Grossman, *The Normative Legitimacy of International Courts,* 86 Temp. L. Rev. 61 106 (2013); and Eric Posner and Miguel F.P. de Figueiredo, *Is the International Court of Justice Biased?* (Coase-Sandor Working Paper Series in Law and Econ., Working Paper No. 234, 2004).
– On the presence on the bench of judges of the nationality of the five permanent members of the Security Council, see Chapters 3 and 5 in this book; and Arun M. Sukumar, *The Significance of Dalveer Bhandari's, and India's, Recent Election to the ICJ*, Lawfare (Dec. 13, 2017).
– On the ability of ICJ judges to engage in extrajudicial activities such as serving as arbitrators in inter-state or investor-state disputes: Articles 16–17 of the Statute; and *Speech by H.R.MR. Abdulqawi A. Yusuf, President of the International Court of Justice, on the occasion of the twenty-third session of the United Nations General Assembly* (25 Oct., 2018).
– On gender-balance at the ICJ: Nienke Grossman, *Sex on the Bench: Do Women Judges Matter for the Legitimacy of International Courts*, 12 Chi. J. Int'l L. 647 (2012); Gleider Hernandez, *Impartiality and Bias at the International Court of Justice*, 1 *Cambridge J. Int'l & Comp. L.* 183 (2012); and Ruth Mackenzie, Kate Malleson, Penny Martin, and Philippe Sands, Selecting International Judges: Principle, Process, and Politics (OUP, 2010), at 47 and 161–65.
– On judicial activism at the ICJ: H.E. Judge Pieter Kooijmans, *The ICJ in the 21st Century: Judicial Restraint, Judicial Activism, or Proactive Judicial Policy*, 56 Int'l & Comp. L.Q. 741 (2007); and Fuad Zarbiyev, *Judicial Activism in*

216   CHAPTER 7

International Law – A Conceptual Framework for Analysis, J. Int'l Dispute Settlement 1 (2012).

Discussion questions:
- Do you find the procedure at the ICJ easy or complex to navigate? Should it be easier or more complicated? Why or why not?
- Should contentious jurisdiction remain a forum exclusively reserved to states or should non-state actors (like intergovernmental organizations or multi-national corporations) be able to access the Court as well?
- How do you reconcile the importance of geographic distribution and the appointment of judges *ad hoc*, on one hand, with Article 2 of the Statute that requires that the Court be composed "of a body of independent judges", on the other hand? Compare this situation with that of domestic judges. Are ICJ judges more likely to be biased than ICJ judges? Is it reasonable to expect judges – at the ICJ or elsewhere – to be unbiased?
- How would an increased presence of women on the Court affect the Court's decisions or decision-making process, if at all?

Lessons 5 and 6 – The Court and the United Nations: Advisory Jurisdiction
Switching to the Court's other type of jurisdiction, these two lessons examine the history of advisory jurisdiction (how it was carried over from the PCIJ) and its substance (including the difference between jurisdiction and propriety). The first lesson analyzes the unique features and inherently more flexible nature of the Court's advisory jurisdiction. At the end of this class, students should feel comfortable explaining nature of advisory jurisdiction and contrasting it with contentious jurisdiction.

In the second lesson, the discussion goes beyond the nature of advisory jurisdiction to consider its impact on the authority of the Court, the UN, and international law. This lesson can be supplemented with a discussion of how the Court's advisory jurisdiction influenced other courts that have embraced this unique function (such as the Inter-American Court of Human Rights and the European Court of Human Rights). Further insights can be gained from an analysis of the data presented in Chapter 5, which sheds light on how states view the advisory function and their patterns of behavior in advisory proceedings.

Reading material:
- In this book, Chapters 3 and 5 (Section A(5)).
- UN Charter, Article 94; ICJ Statute, Article 65.
- For a general overview of advisory opinions: *How the Court Works*, available at http://www.icj-cij.org/en/how-the-court-works.

TEACHING THE INTERNATIONAL COURT OF JUSTICE

– For suggestions on how to increase the use of the Court's advisory jurisdiction: Stephen M. Schwebel, *Widening the Advisory Jurisdiction of the International Court of Justice without Amending Its Statute*, 33 Catholic U.L. Rev. 355, 360 (1984) (suggesting that right to request advisory opinions be extended to the United Nations Secretary-General). See also *Preventive diplomacy, peacemaking and peace-keeping, Report of the Secretary-General pursuant to the statement adopted by the Summit Meeting of the Security Council on 31 January 1992* (June 12, 1992), para. 38.

– For an analysis of whether the Court has jurisdiction and whether there might be compelling reasons to decline to answer the request for an advisory opinion, consider the following:
  – *Legal Consequences of the Construction of a Wall in the Occupied Palestinian Territory*, Advisory Opinion (2004), paras. 36–65;
  – *Legality of the Threat or Use of Nuclear Weapons*, Advisory Opinion (1996), paras. 10–19, 24–33, 37–50;
  – *Accordance with International Law of the Unilateral Declaration of Independence in Respect of Kosovo*, Advisory Opinion (2010) (which can also serve to initiate a discussion of the political aspects of advisory opinions).

– On the binding or non-binding nature of advisory opinions: Roberto Ago, *"Binding" Advisory Opinions of the International Court of Justice*, 85 AM. J. INT'L L. 439 (1991).

– On the use of advisory jurisdiction as a means of interacting with other courts: Tullio Treves, *Advisory Opinions of the International Court of Justice on Questions Raised by Other International Tribunals, in* MAX PLANCK U.N. Y.B. 215 (J.A. Frowein and R. Wolfrum eds., 2000).

Discussion questions:
– What important function(s) do advisory opinions fulfill?
– Should there be additional limits to the Court's advisory competence or, on the contrary, should its use be encouraged? In particular, should organizations outside of the UN system be able to request advisory opinions?
– Does the fact that advisory opinions are not binding reduce the Court to an inferior position? Should advisory opinions be binding? Why or why not?

Lesson 7 – The Role of the Court in Advancing Peace and Security

This session examines the Court's various roles – as a court of law, a law-making institution, an arbiter of states' disputes, and a guardian of international peace and security – and assesses its ability to perform those functions all at once.

Though it is helpful to discuss these various roles as an introductory matter, the session ultimately focusses on the impact of the Court's involvement in appeasing international tensions.

The class also explores the concept of compliance in the context of the ICJ: first, how compliance ought to be measured and its importance in assessing the Court's record, and, second, the inevitable challenge of ensuring compliance with the Court's judgments in a decentralized legal system dominated by sovereign states. This class may also address the relationship between the Court and the Security Council as two separate institutions in the UN system with overlapping influence, and the role of the Security Council in enforcing ICJ judgments. At the end of the class, students should feel comfortable explaining the various functions fulfilled by the Court and share personal opinions on their respective importance, achievements, and limitations. They should also understand the inherent weaknesses of the concept of compliance as a benchmark to assess the Court's record, and suggest alternative methods for measuring the Court's effectiveness.

Reading material:
- In this book, Chapter 5(C).
- UN Charter, Article 94.
- On compliance and effectiveness of ICJ decisions: Colter Paulson, *Compliance with Final Judgements of the International Court of Justice since 1987*, 98 AM. J. INT'L L. 434 (2004).
- On the compliance of ICJ decisions by states, or lack thereof: Aloysius P. Llamzon, *Jurisdiction and Compliance in Recent Decisions of the International Court of Justice*, 18 European Journal of International Law 815 (2008).
- On the interaction between the Court and the UN Security Council: Ken Roberts, *Second-Guessing the Security Council: The International Court of Justice and its Powers of Judicial Review*, 7 PACE INT'L. L. REV. 281 (1995); and Dapo Akande, *The International Court of Justice and the Security Council: Is There Room for Judicial Control of Decisions of the Political Organs of the United Nations?*, 46 Int'l & Comp. L.Q. 309 (1997).

Discussion questions:
- How does the issue of compliance impact the authority of the Court, if at all?
- What mechanisms can be put in place to ensure the enforcement of the Court's judgments?
- How can the decision-making process at the ICJ, and the decisions themselves promote compliance?

Lesson 8 – The Role of the Court in Developing International Law

One of the more disputed aspects of ICJ jurisprudence is whether the decisions of the Court amount to court of law judgments or equity determinations. How does the Court combine the application of legal principles with the development of international law? Decisions such as *Reparations for Injuries* and *Kosovo* (in the realm of advisory opinions), and *Maritime Dispute (Peru v. Chile)* or *Case Concerning Application of the Convention on the Prevention and Punishment of the Crime of Genocide* and *Case Concerning Avena and Other Mexican Nationals* (in contentious proceedings) can be contrasted to highlight the difference between win-win judgments and those that identify a clear "winner" and "loser". Students should reflect on how "win-win" outcomes affect the role and legitimacy of the Court.

Reading material:

- ICJ Statute, Article 38.
- On the concept of equity in international law: Francesco Francioni, *Equity in International Law*, Max Planck Encyclopedia of International Law (2013); and Shabtai Rosenne, *The Position of the International Court of Justice on the Foundations of the Principle of Equity in International Law*, in Forty Years International Court of Justice – Jurisdiction, Equity and Equality 85 (Bloed A.; van Dijk P., eds.) (1988).
- On the impact of ICJ decisions on international law, in general: Hersch Lauterpacht, The Development of International Law by the International Court 3–23 (1958).
- On equity in the jurisprudence of the ICJ: Prosper Weil, *L'Equité dans la Jurisprudence de la Cour Internationale de Justice*, in Essays in Honor of Robert Jennings, Fifty Years of the International Court of Justice (Vaughan Lowe and Malgosia Fitzmaurice, eds., 1996), at 121.
- On assessing the effectiveness of the Court: Laurence Boisson de Chazournes, *Testing the Effectiveness of the ICJ: The Nuclear Weapons Case*, 91 ASIL Proceedings (1997).
- On the legitimacy and authority of ICJ decisions considered attempts to provide "win-win" outcomes: Nienke Grossman, *Solomonic Judgments and the International Court of Justice*, in Legitimacy and International Courts 43 (Nienke Grossman, Harlan Grant Cohen, Andreas Follesdal and Geir Ullfstein eds., 2018).
- For an IR perspective, Krista E. Wiegand and Emilia Justyna Powell, *Past Experience, Quest for the Best Forum, and Peaceful Attempts to Resolve Territorial Disputes*, 55 Journal of Conflict Resolution 33 (2011).

Discussion questions:
- How has the ICJ helped develop international law? Where has the Court hindered or impeded the expansion of international law? Why would the Court do so?
- Does the ICJ decide in equity or in law?
- Can the various roles of the Court – settling disputes, developing international law, promoting peace and security, advising the UN – be reconciled?
- How does the perception of winning the case affect the likelihood of states to make use of the Court again in the future?

Lesson 9 – The Relationship of the ICJ with other International Courts and Tribunals

From the only international judicial body in 1945, the ICJ became one of many international courts and tribunals. This class focuses on the expansion of international adjudicatory mechanisms and the inevitable friction, as well as cooperation, between these courts. At the end of this class, students should be able to critically discuss the expansion of the international judicial system as well as the concept of fragmentation. If time allows, this class may also analyze the relationship between the Court and national courts.

Reading material:
- In this book, Chapter 4. If time allows, this class can also examine the relationship of the ICJ with national courts, academia, and/or non-state actors.
- On the proliferation of international courts: Anne-Marie Slaughter, *A Global Community of Courts*, 44 Harv. Int'l L. Rev. 191 (2007); Thomas Buergenthal, *Proliferation of International Courts and Tribunals: Is it Good or Bad?*, 14 Leiden J. Int'l L. 267 (2001); Pierre-Marie Dupuy, *The Danger of Fragmentation or Unification of the International Legal System and the International Court of Justice*, 31 Int'l L. & Pol. 791 (1999); Gerhard Hafner, *Pros and Cons Ensuing from Fragmentation of International Law*, 25 Mich. J. Int'l L. 849 (2004); and Firew Kebede Tiba, *What Caused the Multiplicity of International Courts and Tribunals?*, 10 Gonz. J. Int'l L. 202 (2007).
- On methods available to assess the effectiveness of the Court: Yuval Shany, *Assessing the Effectiveness of International Courts: A Goal Based Approach*, 106 Am. J. Int'l L. 225 (2012).
- For an IR perspective: Karen Alter, *The Multiple Roles of International Courts and Tribunals*, in Interdisciplinary Perspectives on International Law and International Relations: The State of the Art 345 (J. Dunoff and M. Pollack, eds., 2012).

Discussion questions:
- Is the international legal system truly "fragmented"?
- If fragmentation is real, what are the advantages and disadvantages of this phenomenon?
- What type of interaction does the ICJ have with other international courts and tribunals? Can you identify areas of competition in their respective jurisdictions? Is there anything akin to a hierarchy in the international judicial system?
- Are international courts effective mechanisms for international governance?
- Are domestic courts effective mechanisms for the enforcement of ICJ decisions?

Lesson 10 – A Need for Reform of the ICJ?

The ICJ has remained largely unchanged since its creation in 1945. The Rules of the Court were amended in 1972, but that does not really amount to a reform of the Court. Meanwhile, other organs of the UN have been reformed – such as the Commission on Human Rights, the UN Administrative Tribunal, and even the Security Council whose membership was expanded on two occasions. In this lesson, students should reflect upon these contrasted approaches. What would an ICJ reform look like? *First*, procedurally, what would be needed for the Statute to be amended? According to the ICJ Statute, an amendment of the Statute is akin to an amendment of the UN Charter. *Second*, why has such a reform not taken place? This can be interpreted either as a show of confidence – or mere indifference – for the Court.

Reading material:
- In this book, Chapter 5, Sections A, B, and Conclusion.
- Rules of the Court, available at https://www.icj-cij.org/en/rules.
- UN Charter, Articles 108 and 109; ICJ Statute, Articles 69 and 70.
- On the purpose of the Court's unique role in the changing international legal landscape: Joan E. Donoghue, *The Role of the World Court Today*, 47 Ga. L. Rev. 181 (2012).
- On a possible reform of the ICJ: *Reforming the United Nations: What About the International Court of Justice*, 5 Chinese J. Int'l L. 39 (2006). The recommendations of the International Law Association's American Branch Committee on Intergovernmental Settlement of Disputes for a potential reform of the ICJ are reproduced therein.

Discussion questions:
- What aspects of the ICJ are most susceptible to reform? What functions and features are enduring? What would need to change?

222   CHAPTER 7

– Are states satisfied with the Court? Has the Court succeeded in providing its
  services to an enlarged constituency?

Lessons 11 and 12 – Moot Court Exercise
The course ends with a very practical exercise, built on the model of the
Philip C. Jessup International Law Moot Court Competition. Its goal is to
expose students to international adjudication in an interactive and interesting
way. As the title of Chapter 6 indicates, it literally aims at bringing the ICJ into
the classroom. From personal experience, and the work involved in preparing
Chapter 6 certainly is a testament to that, setting up a moot court requires
a significant investment of time and resources. Teachers may not have the
time needed to prepare their own moot court. Hopefully this book will make
that easier.

The recommendation is to devote the two last lessons of the course to the
moot court exercise. Several moot court scenarios are offered in Chapter 6,
touching on different areas of international law to account for personal preferences, and are accompanied with a practical guidance on how to set up a
successful moot court. Most of the preparation will take place outside the
classroom as students research and draft their materials, but it is suggested
that at least one class include a discussion of the case and an overview of
the process. By taking the law (and the ICJ) out of the books, these last lessons will provide students with a hands-on approach to ICJ work and
invaluable insights into the complexities of international law and the inner
workings of the Court. The performance of the students may be graded by
the teacher.

Reading material:
– In this book, Chapter 6 (a facilitator's guide is available upon request from
  the Publisher at worldcourt@brill.com).
– ICJ Statute, available at http://www.icj-cij.org/en/statute.
– UN Charter, available at http://www.un.org/en/charter-united-nations/.
– Vienna Convention on the Law of Treaties, available at http://legal.un.org
  /ilc/texts/instruments/english/conventions/1_1_1969.pdf.
– On the importance of holding moot court exercises as an effective tech-
  nique of teaching international law in political science departments:
  Edward Collins and Martin Rogoff, *The Use of an Interscholastic Moot Court
  Competition in the Teaching of International Law*, 24 Pol. Sci. & Pol. 516 (1991).

It is hoped that the present chapter will facilitate teaching of the ICJ, and that
attention will be devoted to the institution and its workings, alongside its

jurisprudence. In addition to the suggested syllabi above, each chapter includes multiple references to the cases and doctrine (which appear in grey boxes), as well as recommendations for further reading. Teachers are encouraged to look through these as additional sources, use them in their frontal lectures, incorporate them in exam questions, and include them in their syllabi.

Index

Page numbers in *italic* refer to illustrations and figures. Page numbers followed by a *t* refer to tables.

academia
  and fragmentation of legal order   156
  ICJ's referencing of   143–146
  scholarly critiques of ICJ by   147–148
Accordance with International Law of the Unilateral Declaration of Independence in Respect of Kosovo advisory opinion   89, 147, 151
advisory opinions
  of African Court on Human and Peoples' Rights   115–116
  of ECHR   111–112
  of IACHR   113–115
  of ICJ. *see* advisory opinions of ICJ
advisory opinions of ICJ
  in general   80
  and advising on disputes   94–98
  compared to
    African Court on Human and Peoples' Rights   115–116
    ECHR   111–112
    IACHR   113–115
  and consent   96
  declining of   97–98
  function of
    development of international law   88–90
    facilitating UN activities   87
    protection of UN system   90–92
  limited use of   169
  list of   118–120t
  non-binding character of   84–85
  and non-members/international organizations   84–85
  request procedure for
    in general   81–83, 165, 187
    State participation in   168–170, *168*
    timelines for   108–110, 110t
  requests for
    by other UN organs   106
    by UNGA   105–108

    voting on   165–167, *167*
    scope of   80–81, *82*
advisory proceedings of ICJ
  in general   84, 165, 187
  State participation in   168–170, *168*
  timelines for   108–110, 110t
Aegean Sea Continental Shelf case   101n56
Aerial Incident at Lockerbie case   103–104
African Court on Human and Peoples' Rights   115–116
agorae   147
Albania *v.* UK, *Corfu Channel* case   101, 180–181
Alleged Violations of Sovereign Rights and Maritime Spaces in the Caribbean Sea case   131
American Convention on Human Rights   113
American Journal of International Law   147
Ammoun, Fouad   144
Amr, Mohamed Sameh M.   170
Ancient Greece   4–5
Application for Review of Judgment No. 333 of the United Nations Administrative Tribunal advisory opinion   108–109
Application of the Convention on the Prevention and Punishment of the Crime of Genocide case   125–126, 130
Application of the International Convention on the Elimination of All Forms of Racial Discrimination case   69–70, 144
arbitration. *see* international arbitration
Argentina *v.* Uruguay, *Pulp Mills on the River Uruguay* case   74, 125, 131
Argos   5
arguing, before ICJ   61–66
Armed Activities on the Territory of the Congo case   125
  and ICJ's jurisdiction   38–40
Arrest Warrant case   75, 137

A

Australia
- international law in 138
- *v.* Japan, *Whaling in the Antarctic* case 182–183

Avena case 33, 134–135, 147, 180

Azevedo, Philadelpho 27

B

Barcelona Traction case 33, 79

Bedjaoui, Mohammed 104

Beit Surik case 140

Belgium
- filling of preliminary objections by 175
- and ICJ's review of decisions of UNSC 102–103
- *v.* Congo, *Arrest Warrant* case 75, 137
- *v.* Senegal, *Questions Relating to the Obligation to Prosecute or Extradite* case 75
- *v.* Spain, *Barcelona Traction* case 33, 79

Bentham, Jeremy 7

Berman, Franklin 90

Bogdandy, Armin von 66

Bonafé, Beatrice 43

Bosnia *v.* Serbia & Montenegro, *Application of the Convention on the Prevention and Punishment of the Crime of Genocide* case 125–126, 130

Brazil 166

Breard case 75, 129, 134–135

Buergenthal, Thomas 39

C

Cambodia *v.* Thailand, *Temple of Preah Vihear* case 56, 76–77, 183–184

Cannizzaro, Enzo 43

Case Concerning Avena and Other Mexican Nationals 33, 134–135, 147, 180

Čelebići case 129–130

Central American Court of Justice 125

CERD. *see* International Convention on the Elimination of All Forms of Racial Discrimination

Certain Expense of the United Nations advisory opinion 88, 91–92

Certain Questions of Mutual Assistance in Criminal Matters case 59–61

Chad *v.* Libya 184

Chagos Archipelago Separation from Mauritius advisory opinion 89, 106

Charter of the United Nations
- adoption of 22
- on advisory opinions 94
- creation of 25
- on methods of dispute settlement 30
- on national courts 134
- on status of ICJ 26

China 167, 173, 188

Colombia
- *v.* Nicaragua, *Alleged Violations of Sovereign Rights and Maritime Spaces in the Caribbean Sea* case 131
- *v.* Peru, *Haya de la Torre* case 179–180

"A Comment on the Current Health of Advisory Opinions" (Higgins) 86

Commission on Human Rights on the Independence of Judges and Lawyers 84

Compatibility of Draft Legislation advisory opinion 114

competence-competence principle 37

compliance
- with judgement of ICJ
  - in general 178–179
  - appearance of 182–183
  - defining of 179–180
  - and legitimacy 183–184
  - for other reasons 181–182
  - and timing issue 180–181

compromissory clauses 48

Compulsory Arbitration of International Disputes (Cory) 8

compulsory jurisdiction
- and ICJ 27
- objections to 9
- and PCIJ 14–15

Compulsory Jurisdiction and Defiance in the World Court: A Comparison of the PCIJ and the ICJ (Scott & Csajko) 18

Conditions of Admission of a State to Membership in the United Nation advisory opinion 91

Congo
- *v.* Belgium, *Arrest Warrant* case 75, 137
- *v.* Rwanda, *Armed Activities on the Territory of the Congo* case 39–40
- *v.* Uganda, *Armed Activities on the Territory of the Congo* case 38–39, 125

INDEX

consent
  and advisory opinions   96
  and ICJ's jurisdiction   36–37, 37–40
  by implication   59–60
  principle of   35–36
context, interpretation of term   42, 43
Continued Presence of South Africa in Namibia
  advisory opinion   88, 92, 109
*Controlling Interlocutory Aspects of
  Proceedings in the International Court of
  Justice* (Rosenne)   72
Convention for the Pacific Settlement of
  International Disputes (1899)   9–10
Convention on Mutual Assistance in
  Criminal Matters (1986; France and
  Djibouti)   60
Convention on Privileges and Immunities of
  the United Nations   81n3
Convention on the Prevention and
  Punishment of the Crime of Genocide
  (1948)   48
Corfu Channel case   101, 180–181
Cory, Helen May   8
Costa Rica   114
courts. *see* international courts/tribunals;
  national courts
Couvreur, Philippe   23, 26, 102–103
Covenant of the League of Nations
  (1919)   12–13, 14, 25, 94
Csajko, Karen D.   18
Cuba   162, 168
Cumaraswamy, Dato Param   84
Czech Republic   167, 169

De Jure Belli ac Pacis (Grotius)   12
Democratic Republic of the Congo (DRC).
  see Congo
*The Development of International Law
  by the International Court of Justice*
  (Lauterpacht)   65
*Developments in Dispute Settlement
  Inter-State Arbitration Since 1945* (Gray &
  Kingsbury)   7
*Diplomatic Protection and the International
  Court of Justice* (Donoghue)   30–31
disagreements   17, 45–46
disputes   17, 46

Djibouti *v.* France, *Certain Questions
  of Mutual Assistance in Criminal
  Matters*   59–61
domestic law   135–141
Donoghue, Joan E.   30–31
DRC (Democratic Republic of the Congo).
  see Congo
Dumbarton Oaks Conference (1944)   21

Eastern Carelia advisory opinion   17, 87n20
ECHR. *see* European Court of Human Rights
effective control tests   126, 130
Eichmann case   136–137
El Salvador   174
Elaraby, Nabil   40
Electricity Company case   17
equality, principle of   61–63
Estonia, and ICJ, optional clause declaration
  of   53
Ethiopia *v.* Liberia, *South West Africa*
  cases   71, 88, 152n105
European Convention for the Peaceful
  Settlement of Disputes   49
European Convention on Human Rights and
  Fundamental Freedoms   111–112
European Court of Human Rights
  (ECHR)   111–112

forum prorogatum doctrine   59–61
forum shopping   127
*Fragmenting International Law through
  Compromissory Clauses? Some Remarks on
  the Decision of the ICJ in the Oil Platforms
  Case* (Cannizzaro & Bonafé)   43
framework agreements   51–52
France
  and ICJ
    in general   173
    advisory proceedings, voting
      on   166–167
    filling preliminary objections by   175
    optional clause declarations of   56,
      174
    as respondent   159
  v. Djibouti, *Certain Questions of Mutual
    Assistance in Criminal Matters*   59–61
  v. Turkey, *Lotus* case   36
Free Zones case   17

From the Consensual to the Compulsory Paradigm (Romano)   56–57

General Act for the Pacific Settlement of Disputes (1928)   49
Gent, Stephen E.   5
Georgia *v.* Russia, *Application of the International Convention on the Elimination of All Forms of Racial Discrimination*   69–70, 144
Germany
  and ICJ
    filling preliminary objections by   175
    optional clause declaration of   55
    v. Italy, *Jurisdictional Immunities of the State* case   137
    v. UK, *S.S. Wimbledon* case   14
    v. US, *LaGrand* case   75, 129, 134–135
Gray, Christine   7
Greece
  optional clause declaration of   54
  v. Turkey, *Aegean Sea Continental Shelf* case   101n56
Grotius, Hugo   12
Guatemala
  as non-appearing respondent   177
  v. Liechtenstein, *Nottebohm* case   144, 177
Guerrero, José Gustavo   23
Guggenheim, M.   144
Guillaume, Gilbert   127–128

Hafner, Gerhard   46
Hague Peace Conference (1899)   8–9
Harvard Law Review   147
Haya de la Torre case   179–180
Henkin, Louis   144
Herzegovina *v.* Serbia & Montenegro, *Application of the Convention on the Prevention and Punishment of the Crime of Genocide* case   125–126, 130
Higgins, Rosalyn   25
  on advisory opinions   86
  on consent   40
  on fragmentation of international law   125–126
  opinion of, in *Oil Platforms Case*   44
The History of the Peloponnesian War (Thucyclides)   5

Honduras   175
Huber, Max   13–14

IACHR. *see* Inter-American Court of Human Rights
ICC. *see* International Criminal Court
ICJ. *see* International Court of Justice
ICSID. *see* International Center for the Settlement of Investment Disputes
ICTY. *see* International Criminal Tribunal for the Former Yugoslavia
ILC. *see* International Law Commission
India
  and ICJ
    in general   187–188
    advisory proceedings, participation in   166, 169
    preliminary objections by   175
  and international law   139–140
"The Influence of Teaching of Publicists on the Development of International Law" (Sandesh)   146
Informal Inter-Allied Committee on the Future of the Permanent Court of International Justice   20–21
Inter-American Court of Human Rights (IACHR)   113–115, 129
international adjudication
  characteristics of   5
  early forms of   4–7
  ICJ's role within   30–31
  vs. international arbitration   5
  see also under specific courts
international arbitration
  as barrier against conflict   8
  characteristics of   5
  genesis of modern   5–7
  vs. international adjudication   5
  and PCA   9, 10–11
  principle of consent in   36
  process of   8
International Center for the Settlement of Investment Disputes (ICSID)   122
International Convention on the Elimination of All Forms of Racial Discrimination (CERD)   70
The International Court of Justice and the Effectiveness of International Law (Couvreur)   102–103

INDEX

229

International Court of Justice (ICJ)
  in general   2–3, 136
  activity by decade of   *20*
  admissibility to, of legal disputes   45–47
  advisory function of. *see* advisory
    opinions of ICJ
  annual report of   106
  arguing before   61–66
  assessment of
    in general   156–157
    advisory opinions, state
      participation   168–170, *168*
    advisory opinions, voting on
      165–167, *167*
    applicants   158–159, *158, 159, 160*
    compliance with   178–185
    intervention patterns   161–163
    non-use of   172–173
    optional clause declaration   163–165,
      164, 173–174
    preliminary objections   174–175, *174,
      175*
    respondents   159–160, *160, 161*, 176–178
  competence of   37, 42, 46
  composition of   23–24
    see also judges of ICJ; Registrars of ICJ
  as court of appeal   140–141
  and development of international
    law   65
  and equality, principle of   61–63
  establishment of   2
  and international organizations   31–32,
    33–35
  judgement of. *see* judgements of ICJ
  judges of. *see* judges of ICJ
  jurisdiction of. *see* jurisdiction of ICJ
  jurisprudence of, decisions of national
    courts in   135–138
  Practice Directions of   151–152
  premises of   *29, 58*
  press release of   132
  proceedings of
    in general   66–67
    advisory opinions. *see* advisory
      proceedings of ICJ
    preliminary objections   67–73, *67*
    provisional measures   73–77
  relationship of

    with academia   143–148, 156
    with ICTY   130–131
    with national courts. *see* national
      courts
    with non-state actors. *see* non-state
      actors
    with other courts and
      tribunals   121–123
    with States. *see* States
    with UN. *see* advisory opinions of ICJ
    with UNGA   105–108
    with UNSC   99–105
  role of   2, 30–31
  Rule of Court of. *see* Rules of Court (of ICJ)
  scholarly critiques of   147–148
  similarities between PCIJ and   18
  status of   25, 26, 27, 155–156
  Statute of. *see* Statute of the International
    Court of Justice
  teaching of
    courses overview   210–228
    see also moot court
  on UNGA resolutions   106–108
  and value of legal precedents   63–66
international courts/tribunals
  and ICJ   121–123
  proliferation of
    in general   122–123
    and absence of hierarchy   129–130
    and forum shopping   127
    and international law   124–132
    and variance in
      interpretation   127–128
International Criminal Court (ICC)   122, 125
International Criminal Tribunal for the
  Former Yugoslavia (ICTY)   122, 126, 129
International Labor Organization   150
international law
  and changing views on war   12
  development of
    and advisory opinions   88–90, 114
    ICJ's role in   65
    PCIJ's role in   13–14, 16–18
    and proliferation of courts and
      tribunals   124–132
    and teachings of publicists   146
  and domestic law   135–141
  fragmentation of

230 INDEX

international law (cont.)
    in general   124–132
    and loss of scholarly interests   156
    principle of consent in   36
International Law Commission (ILC)
    145–146
International League of the Rights of
    Man   152n105
*International Legal Argument in the
    Permanent Court of International Justice*
    (Spiermann)   17
international organizations   33–34, 149
International Status of South West Africa
    advisory opinion   152n105
International Tribunal for the Law of the Sea
    (ITLOS)   121–122
International Whaling Commission
    (IWC)   183
*Interpretation of Peace Treaties with
    Bulgaria, Hungary and Romania* advisory
    opinion   87, 97–98
intervention patterns   161–163
Iran
    Treaty of Amity with US   41–42
    v. US
        Oil Platforms case   37, 41–44, 48
        *United States Diplomatic and Consular
        Staff in Tehran* case   46–47, 75, 182
Islamic Conference   151
Israeli Supreme Court   140
Italy *v.* Germany, *Jurisdictional Immunities of
    the State* case   137
ITLOS. *see* International Tribunal for the Law
    of the Sea
IWC. *see* International Whaling Commission

Japan
    party to Statute of ICJ   32
    v. Australia, *Whaling in the Antarctic*
        case   182–183
Japanese Whale Research Program under
    Special Permit in the Antarctic
    (JARPA II)   182–183
Jay Treaty (1794; UK and US)   5–6
Jennings, Robert   17, 122
joint committees   5–6
judgements of ICJ   79
    compliance with

    in general   178–179
    appearance of   182–183
    defining of   179–180
    and legitimacy   183–184
    for other reasons   181–182
    and timing issue   180–181
judges of ICJ
    in general   23, *24*
    ad hoc   23, 24
    appointment of   107
    backgrounds of   143–144
    per state   *189*
    scholarly referencing by   144–145
jurisdiction of ICJ
    broadness of   35–36
    compulsory   27, 37, 44
    conferring of
        in general   47
        under *forum prorogatum*
            doctrine   59–61
        by optional clause declaration
            52–54, 58–59
        by treaties, after dispute arises
            50–54, *51*
        by treaties, before dispute
            arises   48–49
        by consent   36–44
*Jurisdiction of the International Court of
    Justice* (Xue)   177
Jurisdictional Immunities of the State
    case   137

Kingsbury, Benedict   7
Kooijmans, Pieter   40
Kosovo, and *Accordance with International
    Law of the Unilateral Declaration of
    Independence in Respect of Kosovo*
    advisory opinion   89, 147, 151

LaGrand case   75, 129, 134–135
Lauterpacht, Hersch   65
Lawmaking through Advisory Opinions?
    (Oellers-Frahm)   88
League of Arab States   151
League of Nations
    central political organs of   11–12n16
    Covenant of   12–13, 14, 25, 94
    creation of PCIJ by   2, 4, 13

INDEX

dissolvement of   24
establishment of   11
UN replacing of   22
Legal Consequences of the Construction of a Wall in the Occupied Palestinian Territory advisory opinion   84, 98, 140, 146, 151
legal precedents, value of   63–66
Legality of the Use by a State of Nuclear Weapons in Armed Conflict advisory opinion   108–109, 152n105
Liberia *v.* Ethiopia & South Africa, *South West Africa* cases   71, 88, 152n105
Libya
  v. Chad   184
  v. UK & US, *Aerial Incident at Lockerbie* case   103–104
Liechtenstein
  party to Statute of ICJ   32
  v. Guatemala, *Nottebohm* case   144, 177
Lockerbie bombing   103–104
Lotus case   36

Magritte, René   2–3
Mara'abe case   140
Mavrommatis case   17
Mexico
  optional clause declaration of   58–59
  v. US
    Avena case   33, 134–135, 147, 180
    Breard case   129
Milanović, Marko   130–131
Military and Paramilitary Activities in and against Nicaragua case
  compliance in   181–182
  effective control test in   126
  merits in   63
  provisional measures in   75, 76
  and UNSC   100, 101
  withdrawal optional clause declaration in   55–56
Montenegro *v.* Bosnia & Herzegovina, *Application of the Convention on the Prevention and Punishment of the Crime of Genocide* case   125–126, 130
Montreal Convention for the Suppression of Unlawful Acts against the Safety of Civil Aviation (1971)   103
Moore, John Norton   144
moot court

in general   190–191
oral pleadings phase
  addressing the court   194–195
  conclusion   195
  oral pleadings   193–194
  overview   193
  room setup   193–194
  timekeeper   194
problems   197–205
recap session   196
written pleadings phase
  judges' notes   192
  memorial   191–192
  overview   191

NAFTA. *see* North American Free Trade Agreement
Namibia. *see Continued Presence of South Africa in Namibia* advisory opinion; *South West Africa* cases
National Bank of Albania   181
national courts
  relationship with ICJ of
    in general   134
    complying with ICJ decisions   134–135
    decisions of ICJ in jurisprudence of national courts   138–141
    decisions of national courts in ICJ's jurisprudence   135–138
Nauru   32
Netherlands   169
neutral third party   5, 6
New Scientific Whale Research Program in the Antarctic Ocean (NEWREP-A)   183
Nicaragua
  and ICJ, as respondent   159
  v. Colombia, *Alleged Violations of Sovereign Rights and Maritime Spaces in the Caribbean Sea* case   131
  v. US, *Military and Paramilitary Activities in and against Nicaragua* case   37, 55–56, 75, 76, 100, 101, 126, 181–182
Nicolas II, Tsar of Russia   8–9
No Thanks, We Already Have Our Own Laws (Posner)   139
non-appearing respondents   176–178, *176*
non-legal disputes, *v.* legal disputes   45

232 INDEX

non-state actors
  and ICJ
    in general   31–32, 33–35, 148–149
    in advisory proceedings   150–152
    in contentious proceedings   149
  and PCIJ   150
North American Free Trade Agreement
  (NAFTA)   122
North Sea Continental Shelf case   144, 145
Norway   175
Nottebohm case   144, 177
Nuclear Tests cases   56
Nuclear Weapons advisory opinion   108–109,
  152n105

OAS. *see* Organization of American States
OAU. *see* Organization of African Unity
Oda, Shigeru   76
Oellers-Frahm, Karin   88
Oil Platforms Case   37, 41–44, 48
On the Functions of International Courts: An
  Appraisal in Light of Their Burgeoning
  Public Authority (Bogdandy &
  Venzke)   66
optional clause declaration
  in general   15–16, 52–53, 55–56, 58–59
  assessment of   163–165, *164*
  limited use of   56–57
  States not making use of   173–174
  temporal reservation to   53
  withdrawal of   55–56
Organization of African Unity (OAU)
  115–116
Organization of American States (OAS)   49,
  113–114
overall control tests   126, 130
Owada, Hisashi   40

Pakistan   175
Palestine
  and *Legal Consequences of the*
    Construction of a Wall in the Occupied
    Palestinian Territory advisory
    opinion   84, 98, 140, 146, 151
  v. US, *Relocation of the United States*
    Embassy to Jerusalem case   34, 149
Paraguay *v.* US, *Breard* case   75, 129, 134–135
Passage through the Great Belt Case (Finland
  v. Denmark)   31

PCA. *see* Permanent Court of Arbitration
PCIJ. *see* Permanent Court of International
  Justice
Peace Palace (The Hague)   *29, 58*
peer-based justice   5
Permanent Court of Arbitration (PCA)   9,
  10–11, 107
Permanent Court of International Justice
  (PCIJ)
  achievements of   16–19
  adjudicative function of   13
  advisory function of   80–81, 94
  and compulsory jurisdiction   14–15
  disputes handled by   16
  dissolvement of   23
  establishment of   2, 4, 13
  and international law   13–14, 16–18
  jurisprudence of, decisions of national
    courts in   137
  and non-state actors   150
  and optional clause mechanism   15–16,
    52
  on principle of consent   36
  Rules of Court of   72, 155n2
  as separate entity   14, 16
  similarities between ICJ and   18
  Statute of   15–16
The Perplexities of Modern International Law
  (Rosenne)   12
Peru *v.* Colombia, *Haya de la Torre*
  case   179–180
The Physiognomy of Disputes and the
  Appropriate Means to Resolve Them
  (Hafner)   46
Pinochet cases   136–137
Plant, Brendan   144
Poland   167, 169, 184
political disputes, *v.* legal disputes   46
The Politics of International Arbitration and
  Adjudication (Gent)   5
Posner, Richard   139
Practice Directions of ICJ   151–152
preliminary objections   67–73, 67, 174–175,
  174, 175
Present-Day Relevance of the Jay Treaty
  Arbitrations (Schwarzenberg)   6
Prosecutor v. Thomas Lubanga Dyilo
  case   125

INDEX

Protocol to the African Charter on Human
  and Peoples' Rights   115
provisional measures   73–77
*Provisional Measures the Practice of the
  International Court of Justice* (Oda)   76
Pulp Mills on the River Uruguay case   74,
  125, 131

*Questions Relating to the Obligation to
  Prosecute or Extradite* case   75

Registrars of ICJ   23, 24, 26, 150
*Relocation of the United States Embassy to
  Jerusalem* case   34, 149
Reparation for Injuries advisory opinion   88
respondents
  in general   159–160, *160, 161*
  non-appearing   176–178, *176*
Riddell, Anna   144
*The Role of the International Court of Justice
  as Principal Judicial Organ of the UN*
  (Amr)   170
Romano, Cesaro   56–57
Rosenne, Shabtai   1, 12, 72
Rules of Court (of ICJ)
  amendments to   72, 155–156n2
  on international organizations   149
  on judges *ad hoc*   24
  on preliminary objections   68
Rules of Court (of PCIJ)   72, 155n2
Russia
  and ICJ
    in general   173
    advisory proceedings, participation
      in   168
    advisory proceedings, voting on   167
    filling preliminary objections by   175
    v. Georgia, *Application of the International
      Convention on the Elimination of All
      Forms of Racial Discrimination*   69–
      70, 144
Rwanda *v.* Congo, *Armed Activities on the
  Territory of the Congo*   39–40
Rycroft, Matthew   96

San Francisco Conference (1945)   22, 102
San Marino   32
Schwarzenberger, Georg   6
Schwebel, Steve   104

Scotland   103–104
Scott, Gary L.   18
Secretary-General's Trust Fund to Assist
  States in the Settlement of Disputes   62
Security Council Resolutions   32
Senegal *v.* Belgium, *Questions Relating to
  the Obligation to Prosecute or Extradite*
  case   75
Serbia
  filling preliminary objections by   175
  v. Bosnia, *Application of the Convention on
    the Prevention and Punishment of the
    Crime of Genocide* case   125–126, 130
Simma, Bruno   40, 131, 144
Singapore   175
Sivakumara, Sandesh   146
South Africa
  and ICJ
    filling preliminary objections by
      175
    optional clause declaration of   56
    and international law   139–140
    v. Liberia, *South West Africa* cases   71, 88,
      152n105
    *see also Continued Presence of South Africa
      in Namibia* advisory opinion
South West Africa cases   71, 88, 152n105
Spain
  filling preliminary objections by   175
  v. Belgium, *Barcelona Traction* case   33,
    79
Sparta   5
Spiermann, Ole   17
S.S. Wimbledon case   14
State Responsibility for Genocide: A Follow Up
  (Milanović)   130–131
States
  and costs of international litigation   62
  and ICJ
    in general   30, 171, 186–187
    advisory proceeding. *see* advisory
      opinions of ICJ
    as applicants   158–159, *158, 159, 160*
    applications of intervention
      by   161–163
    compliance with judgement of. *see*
      judgements of ICJ
    filling preliminary objections
      174–175, *174, 175*

States (cont.)
    and interest of individual 33
    not making use of 172–173
    optional clause declaration of. *see*
      optional clause declaration
    as respondents 159–160, *160, 161*
    as respondents, non-appearing
      176–178, *176*
    without UN membership 32, 34
Statute of Permanent Court of International
  Justice 15–16
Statute of the International Court of Justice
    adoption of 22
    on advisory opinions 96
    on applications of intervention by 161
    on composition of ICJ 24
    creation of 25
    on highly qualified publicists 142–143
    on international organizations 150
    on judicial continuity with the PCIJ 27
    on jurisdiction of ICJ 35, 36
    on legal precedents 64
    on non-appearing respondents 176
    on non-state actors 148
    optional clause declaration in 52
    on provisional measures 74
    on relationship with national
      courts 135–136
    on requests for advisory opinions 83
    on specialized chambers 170–171
    States party to 31–32
    on status of ICJ 26
Sweden 169
Switzerland 32

Tadić case 126, 130
Targeted Killing case 136–137
teaching of ICJ
    courses overview 206–223
    see also moot court
Temple of Preah Vihear case 56, 76–77,
  183–184
Thailand
    optional clause declaration of 56
    v. Cambodia, *Temple of Preah Vihear*
      case 56, 76–77, 183–184
"The Treachery of Images" (Magritte) 2–3
Thucyclides 5

treaties
    compromissory clauses in 48
    see also under specific treaties
Treaty of Amity, Economic Relations, and
  Consular Rights (US and Iran) 41–42
Treaty of Friendship and Co-operation (1977;
  France and Djibouti) 60
tribunals. *see* international courts/tribunals
Tripartite Commission for the Restitution of
  Monetary Gold 181
Turkey
    optional clause declarations of 174
    v. France, *Lotus* case 36
    v. Greece, *Aegean Sea Continental Shelf*
      case 101n56

Uganda *v.* Congo, *Armed Activities on the*
  Territory of the Congo case 38–39, 125
UNESCO World Heritage sites 76–77, 184
United Kingdom (UK)
    and ICJ
      in general 173
      advisory proceedings, voting on
        167
      filling preliminary objections
        by 174–175
      optional clause declaration of
        54
      as respondent 159
    Jay Treaty with US 5–6
    v. Albania, *Corfu Channel* case 101,
      180–181
    v. Germany, *S.S. Wimbledon* case 14
    v. Libya, *Aerial Incident at Lockerbie*
      case 103–104
United Nations Convention on the Law of
  the Sea 121–122
United Nations General Assembly
  (UNGA) 81, 106–108
United Nations Security Council (UNSC)
    and ICJ
      overview 99–105
      advisory function of 81
      judges' appointments 107
      and judicial review 102–103
United Nations (UN)
    Charter of. *see* Charter of the United
      Nations

INDEX 235

establishment of 20–22
General Assembly of 106–108
and ICJ's advisory function. *see* advisory opinions of ICJ
and Statute of the International Court of Justice. *see* Statute of the International Court of Justice
United States Diplomatic and Consular Staff in Tehran case 46–47, 74, 182
United States (US)
 and ICJ
  in general 173
  advisory proceedings, voting on 167
  filling preliminary objections by 174
  optional clause declarations of 55–56, 174
  as respondent 159
 international law in 138
 Jay Treaty with UK 5–6
 Treaty of Amity with Iran 41–42
 v. Germany, *LaGrand* case 75, 129, 134–135
 v. Iran
  Oil Platforms case 37, 41–44, 48
  United States Diplomatic and Consular Staff in Tehran case 46–47, 75, 182
 v. Libya, *Aerial Incident at Lockerbie* case 103–104
 v. Mexico
  Avena case 33, 134–135, 147, 180
  Breard case 129
 v. Nicaragua, *Military and Paramilitary Activities in and against Nicaragua* case 37, 55–56, 75, 76, 100, 101, 126, 181–182

 v. Palestine, *Relocation of the United States Embassy to Jerusalem* case 34, 149
 v. Paraguay, *Breard* case 75, 129, 134–135
Uruguay *v.* Argentina, *Pulp Mills on the River Uruguay* case 74, 125, 131
The Uses and Abuses of Advisory Opinions (Berman) 90

Venzke, Ingo 66
Vienna Convention on the Law of Treaties between States and International Organizations or between International Organizations (1986) 34, 42
Vienna Conventions on Diplomatic and Consular Relations (1961/1963) 49, 129, 135, 180
Visscher, Charles de 102
voting, on advisory opinions 165–167, *167*

war, changing views on 12
Western Sahara advisory opinion 95, 97
Whaling in the Antarctic case 182–183
Winiarski, Bohdan Stefan 184
withdrawal, of optional clause declarations 55–56
World Court. *see* International Court of Justice
World Trade Agreement 128–129
World Trade Organization's Dispute Settlement Body 122, 128–129

Xue, Hanquin 177

Yugoslavia 174n17

Printed in the United States
by Baker & Taylor Publisher Services